DEEPENING WITCHCRAFT

ADVANCING SKILLS & KNOWLEDGE

GREY CAT

DEEPENING
WITCHCRAFT

ADVANCING SKILLS & KNOWLEDGE

GREY CAT

ECW PRESS

Published by ECW PRESS
2120 Queen Street East, Suite 200, Toronto, Ontario, Canada M4E 1E2

NATIONAL LIBRARY OF CANADA CATALOGUING IN PUBLICATION DATA

Grey Cat
Deepening Witchcraft: advancing skills and knowledge
ISBN 1-55022-495-6
1. Witchcraft — Handbooks, manuals, etc. 1. Title.
BF1566.G74 2002   133.4'3   C2201-903579-9

Acquisition Editor: Emma McKay
Copy Editor: Jodi Lewchuk
Cover and Interior Design: Guylaine Régimbald—Solo Design
Typesetting: Wiesia Kolasinska
Production: Heather Bean
Printed by: Transcontinental

This book is set in Electra and Europa Arabesque.

The publication of *Deepening Witchcraft* has been generously supported by the Canada Council, the Ontario Arts Council, and the Government of Canada through the Book Publishing Industry Development Program. **Canadä**

DISTRIBUTION

CANADA: General Distribution Services, 325 Humber College Blvd., Toronto, ON M9W 7C3

UNITED STATES: Independent Publishers Group, 814 North Franklin Street, Chicago, Illinois 60610

EUROPE: Turnaround Publisher Services, Unit 3, Olympia Trading Estate, Coburg Road, Wood Green, London N22 6T2

AUSTRALIA AND NEW ZEALAND: Wakefield Press, 17 Rundle Street (Box 2066), Kent Town, South Australia 5071

ECW PRESS
ecwpress.com

CONTENTS

Foreword   9

Acknowledgments   13

1 Who Are Ye and Whence Do Ye Come?
   Introduction   15

2 The Butterfly of Thought Is Disturbed
   by the Harsh Stone of Reason
   Analytical Thinking   40

3 In Days of Old, When Knighthood Was in Flower
   History: Creation to Reformation   67

4 Dancing on the Hilltops
   History: Reformation to Gardner   86

5 Wheels, Spirals, Hammers, and Trees
   Neopagan Religious Philosophy   113

6 I See the Moon, the Moon Sees Me
   The Pagan Concept of Deity   135

7 Go Ye Therefore and Sin No More
   Morals and Ethics   151

8 Pluck Your Magic Twanger, Froggie
   Advanced Magic   171

9 Standing Alone in the Center
   Designing and Leading Large Group Ritual   201

10 Blow the Horns and Call the People Here
    Organizing Events   223

11 Pathways to the Future
    Teaching Our Religion   263

12 A Community of Like-Minded People
    Building Community   285

13 Who Am I When I'm By Myself?
    Personal Growth   313

Index   343

FOREWORD

"We the willing, led by the unknowing, are doing the impossible for the ungrateful. We have done so much for so long with so little, we're now entitled to do everything with nothing." These words were written to me years ago in 1977 by my first Craft daughter. She had recently received her third degree and was formally starting her own coven in the Baltimore area.

She had it easier than we did, Grey Cat, for she had elders who had already been there, so to speak, and had at least some knowledge of the early Pagan and public Wiccan pitfalls that existed. Most importantly, she had training. She had been my only student for many years before we opened Ravenwood in Atlanta. I followed the protocol of the times; I arranged for her to be introduced to the leading High Priestess of the area. Lady Morganna, the queen elder, organized a tea for this purpose. These elder priestesses welcomed her and were honor-bound to help her succeed in her endeavors, to be there for her. Of course, in 1977 most all were of traditional background — teaching one-on-one — but were walking silently within the shadows of an upcoming Pagan resurgence and an alarming public attraction to Witchcraft.

And there was no book, no manual, and no experience to indicate how to proceed. The elders at the time knew that things were changing and indeed there was a need to address those many seekers who felt themselves born to be witches, to direct them to positive information and leaders that would have the knowledge, ethics, and personal accountability to address their needs. Thus began a new and frightening era.

And those of us who were on the front lines knew that we could never give up, that we had to stand fast with absolute tenacity. If we failed it would mean a failure for all. And for twenty-six years we have provided many with an education of what Wicca is — and is not.

We of Ravenwood have long worked with our neighbors, community activists, police department, city council members, and zoning committees on special use procedures and other regulations. We were the first Wiccan church to receive property insurance, and we managed to open a Wiccan church bank account. In the south, no less. And we were one of the earliest Pagan organizations to receive federal tax-exempt status. Ultimately, after long court hearings, we were the first Wiccan group in the country to win a property tax exemption.

We indeed spent many years enduring numerous trials, persecutions, and terrorist attacks. But we prevailed; we honored our tradition, we were accountable to the Craft elders at large, and we were productive members in our daily lives within our community. By our deeds we were known.

This book is most timely; Grey Cat has done hands-on work in the field for many years. I have known her and her work for over a decade, and she has done in-depth research and has learned through her contact with many diverse groups and traditions. Within this book you will find the necessary information for addressing some of the many facets involved in being a member of the clergy. It does a truly in-depth and thorough job of presenting what it takes to teach, lead, and train an aspirant to the priest/esshood.

This is an awesome responsibility, and it is only from diligent day-to-day, year-to-year experience that one could pen this wisdom. This book is born of learning by doing and having the tenacity to stick and stay. By example it says let naught turn you aside, in spite of your own doubts; grow stronger with purpose as you find yourself speaking with the Voice of the Great Mother as Her veil enfolds you.

For the past thirty years I have walked this path as a teacher and mentor and as a public spokesperson and civil rights activist who also represents the traditional aspects of the old religion. Grey Cat, along with many other leaders, agrees that our purpose is not to further the numbers within Wicca, for we believe Wicca not to be the way of the masses. To us, only individuals who have already demonstrated leadership, ethics, and people skills, only individuals who have made positive contributions to their own communities, only individuals who are emotionally healthy and stable, and only individuals who are applying the basic tenets (tools) to their own lives and are leading by example are the people to whom we need to give further training. They are our clergy. And they are precious few.

Within the Pagan movement there is much need for good, ethical leaders—indeed, for clergy. Our own clergy. But the calling must be from the soul and of the soul, and if one cannot work in this infinite frontier with total love and dedication and a willingness to serve all humanity, then one is not of the old law.

For thirty-some years I have walked the old ways of the Mother Goddess. I'm of those who believe themselves to have derived from a traditional Craft background. I consider myself a traditional Witch; I had the blessings of early teachers who gave to me the many grains of ancient truths, which were planted within my heart and soul with their love and trust. And most of all, with their example. To my early elders, the Craft was their way of life; everything was related to the all. An individual who was called to this sacred keep was one of unique individuality, and that unique individuality was sacred. Those elders worked with the individual one-on-one, as needed, giving the language of the ancients in a form the individual could truly relate to. "Begin with yourself; know yourself." The Craft was a sacred journey for each and was shared with only a few who lived its ethics and tenets in love and trust, grace and honor with the old gods, our ancestors, and the Mother Goddess Herself.

This book is a manual of personal experience and addresses some of the many aspects that are required of one who is seeking to attain further knowledge about becoming a leader, teacher, counsel to the Goddess's children.

Remember, this knowledge and these facts have been learned through experience. That is the basis of our learning: knowing and doing. By your deeds you are known. Apply to all aspects of your life the tenets of the old ways, thus attaining inner consciousness of the Law of One, whereby the seeker progresses from knowing and doing to Being and Becoming.

Blessed be to all sincere seekers who partake of the holy well. May it bring you to the glade of understanding.

LADY SINTANA
Founder/Elder Queen Mother
Ravenwood Church and Seminary
www.ravenwoodchurch.org

ACKNOWLEDGMENTS

No book such as this one is ever written alone. My publisher, however, isn't going to let me thank every Pagan I've ever met for their help so I'll have to cut this down to just those who have aided me in this work over the last six months. Michael Ragan, my teacher, straightened me out on some tricky points and always keeps me straight. The people of NorthWind Tradition of American Witchcraft supported me, particularly Wren, as always my right-hand woman; Ceffyl Starr read most of the book and commented, and helped me find references; Mel looked some things up for me; and Moonstone knew I could do it. My readers group — Dave, Patty Erion, my "brother" Robert and his wife Areill, Phoenix, and Lady Weaver — was helpful. M. Macha Nightmare read several chapters and helped me say what I meant, and introduced me to her publisher. Rhiannon Ruadh contributed greatly to Chapter 10 and was there for me personally and professionally throughout. John Wisdom Gonce patiently answered dumb questions about Ceremonial Magic and Chas. Clifton did the same for the history of Wicca in the US. Members of the SEWN, PagTen, and pagan-clergy mail lists answered some difficult questions and/or shared their opinions on certain points, and the Internet in general provided opportunities for research and ease in ordering needed books. Judy Harrow recommended books — and her own was most helpful. Isaac Bonewits's organized and on target analysis of Neopagan beliefs was also valuable. Lady Sintana and Lord Merlin, Clergy Emeritus of Ravenwood, answered questions. Rabbit learned to be a literary agent at my request and without her support I couldn't have done it. B. Stevens uncomplicated my baroque prose, put the commas in the right places, and helped with Chapter 11. My daughter did everything from washing the dog to getting my groceries so I could devote all my good time to writing. And finally there's Jodi, my editor: we fought over every comma and capital and ended up with a much better book.

CHAPTER ONE

See them dancing on the hilltops,

Whirling wildly in the dark of night.

Hear them chanting of the Goddess,

Tall, serene and full of light.

Hear them baying at the shadows

Dressing trees with ebon robes.

Feel them calling to the hidden

Children of the ancient Gods.

GREY CAT

WHO ARE YE AND WHENCE DO YE COME?

Introduction

How and when did you find out about Witchcraft or Neopaganism?[1] For me, it was finding a listing for *Drawing Down the Moon*[2] in a catalog from The Bear Tribe I got from a holdover hippie friend. It was a revelation to me that there were actually other people who thought the way I did about religion. I felt as if I'd found my home. In my early twenties I'd wandered through Christianity trying to find the place where I fit — without success. Long before the early 1980s, when I found the book, I'd given up on finding my niche in any religion and had done quite well during the intervening years essentially without a religion.

At first, I must admit, I was a lot more interested in doing magic than I was in the religious aspect of Witchcraft. In fact, the idea that Witchcraft was somehow connected with religion, of all things, seemed very peculiar to me then. My, how times (and people) do change. As it happens with so many newcomers, the religious aspect soon became a lot more important to me than any sort of magic.

I proceeded to read everything I could find on the subject — and plenty of that wasn't quite on it. At the point I quit keeping track, there were 225 titles on my book list. In my old office space, there are five or six notebooks full of information taken from these books. Some of those notes appear in this book. I suppose I stopped keeping a list because it was getting rather difficult to find any material that was really new.

When I finally decided that it was time to start this book I ended up buying over twenty-five more books covering a variety of subjects. In fact, more than half of them didn't appear on the surface to have anything to do with Neopaganism. Believe it or not, those are the ones I've gotten the most from. I've been a Witch and Priestess for almost twenty years and in those years I've been faced with a lot of challenges. Because I felt that it was my calling to work for the good of the community, I attempted to learn about all the various things that students and others seemed to demand of me. Since that covers everything from first aid to divination, I've come to the realization that all of us need to specialize to some extent. Nobody can do everything really well.

It is my hope that this book will assist you in your attempt to learn about the things those in your community are demanding of you.

Who comprises the Neopagan clergy: priest/esses, leaders, writers? The work of religious clergy summons very unusual people: those within whom a deeply mystic river flows and within whose ears the call of the God/dess sounds; those with sight powered by the energies of the universe; those with an abundance of practicality and dedication; those willing to work their butts off. Such are the individuals needed for the health of our religion and we must respect and nurture them, as they work for us all.

But how do we prepare these people to be clergy in the Neopagan community? For many years, the creation of a Wiccan University, Seminary (Oviary?), or some other sort of training school for those who have already learned basic Wicca has been the dream of some leaders in the American Craft. These dreams are little closer to realization than they were fifteen years ago when Amber K* first published her magazine titled *Priest/ess*. Several of these projects have been furthered by an assortment of in-person and on-line courses intended to help our clergy prepare for the demands of leadership.

Groups have worked on setting up study programs in an attempt to more carefully define the process of moving from initiation to leadership and some have prepared materials to help their students through this process. Ár n'Draiocht Féin developed an ambitious study program intended to turn out PhD-level clergy. As a member of the committee that worked on the program, I can say that completing it would require spending a good deal of time and money, but you'd finish a very well-educated Druid. ADF's motto, "Why Not Excellence?" is all the justification its program requires; however, such ambitious and scholarly demands may not be the best solution for everyone.[3]

In reality, most Neopagan leaders and teachers juggle a full-time job, a family, and the needs of their group and students — not to mention community activities. Time and resources for taking university courses, learning a new language, and performing rigorous historical research are difficult to find. While I can easily agree that it would be really fine to have leaders with advanced general education as well as training targeted to specific needs, it's unrealistic to freeze ourselves into this ideal. I have completely failed to note any extreme of difference in the effectiveness of Christian clergy related to the number of years they have spent in college. In fact, my recent reading in Christian sociology shows that such training isn't necessarily a good thing.

For lack of any better alternative we buy and read virtually every new beginning Wicca book, all of which chew over the same stuff (sometimes more and sometimes less accurately). We hope that there will be a new thought or approach, something that will give us a hint of an interesting or worthwhile path to take. We read, study, and do historical research and we go to gatherings and attend the few leadership workshops offered. Best of all, we talk with our peers who are leaders of other groups — people who face the same problems and demands that we face.

We learn from each other, not as the blind leading the blind, but perhaps as the lame carried by the blind for whom the lame sees. But a few weekends a year is not sufficient to complete our education. Neither is this book, no matter how successfully I complete my task. With luck I can point out some directions for you to take in your search for competency and professionalism.

No! *Professionalism* is not necessarily a bad word. It just means knowing that you know your job, that you do it well, and that you are able to meet your responsibilities and fulfill the reasonable expectations of your students, initiates, group members, and peers. It doesn't mean that you'll always be able to answer every question and heal any ill (psychological or physical) or that you'll be the perfect teacher and priest/ess. What you can do is add to your education and experience and depend on them and the hand of the God/dess to make you good enough.

Remember that our mythology is very, very important: it gives us the vision and the elemental spark to make our work successful. If we include in this mythology the picture of the perfect priest/ess — one who knows all, helps all, saves all — we're doing ourselves a great disservice. It's quite inaccurate (as most of us fully realize) to picture our ancestors as having primitive minds; it's also inaccurate to picture any of them as representing perfection. The myths of the Noble Savage and the Golden Age existed in Ancient Greece as they do today — and were no more true.

However, there's another myth that you should never ignore or forget: the Goddesses, the Gods — they don't leave you to work alone. From my own experience I can assure you that they are there for you and they will whisper to your mind when you have need. You may not hear voices, but at just the right moment you'll realize that you *know* — you know what to say or, as happens more often with me, you'll realize what's really going on, what's really wrong. What you must do is listen and act. As one of my initiates commented, "I'm a High Priestess, I know things." It's frightening the first time you receive this guidance and it's a mistake to become dependent upon it, but it *is* there for you.

The first question to arise with respect to training is frequently about initiation. Of course, outside of Witchcraft and/or Wicca, few of the Pagan groups have initiations at all. The controversy about initiation into Wicca isn't likely to die down anytime soon — if ever. Do you have to be initiated only by someone who was initiated by someone who was . . . ? My personal opinion is that it can help but it's not the only way. Instead of going into all the timeworn arguments, let me give you my position.

Wicca is a mystery religion. A *mystery* is generally defined as a *secret* although it comes from the Greek word referring to the rites of Demeter (among others), which were not spoken of to those who had not experienced them. In fact, although the law protected the secrecy of the specific activities taking place at these rituals, only those details were protected — no penalty was prescribed for publicizing the inner mystery that the rituals were intended to reveal. The reason behind this practice is simple: the mystery could not be expressed in language. The mystery is not a secret because a secret can be told; it's a mystery because it can only be experienced. Initiation rites are one way of bringing people to the mystery.

It's almost impossible to discuss the secrets of an initiatory religion, much less reveal them. Just trying to figure out if their student has "got it" keeps Wiccan teachers awake at night. When a new Wiccan is being trained, much of the process is aimed at getting them to experience the mystery — particularly difficult as there's no knowing just where to aim! And no, we don't always succeed, although initiation at the right time frequently will finish the task. The individual forced by failure to find a congenial teacher (or any other teacher at all) or by a preference to work as a solitary is obviously going to have a more difficult time than the individual with a good teacher. However, the task's level of difficulty does not preclude its accomplishment if for no other reason than that the Goddess knows her own.

Formal initiation is by no means necessary for someone to be a "real" Witch. I've learned that initiations can happen whether or not there's a human to preside at them. I guess I ought to warn all my readers that even having a formal third degree initiation won't protect you from suddenly realizing that you're undergoing yet another initiation with all the accompanying bells and whistles, including anything from adopting a new name to having the unprocessed fecal matter strike the revolving air impeller.

Initiation, regardless of how and when it happens, is an internal event knowable only by the individual and only the gods may judge if the individual is correct or incorrect in their analysis. Of course, I'm definitely an iconoclast; I also believe that the initial initiation cannot be repeated. It's like being pregnant: either you are or you aren't. When someone has an initiation, formal or not, and wishes to work with my group, we do determine whether or not their training fulfills our definition and then we *adopt* the individual — after they have reviewed our training materials.

Unfortunately, some charlatan claiming to be a Witch may initiate a newcomer in return for sexual or other favors. The victim is told that they are now a Witch or even a High Priest/ess. However, most groups feel that education, training, and inner development are all crucial ingredients in the making of a Witch. While a few groups perform an initiation before sharing much information, it is understood that the further training required after the initiation is part of the process. Abusers, however, may make no gesture whatsoever at providing any training (one suspects they have little, if any, themselves) but flatter their victim instead by telling them that they are a "natural" or have already learned more from their reading than most Witches know. The poor victim then enters the Pagan community feeling secure in their initiation only to realize, sooner or later, that they have been cheated and made a fool of by an unprincipled fraud.

Lack of a formal initiation, preferably by a group people have heard of, does not disqualify you from working with the material in this book. Humans are as likely as chickens to get caught up in pecking orders, particularly if a few individuals feel the need to assert their superiority over others despite teachings which attempt to remind people that neither knowledge nor time in service nor native talent nor legitimate skills can make one human superior to another.

As long as I've gotten into it, I'll go on to say that it's not accurate to refer to most Witchcraft groups as *nonhierarchical*. Where there are students there are also teachers and this situation is innately hierarchical. On the other hand, since the Craft recognizes the inalienable right of anyone to "vote with their feet," no group is able to maintain for long a farther-reaching and more oppressive hierarchy while maintaining its membership numbers. If we weren't innately rebels, we wouldn't be Witches.

A Priestess's Litany for a New Day

I come to the East. I ask the wind to clear away preconceptions and muddy reasoning. At this moment of sunrise, the beginning of a new day, I come to thee seeking the wisdom I may need.

I come to the South. I ask the fire and the full light of noon to give me courage and energy. Burn from me all my angers and smallness of mind. I come to thee seeking right action and protection in whatever I am called to do.

I come to the West. I ask the still waters to hold me sensitive to the material needs of my world. Let the moving waters wash from me the busyness of mundane concerns. I come to thee seeking the quiet sensitivity of thy flow in twilight.

I come to the North. I ask the earth and stones for wisdom, stability and endurance. Absorb from me all stolid heaviness. I come to thee seeking growth and the quiet of thy night.

I come to the Center. Let me never forget that all things find their source in spirit and to spirit shall all return. I come to thee seeking balance.

I come to the silver light of Moon, the golden light of Sun. May I, this day and this night, find my path and walk it with grace, serenity, hope.

I begin.

— Grey Cat

Say the words "Wiccan (or Pagan or Witchcraft) clergy" at a gathering or on the Internet and immediately people are up on their feet screaming. The loudest screamers will be saying that "Pagans don't need clergy to mediate between themselves and the Gods." I don't know who told these people that this is the only or even the primary job of *any* clergy, although it's true that at times the Roman Catholic establishment has made this claim. Certainly no Pagan leader I'm aware of ever has professed this ability. (The extraneous allegation is a classic example of misdirection, which you will find described in Chapter 2.)

Nonetheless, we're generally very uncomfortable with the clergy label. I've looked at most of the possible substitutes: *ecclesiastic* is impossible to pronounce and spell and the dictionary meanings are identical to *clergy*; *minister* has a meaning almost identical to *clergy*, as does *priest. Priest* is the word most Pagans are willing to use but in majority society the word's meaning is more specific, applying to the clergy of the several catholic denominations rather than to all clergy. Consequently, the word *priest* can be somewhat of a problem. *Clergy* is the word preferred by lawmakers and one reason for needing a specific term by which to call ourselves relates to achieving acceptance by the majority society.

One misconception we hold about the word *clergy* is that accepting the title means that we seek to achieve our full living from that work alone. Quite outside of the serious question about the implications of paid clergy to the Pagan world, few of our groups can realistically be asked to support clergy. When Isaac Bonewits wanted to find the time and energy to research and then design and write materials for a historically based Druidic tradition, he suggested that people who were interested in his end result might help by contributing a small sum a year to his mundane support. In return, he would devote his time thus freed to this work. Do I need to tell you that there were very few takers?

Our Pagan culture is rightfully notorious for the unwillingness of so many of its members to put their money where their mouth is. In a very real way, we do not walk our talk. The assumption that one of our leaders could instantly be transmuted from a serious Pagan researcher into a Jim Bakker greatly overstates the magical power of money. Worse, not only are we unwilling to support our local high priest/ess, we routinely find that the prices charged by our Neopagan craftsmen are "too high" and we ask them to sell their labor much below minimum wage to satisfy our whim for dirt cheap magical tools. In a private letter Judy Harrow says:

> I'm opposed to paid clergy, for a lot of reasons. But when we avoid paid clergy, we need to consider this: in our society, besides being a way of meeting our material needs, money is a way of showing appreciation. I personally neither want nor need extrinsic *compensation* for the work I do for love. Being human, I do still need to know that what I do matters, is helpful to people. I need appreciation. If we aren't giving each other material rewards, we need to find other ways to express our appreciation. People who do not feel appreciated are at much greater risk for burnout.4 (Harrow's emphasis)

I am not at all suggesting that we imitate the New Age movement and charge huge prices for weekends and workshops. What I am urging is that our people have more respect for what they are given and that they honor their teachers and leaders by *at least* making sure that the group isn't costing those teachers and leaders any money. If our students and participants can't take responsibility for this much, I could easily wonder if what we're doing is worth it. I will return to the money issue later.

I'm a rather practical person. I see that there are a whole lot of people who are being asked to teach, to lead rituals, to initiate, to counsel, to show the way. These teachers, ritual designers and leaders, initiators, counselors, pathfinders, and (yes) writers *are* acting as clergy. There is a strong movement in Paganism that believes in total egalitarian ideals (as defined by each believer). This movement also believes that leadership is not only unnecessary, but that it is demeaning to those being led and surfaces only because of individuals with overdeveloped egos. These beliefs are based on an inaccurate interpretation of equality that demonstrably doesn't work! Letting a word accumulate more emotional overtones than is necessary can practically cut off communication. Clergy are actually just the house servants who keep a religion functioning. Without those individuals willing to devote time and energy for the benefit of all in our community, the Neopagan movement would have no public presence at all.

If every Pagan actually did prefer to come up with their own individual cosmology and structure of spiritual growth, to do all their celebrating alone, to need no Neopagan books for outside information . . . well, then I guess there'd be no job for Neopagan clergy. But regardless of what I've seen in chat rooms and on mail lists, I do note that a whole lot of people turn up at gatherings and festivals seeking teachers and generally demanding a Pagan equivalent to clergy.

I'm actually not making the usual differential between *clergy* and *congregation* or *laity* because while that's the way Christians do things, it's not the only way. I think most of us expect everyone attending a ritual or a gathering to be full participants rather than passive observers. We don't always design rituals that make it clear, but I do believe that shared participation is the goal of almost all our leaders.

The word *equal* is widely misunderstood these days. It has never meant that all people have the same amount of intelligence, ability, knowledge, etc. People just aren't all equal in that sense; my daughter can draw better than I can and I can remember unimportant facts better than she can. An ideal equality exists when all people have equal opportunities to make the most of themselves, *not* when they can all do each other's jobs equally well.

Some opportunities require teachers and leaders to provide guidance, information, and support. Most opportunities require that the individual have the inner fire to pursue and achieve them. Certainly there's a need for Pagans who can and will teach, organize group events, design group celebrations for the wheel of the year and phases of the moon. People are needed to provide an ear to those with problems that possess a spiritual, religious aspect and cannot be properly handled by either nonreligious ears or counselors who walk a different religious path.

At a small gathering in Tennessee, I asked what jobs Pagan leaders may be called upon to do. I accumulated the following list of roles that our leaders can expect to be asked to assume:

- Gathering organizer
- Mother
- Friend
- Troublemaker
- Example
- Encyclopedia
- Witch doctor
- Etiquette and ethics coach
- Co-student
- Counselor
- Psychologist
- Healer
- Spell worker
- Magician
- Self-image coach
- Teacher

To put the job mentioned last first, I believe the most important work of almost all clergy — certainly of our clergy — is teaching. As a new-old religion, people don't already know what we believe, what we do, what we are. In the case of Witchcraft, there is a book's worth of group-specific information and practice that the newcomer is expected to learn before they can be considered a full participant. The result is that few of us can manage to be free of students for any significant period of time. Whether we instruct one-on-one or gather our students into a class, a significant portion of our so-called free time is spent teaching.

Of course, one of the best things about teaching is that, in general, the teachers learn more than the students. On the other hand, most of us are not trained as teachers and there's a lot more to teaching than just knowing the material. How do you handle a class containing students with different levels of knowledge, widely different backgrounds, diversity in skills and abilities? While I cannot undertake to give you all the skills of a teacher, I can share the techniques that have helped me. I have also asked one of my reviewers, a trained teacher, to share some of his knowledge with us (see Chapter 11).

The second most difficult and time-consuming job of clergy is counseling. A call can come at three o'clock any morning; students, group members, and even complete strangers feel that they can monopolize us for hours at a stretch, telling us their problems and expecting that we will have solutions and sympathy. And to top it all off, you may have to mention to someone that they've been bending your ear and your patience with the exact same problem for any number of weeks, months, or years without taking action. Then, when you sensibly refuse to listen any more until they've made an attempt to better the situation, they go away and tell everyone they know what an awful, unsympathetic person you are! (A good introduction to pastoral counseling is offered on-line by Cherry Hill Seminary.5)

While these two jobs of Wiccan group leaders are difficult, perhaps our greatest challenge lies in the area of group dynamics. Wiccan groups are notoriously short-lived. We see our students come and go like yo-yos spinning up and down. They leave us for quick initiation in a group with easier requirements and start up their own classes long before they've shown any real signs of actually getting it. Treasured initiates working toward elevation and taking on some of the responsibility for the group's activities will suddenly split for overnight (literally) elevation to third degree from some charismatic High-Muckety-Muck who is building a huge group out of others' hard work.

Alternately, a partnership breaks up and the entire pattern of the group is altered — somebody leaves, somebody new joins. Keeping up with the dynamic balance of a group (which sometimes becomes as close — or closer in some ways — than family) is a never-ending balancing act that cannot, by its nature, always be successful. For group leaders the stress never seems to fade away; time off is rare and far too frequently it's interrupted. We have jobs, children, spouses or lovers, housework, health issues, and our own inner mysteries to concern us as well. Many leaders have understandably faltered when attempting to accomplish it all.

I'll tell you right now that *Mother* is a group leadership role I recommend against assuming, at least in the *Mom* aspect. We cannot, and should not, attempt to compensate adults for the nurture they missed, or feel they missed, as a child. We'd quickly tell half a married couple that it is unrealistic and damaging to expect one's spouse to assume the nurturing parental role. It's even more impossible for us to assume it. The motherly quality of sympathetic understanding can stand you in good stead, but *please* don't overdo it! Just as counseling becomes a part of the problem if the counseled is allowed to become addicted to having a listener, too much sympathy and understanding doesn't encourage an individual to learn to stand on their own two feet.

Perhaps magician is the role that can do us, as individuals, the most harm. It's just too tempting to share the view some of our students hold; that is, they see us as nearly all-powerful, able to fix anything, and eager to bend the cosmos to our wills (their wills, actually)! Gee, nice picture: faster than a speeding germ, more powerful than a tall neurosis, able to lead huge rituals with a single bound. It ain't true! Yet it's a picture many people want to hold of their teacher/leader and it's catching.

There is a tightrope that we must walk and one of the very likely results of that walk is burnout (which is another thing I'll talk about later, in Chapter 13). It's very difficult to live the life of a high priest or priestess. It's nearly impossible to balance all the demands we make of ourselves, not to mention the demands that others pile onto us. Maintaining some kind of personal life and evaluating realistically just how much time we can find and how much energy we're able to spare is extremely important.

I realized a few years ago that if the Roman Catholic Church or the Episcopal Church had ordained women in 1960, I might well have been a Christian priest.[6] I feel strongly that I was *called* to be a priestess; it just took me a while to find out in what religion I was supposed to be a priest. However, there's a good bit more to it than just "wanting" to be a priest/ess. Our better priest/esses have been dragged kicking and screaming to their degree initiations. No one with *any* sense wants the job!

It's my experience that Neopaganism chooses its own leaders. I'm not ignoring the folks who have chosen to set themselves up as Gurus, High-Muckety-Mucks, and the Goddess's gift to the great unwashed masses. There has never been a religious movement free of exploiters and false prophets — Saul of Tarsus comes to mind — and there's no reason why Neopaganism should be exempt. Outside of these few crooks, most people currently functioning as Neopagan clergy are doing the jobs because so many people came to them and begged them to do it. And they are trying to reach a standard that exceeds the best of their abilities. With luck, these are the people this book may assist.

If any of my readers think that it would be neat to be the high priest/ess and get to stand in the middle of the Circle and lead the ritual and all that great stuff, all I can say is that you've got some surprises coming. Ritual is a lot more fun if you are *not* the one in charge. Then you can really get into it because you're not required to pay attention to whether or not anyone is getting overwhelmed by what's going on. You're not gauging when to start raising power and how, and you're not directing the power to the agreed upon target. You're not making sure that all the beginners ground effectively so they aren't wandering around with air under their feet. And let's face it, you're probably not hosting the group, which means you're not responsible for the meal or snacks and the cleanup.

Real high priest/esses are embarrassed at receiving exaggerated deference from the community and are far more focused on getting all the work done than they are on swanning around being important. You'll usually notice that at a gathering they have signed up for work-jobs even though they are also holding two workshops. And they turn up at the right place on time!

No clergyperson has an easy job, although those who work within a religion that has mostly settled on its rules and expectations of clergy probably have it a bit easier. However, the job is intrinsically a difficult one that requires a level of dedication not everyone can maintain. It's very important for those undertaking this job to first examine their life and make sure they have determined just how much time and effort they are willing and able to free up for it. When they reach that limit, they must learn how to say no to any further requests or demands.

Complicating matters is the fact that it's not easy to decide which demands you should try to fulfill and which just aren't part of an appropriate job description. A further problem is that our local hospitals, jails, prisons, or social services agencies may refuse to accept us as "real" clergy. Not to mention that our neighbors just might get hysterical about our presence and/or the clergy of some local group may — for honest reasons (fear) or dishonest ones (increasing their own power and group size) — mount an attack against us from the pulpit.

No, I'm not pushing a vision of nice, cuddly little "churches" of Wicca sprinkled all over supporting a priest and priestess, a Sunday school, and bake sales in front of Wal-Mart to raise funds — or am I? While none of us want to feel that our religion is ordinary, it's not unreasonable to want others to feel that way about it if it will bring us safety and religious freedom. However, I'd certainly hate to see us achieve the smugness, narrow-minded-ness, and top-down hierarchies of so many groups that follow the monotheistic paths.

The next ten years will likely be a balancing act for Pagan groups and their leadership, and we need to prepare ourselves to handle it well. Someone once asked me if we were looking ahead to more burning times or to more acceptance from the majority society. My answer to the question was "Yes." Yes, I expect a few of us to meet vicious and possibly even deadly opposition and yes, I expect that more and more Neopagan groups will find local acceptance from their communities. I expect some of us to have to defend our religion in court and I expect many of us to become members of local clergy groups. And I expect that most of us will do a really good job of whatever we're called upon to do.

Before I leave the subject of Pagan clergy I do want to go a little further into the education of clergy and paid clergy as I see these issues affecting Paganism. Reading *The Churching of America*, a sociological study of the movement of people to and between churches, I learned a lot of interesting things.7 One of them was that when Christian clergy become highly educated and well paid, they usually see the beliefs of their religion differ-ently. They develop a desire to fit in with the more affluent classes of majority society and as a result, their particular church becomes much less attractive to many of the parishioners. These clergy become more inter-ested in the income, social position, and the intellectual pecking order of the church membership and less interested in serving the needs of their members.

There's a reason I link *highly educated* to *well paid*. If we ask someone to attend a university or its equivalent, they are going to spend a lot of money on the school's tuition and on supporting themselves while taking the degree. If I make a big investment in a course of study, I'm going to want it to result in a job — with an income attached. The two *do* go together. And a paid clergyperson doesn't have to be particularly hung up on their exact income nor be into social climbing to realize that they must please the source of that income in order to keep collecting it. These comments have nothing to do with certain greedy evangelists who make millions which they then put to personal use. I'm just talking about the normal attitude that an employee must have.

Living religions change, but when they change in favor of comfort, social acceptability, and dry intellectualism, it isn't a change for the better. Religion ideally addresses the total person and a total person has an emotional and spiritual side as well as an intellectual side. In order to achieve balance, Paganism needs to stay hungry in a sense; it needs to stay fresh enough to provide for the emotional and spiritual needs of its adherents and this goal apparently is not best achieved by paid clergy.

A paid clergyperson must be concerned with numbers and with the relative wealth of the individuals making up those numbers. Thus, they inevitably select followers more by these criteria than by enthusiasm and dedication. This kind of selection process would be deadly for our movement. I believe that we must continue to develop our clergy within the small group organization and that these people must be essentially self-trained, thereby preserving their ability to earn their living at some other endeavor.

However, this does not mean that I think that they should never receive any money! Our leaders devote significant proportions of their time to this work and if those they serve do not make some return of that energy, they will lose most of the benefit of the work. I believe our clergy should receive monetary and other recompense for the actual work they produce for the community. When they perform weddings and funerals, visit Pagans in the hospital or in prison, put on big events, do workshops, or offer basic classes to the public, they should receive pay or some other exchange of energy for these services. When they work a great deal with an individual as a counselor or teacher they shouldn't necessarily be given money, but the recipient of these services should do something to return the time spent.

Our paths do not find virtue in poverty itself and the work of our leaders is not improved when they encounter difficulty in maintaining a reasonably pleasant standard of living.

In planning this book I started from the list of jobs presented earlier in this chapter — and from the demands that, in my experience, are made on Neopagan clergy — and attempted to research and write a dozen chapters (in addition to this one) to help us meet these demands. I've also added some topics no one suggested but for which I perceive a need. Some of these topics may not immediately seem important to you, but rest assured that everything in here is something I've needed to know or have been glad that I knew. This book doesn't cover all the topics I thought of and if enough people buy this volume, the publisher will probably be interested in publishing a second. Each chapter in this book can stand alone and you don't necessarily have to read them in the order that I have given them. The brief descriptions below may help you decide what to read first.

Chapter 2 is highly focused on an important survival skill: analyzing what you hear and read using logic and semantics. Never forget that a particular word may carry a lot of emotional connections for you that it does not carry for the writer or speaker — and vice versa. Things are always being presented to you as having been *proved*. Have they really or does someone just want you to think so? You can find survey statistics that prove everyone prefers a certain brand, but how were the survey questions worded? Any religious leader, even when involved in a religion less contro-versial than ours, needs to know when they are being misled.

In Chapters 3 and 4, the story of Witchcraft, as it is presented by our earliest writers, is compared with the current findings of historians. I hadn't expected to need to spend so much of our time on this subject, but new work by academics makes it important for us to reassess just what is history and what is myth. I am not denigrating the myth; I am just trying to separate out which is which.

As the teachers of our religion and as part of the formal interface between Paganism and the majority society, we need to take a good look at what we believe and why. While Paganism includes numerous different paths, we all have a good deal in common. As Pagans, we share in a cosmology or worldview that differs in a number of ways from others in our society. It's important that we understand these beliefs and differences, so Chapter 5 sets out our philosophy.

We don't actually talk about *God* and *Goddess* a great deal although we talk about individual, named deities. Chapter 6 outlines why it's important for us to realize that we've taken an unprecedented step in how and why we choose a Neopagan deity and religious path.

There is a perception that orders from a threatening deity are required in order to make humans behave well. While moral and ethical behavior present a lot of difficulties for individuals, groups, and society as a whole, I hope that all Pagans can attempt to value truth and refuse to cause unnecessary pain as a baseline for their actions. In Chapter 7 I examine some of the elements that can foster good behavior and how we can encourage more people to adopt such a purpose.

The word *Witchcraft* carries with it the idea of magic, and many other Neopagans also believe in magic. How can we make our magic more effective? How can we make it safer? Is there such a thing as *advanced magic*? Chapter 8 discusses these questions and more.

Since "going to church" in one sense or another is generally a part of any religion, Chapter 9 takes ritual apart and puts it back together again. Any religious ritual may be divided into a number of distinct sections which can be rearranged in a number of ways, some of which are better than others. Additionally, the number of people at a ritual makes a big difference in what does and doesn't work well, and the difference between working and celebratory rituals must be considered. I discuss all of these issues in this chapter.

In Chapter 10 I've been able to give you a lot of advice for putting on a community event, from an open ritual to a week-long Pagan festival. In addition to my own experience with this particular task, I've been able to include the wisdom of a Pagan who has extensive first-hand knowledge in this area. With any luck at all you'll be able to avoid all the glorious learning experiences we had.

I suspect that a lot of us feel quite secure about our teaching, at least when we can teach in the same way that we were taught. But this is a new century; we are being inundated with students and some of us are feeling the need to explore new techniques. Whether it's orientation classes taught jointly by a group of covens, on-line classes, correspondence courses, or traditional one-on-one training, leaders are trying new teaching methods. Most methods work well for some people and few don't work for anyone at all. In Chapter 11 I look at some techniques for teaching and discuss just what our students need to know.

Drawing near to the end of our journey, we reach a scary spot: a discussion of our role in representing Paganism to society at large and our position as leaders within the Pagan movement. In a few cities Pagan leaders have achieved seats on various formal assemblies composed of religious leaders. Is this a good thing? There's disagreement on this point, but I happen to think it's very good. We may be called upon to talk to the local police or educational authorities about Neopagan beliefs or we may be asked to open a city council meeting or a parade with a prayer. Are we ready to take our place as "just another religion"? What is our role in the Neopagan community? What can we do about all the discord we perceive to be present within our movement? Chapter 12 isn't going to solve all these problems but perhaps it will help.

Last of all, in Chapter 13 I want to question how we are going to do our jobs if we don't take care of ourselves, both physically and spiritually. Who will priestess the high priestess? Burnout has deprived too many groups of good leadership. We need to minimize this condition for our own personal good and for the good of all. It isn't selfish to take care of our own needs; in fact, it's one of the most important jobs our God/desses give us. We must learn to keep enough time and space for ourselves so we can continue to grow as individuals and as spirits and preserve enough room for our own practice of our religion.

Throughout this volume I'll be recommending books and Web sites that will help each of you further your own specialized education. Ordination, third degree initiation, tenth circle — whatever — isn't the end of a priest/ess's training. Third is the highest initiation most Witchcraft groups observe formally, but there are more and they're likely to come upon you at inconvenient times, bringing with them all the confusion and upset of your nice, comfortable life that your initial initiation did. As we share with each other — discussing problems, venting frustrations, recounting successes — we add to the body of knowledge needed to create Neopagan leaders prepared to do our part in the development of a new movement that we obviously feel is good and good for people.

We are not limited by the conventional categories, nor would we be, for we are the Witches. We live in the borderlands, the realms of ambiguity, on the edge of the forest and at the edge of the sea, in the dawn and at twilight, in between.[8]

Before I let you go on and actually read the book, I need to make sure you will be able to figure out what is fact and what is opinion. In the history chapters I will write declarative sentences which say this or that happened. While I am not an academic historian, I've been reading history since I was in my late teens and mythology since I was about eight. I've attended college and although I never took a degree, I've read more in history, social anthropology, physical anthropology, sociology, psychology, and archeology than I would have needed to obtain a degree in any of them. Some statements I make are not attributed to any authority with a footnote. In many cases these statements are ideas that have been, and continue to be, accepted by most academic historians. In other cases these statements may be my own conclusions. When I'm actually referring to some other person's conclusions, I cite an authority.

Most of my reading has been done to satisfy my own curiosity and I didn't trouble to pick out quotes I thought were particularly meaningful, nor did I keep records of points to footnote. I probably could, given a pile of the books I've read, find the source of most of the statements and opinions I give — but that isn't going to happen. And no matter how many footnotes to how many respected academic authorities I were to cite, everything I say about history may very possibly be outdated next week by some genius's penetrating analysis of the materials.

The fact that history has already happened doesn't mean that we can know what *really* happened, as the continuing discussion of events like the assassination of JFK proves. I've done all that any person, academic or not, can do: I've been as accurate as possible and have focused my own analytical abilities on each question to produce the best answer I could from the facts in my possession. I've made every attempt to avoid misleading you and have done my best not to reason beyond the facts.

The chapters on Neopagan beliefs, the deities, and ethics represent my best attempt — through reading, conversation, and eavesdropping — to describe our core beliefs accurately and in such a way that we can come close to an agreement upon them. Every group and every individual has beliefs I haven't mentioned and anyone may put a far different emphasis on a specific belief than I have — as it should be, in my opinion. My discussion on morality undoubtedly harks back to a belief in a *natural philosophy*, which is the same belief that Thomas Jefferson and the others who helped write the basic documents of the United States held; that is, there is a standard of behavior that well-meaning humans can accept as right and good without recourse to a belief in the supernatural. I attempt to suggest why this belief exists and why it's worthwhile to attempt to strive, as an individual, for good, right, and moral behavior.

In the practical chapters I share those things which have worked for me and/or for people I have talked to. Some of these things will not work for you — or perhaps for anyone but me. I can't know until a number of people have tried them without success. All I can do is give you the benefit of my own experience and hope that more and more lore about these activities will accumulate so that we can gift those who follow us with better and better advice. S. I. Hayakawa says that words (communication) "come to us as *free gifts from the dead*", that we may learn from them and so have the time to learn more (Hayakawa's emphasis).[9] These words are my gift to you in the hope that you can add to them before passing them on.

May the Lord and the Lady protect and keep you on your journey as they have me.

Blessed Be
Grey Cat

NOTES

[1] In this book, the terms *Wicca, Wica, Witchcraft*, and *the Craft* will mean the same thing: an initiatory religious tradition that includes group ritual practiced in created sacred space termed a *circle*. *Wiccan, Witchen*, and *Witch* refer to a member of such a group. At one time much discussion centered on whether *Wiccan* or *Witch* was the more correct historical term. When we went public with this religion many of us adopted *Wiccan*, a less controversial term. Recently I've seen a lot of discussions assigning a variety of narrower definitions to these terms, none of which is in agreement with any other. I decline to enter into this discussion here.

I will use the word *Neopagan* to refer to the wide spectrum of polytheistic religions that make up a nonconventional religious movement in Western Europe and the Americas. I will refer to ancient polytheistic religions as *pagan*; I will not capitalize the term, as this was not the name those groups used for their religions. Any appearance of the word *Pagan* (capitalized) will be synonymous with *Neopagan*.

[2] Margot Adler, *Drawing Down the Moon*, rev. ed. (Boston: Beacon Press, 1986).

[3] For more information see www.adf.org/training/.

[4] Judy Harrow, personal correspondence with author, 8 July 2001.

[5] See www.cherryhillseminary.org. (Cherry Hill Seminary, RR 1, Box 239, Bethel, VT, 05032.)

[6] I've always tended to think of my self as a *priest* rather than a *priestess*. I think that's partly because I never wanted to be something that ended in *ette* or *enne*, which are suffixes that seem to me to trivialize.

[7] Roger Finke and Rodney Stark, *The Churching of America, 1776–1990: Winners and Losers in Our Religious Economy* (New Brunswick: Rutgers University Press, 1992).

[8] Judy Harrow, *Wicca Covens: How to Start and Organize Your Own* (Secaucus: Citadel, 1999), 10.

[9] S. I. Hayakawa and A.R. Hayakawa, *Language and Thought in Action*, 5th ed. (New York: Harcourt Brace & Company, 1990), 8.

CHAPTER TWO

And Odin tied himself to the World Tree — tightly, as only a God could. The rough bark pressed painfully against His back, devouring His skin, pulling His flesh into its wooden heart. The brilliant winter sun swept across the sky and the first long night began.

What could matter so much to the God that He would offer up all to seek it? What, after all, does a God need? He ponders these questions as the sun comes late into the sky. Too soon the sun sank; so began the second night.

What thoughts went through the God's mind when the sun failed to rise, though He knew the hours had long counted out a night.

After hours so many He'd lost the count, into the God's eyes there came a hint of red. He thought it was His brain, exhausted by the darkness, inventing color to fill the emptiness. But then the fat, red sun jumped above the world's edge — the night had ended. His bonds unraveled and the Tree released Him to fall to the ground.

In His mind He found the Runes shining from within, tumbling through all the knowledge He'd collected since the spheres were made. Had He always known them? Had they always existed? Had they been created just this day? He looks up; light frosts the Tree, drawing black fire from black feathers covering the ravens perched there.

Them He knew: Thought and Memory, Munin and Hugin. The power they brought Him overwhelmed Him — more even than the new-minted Runes they would empower Him.

THE MYTH OF ODIN[1]

THE BUTTERFLY OF THOUGHT
IS DISTURBED BY THE HARSH
STONE OF REASON

Analytical Thinking

We say that we are are a path of intuition and inspiration. Many of us feel
that using the disciplines of analytical thinking and logic conflicts with this
path. Let me be totally clear here: there is much about religion and belief
that is *not* the proper concern of analytical thinking or logic. However, this
fact does not preclude the wise use of analytical thinking with regard to
many aspects of our religion and lifestyle. Even in our society at large, the
education system places very little emphases on this form of wisdom.
Elementary and secondary schools normally tailor their curriculum to the
needs of business and the economic community in general. If analytical
thinking were taught, advertising firms would have to find some new techniques. This is not some obscure and powerful conspiracy; most people
expect the schools to prepare students for life in modern society. For the
most part, their primary failure in this regard is that they prepare tomorrow's
workers for today's marketplace.

Religious *truth* can never be proved — or disproved — by logic. On the
other hand, in addition to being possible, it's also very useful to subject
much of belief to intellectual analysis, as well as submitting it to our own
intuitive apperceptions. What you believe about the nature of deity and
why you have chosen to believe in it should have a logical structure even

though the foundation assumption, that god/desses do exist, must ultimately be accepted or rejected without recourse to logic.

Analytical thinking requires the submission of both facts and conclusions to an examination for accuracy, truth, and logical methodology. While it's perfectly possible to arrive at a true conclusion from false statements *combined* with fallacious logic, this is always the exception.

Forgive me for riding one of my most deeply felt hobbyhorses for a bit. Encouraged by the nightly news, we seem to have discarded almost any awareness of history. A news story saying that the stock market has hit its highest (or lowest) point since May 18 (which was last Wednesday) builds an impression that "history," as it affects modern society, is only worth consulting in the short term. A person with no knowledge of the early history of Islam cannot understand why one group of Middle Eastern terrorists can't, under any circumstance, be cooperating with a specific other group. Therefore, although the chasm of religious sectarianism between Suni and Shiite Muslims is considerably wider than the one between Roman Catholics and Southern Baptists, many people believe that Osama bin Laden probably receives support from Saddam Hussein.

Historical perspective means knowing about things that happened before one was born and remembering what people have said, whether it was six months, four years, one hundred years, or even one thousand years ago. The problems in Israel and Kosovo make a lot more sense if you have some knowledge of the history behind the nations involved. In Israel the damage was really done fifty years ago, but in Kosovo the problems date back over most of the last millennium!

You don't have to watch any particular evening newscast for many days before you hear a statement like "Heavy metal music blamed for gang unrest" (when I was a teen, it was comic books). Our society seems to love such facile and shallow analyses. If you can blame a problem on a single, easily identified cause, then it's very easy to make it appear as if some-thing's being done to correct it. My grandson's school, in line with other schools, has instituted a strict dress code, not to mention that many schools have metal detectors in the halls, police on duty, and the tendency to expel kids on the least excuse. All this just so that no grown-up is faced with the necessity of having to treat students like people. Many of the real experts say that what educators need to do is talk with the students and attempt to decrease bullying and teasing. But neither suggestion seems to be on the list of things our local schools are planning to do.

These situations show a society refusing to apply either analytical thinking or common sense to its problems. Actually, what's going on here is pretty close to what psychologists call *magical thinking*; that is, if you speak as if something isn't there, it won't be. Texas wants there to be truth in the idea that giving wrongdoers long, hard prison sentences reduces crime. The state continues to put thousands of people in prison though it's been totally apparent for years to anyone with sense that this approach *just isn't working*.

Why should you undertake a lot of study and internal work to change the way you read and listen? Well, the best reason is that you will be harder to fool, which is important because we are all citizens of a particular country and of the world. No matter how earnestly advertisers and politicians use tricks to make us believe things that haven't been proved, we can examine their statements and figure out just how much confidence we should place in them. The United Sates once elected a truthful man President; long before Jimmy Carter's four years were up almost everyone hated him. People don't want truth — they want to be comfortable and able to go on living in just the way they want.

I don't believe Witches can afford to believe practically everything folks tell us. As most of us who use the Internet know, hundreds of hoaxes circulate every year and not all of them stay only on the Net — some manage to find their way into newspapers. Of course, it's a bit ironic that our usual news sources — local newspapers and television news reports — are remarkable for their computer ignorance. I've seen and heard some of the least believable Internet virus hoaxes being repeated by these media. I cannot overemphasize the importance of being careful not only with our sources, but in finding confirmation in a second reputable source. It follows that we need always to evaluate carefully all books we read on Paganism, or on sociology or on history. We need to be adept at detecting errors of fact or logic in both print and in discussions, and we need to learn the most common ways that lack of logic is obscured or misused in an argument. We need to use these skills in all aspects of our lives.

I hear people complaining about the inaccuracies in some Pagan books but the reality is that even at university presses, books are not checked extensively for accuracy by the publisher. Until recently at least, no one employed by a university could afford to have a statement called into serious question but it doesn't seem to me that this is so true any longer. At least I myself have seen some highly doubt-able statements made in books. All book contracts have a section saying how any mistakes, misquotes, or accusations of plagiarism are the author's responsibility — the publisher cannot be blamed.

Advertising, of course, is the richest lode from which to mine logical absurdities. We are forever reading and hearing claims like "dentists recommend" a particular product. But how many dentists: two retired men on the toothpaste company payroll? a couple of dental school graduates doing internships for the company? Further questions might include: what's their training? how experienced are they? why are they recommending the product? what proof is there that they are right? The trick being pulled in this sort of commercial involves appealing to what appears to be an authority. By saying that "dentists recommend" its brand, a company hopes to create in your mind a picture of your own dentist telling you that it will make your teeth better. It also *implies* that a large number of dentists agree on this recommendation — but it doesn't *say* that. Listening to experts certainly can be a very good way of deciding between alternatives; however, it's necessary to know something about the experts in question in order to properly evaluate their recommendation.

Similarly, in many books about Witchcraft the author will footnote a statement of fact to, for instance, *The White Goddess* by Robert Graves.[2] Graves wrote this book in a short period, not as history, but as an exploration of his poetic muse. Graves was not a historian, he was a poet. His book, which has outlived his poetry it seems, is about poetic vision — it is not a scholarly examination of pre-Christian religion.[3] In fact, it's probable that the threefold goddess recognized by most Witches and Pagans was Graves's own invention, as it certainly isn't a feature of the pagan religions we commonly study.[4] Graves may well be correctly cited as a source for a mythology or a belief, but not for a historical fact.

One way in which misinformation can appear to be true is when an author cites only books published ten, twenty, or thirty years ago. Knowledge changes and grows. You're doing yourself a disservice if you don't check references, ensure that the book really does say what is claimed, and determine that the author is up-to-date and really does know what they are talking about. This does not mean you have to personally check every footnote; check any notes for which you have the source book handy and try to check notes that your intuition or general knowledge put into doubt. You can also discuss the book or author with a person that you know has some expertise. The current tendency for many books about the Craft to cite each other has placed many beginning Wicca volumes onto a merry-go-round of antiquated and sometimes incorrect information.

Appealing to an expert is the most usual way to support one's ideas and I do not want to suggest that there is anything wrong with it. However, not all scholarly sounding books are equal. It's important to evaluate each book you use. Ask yourself: when was it published? what are the copyright dates of the books cited? how radical a thesis does the author put forward? Keep an eye open for anything that may have been left out. Even the most particular of researchers has their own blind spot which can cause them to overlook pertinent material.

The most common way to refute a legitimate appeal to an expert is with a tactic called *poisoning the well*; that is, saying that the cited authority shouldn't be believed because they're a bad person, went to the wrong school, is male or female, or advocates a political party unpopular with the listener. Any of these things may be true but they don't necessarily mean that the authority is wrong in all cases. We see this tactic used pretty often by Pagans who suggest that it's wrong to accept the Aesir of the Northern European tribes because Hitler's SS is reported to have worshiped them.

An easy way to win an argument is to attack the speaker; never mind whether they're right or not, they're an idiot and nobody should listen to them! This sort of attack can take a hidden form in phrases like, "I'd be glad to explain further but you don't have the background" or "Oh, you wouldn't be interested in all that." Though these attacks are aimed at the speaker personally, they aren't direct. You can even find this patronizing attitude in books and on the lips of teachers. (Because Witchcraft is a mystery religion, we are stuck with having to tell our students, "Please just try it, you'll understand it later." This can sound patronizing to the student. Being sensitive to this situation can probably help, although it's a hot spot without good solution, as are the following questions: who is really Wiccan? how old is an "elder"? do you have to be initiated?)

Lauren Hutton says that she's been taking hormone therapy for ten years and her "hot flashes are a thing of the past." Well, ten years after menopause, *everyone's* hot flashes are gone, with or without hormone therapy. This is a situation where a fact is used to "prove" something for which the fact in question doesn't apply; if the statement itself is true, you usually don't consider whether or not it actually applies to the conclusion.

Informal logic examines the multitude of ways that people, through voice or print, can lead others to accept their ideas whether or not there are facts to back them up. There are hundreds, if not thousands, of different techniques identified and this doesn't seem to be the place to try to discuss them all. What I hope to do is to help you develop a way of thinking that will make you much harder to deceive and persuade.

No more than you can believe the headlines in *The Star* or *Enquirer* can you really afford to accept anything without checking it against your knowledge of the source and the general subject. But that's not the only way of investigating what people are saying and writing: you can begin by examining exactly what is said or written and how. Give new information some time to settle into your brain. I frequently find that what sounded great yesterday has developed holes and runs by today or tomorrow.

Deductive logic is the formal organized system of logic developed by Aristotle. It arranges two true statements into a formal pattern that, when used correctly, produce a true conclusion. Here's an example:

All cats are mammals.
Super Fuzz is a cat.
Therefore, Super Fuzz is a mammal.

In the example above, deductive logic produces a true and a valid conclusion. However, watch what happens with a very small change:

Some mammals are cats.
Super Fuzz is a cat.
Therefore . . .

We do not get a valid answer since our initial statement, "Some mammals are cats," does not say whether or not all cats are mammals. Arriving at a conclusion from these statements means that you have to guess, which is not something you do in formal logic. This formal arrangement of two statements followed by a conclusion is called a *syllogism*. If you combine all the possible combinations of *all*, *some*, and *no* statements that fit into this formal pattern, there are a possible 256 arrangements out of which exactly 16 can produce a valid conclusion. The first time one attempts to study formal logic it gives the appearance of being a very complicated and difficult concept. This is partly due to the fact that it is taught by substituting symbols for the specific words in the statements. This substitution actually makes it far easier to analyze the statements, just as reducing a written algebra problem to symbols is the necessary first step in solving the problem. I can't go into a full explication of this logical method in this book but I do recommend that you spend some time learning more about it.[5]

Words are magic and like all magic, they must be used with care. Not only is it important sometimes to check on the dictionary definition of a word, it is important to know that a lot of words have slippery meanings, which is extremely useful to those interested in pulling a fast one. The meaning of language can also be deliberately changed using careful word choice. For example, in saying *police action* for *war*, *sanitary engineer* for *garbage collector*, and *substandard housing* for *slums*, we change the picture in an individual's mind and, by so much, have changed reality. Linguist S. Morris Engel explains why it is crucial to understand how language works:

> To realize how people's use of language reveals them is to come to realize for the first time how exposed we all are. Because this has become more and more a world of words, and because a good deal of our life is now led in this more rarefied verbal atmosphere, we owe it to ourselves to learn everything we can about the subtle ways in which language operates. We cannot afford to let our own words betray us. Still less can we afford to let other people's words betray us.[6]

When used unconsciously, ambiguous words and even more, sentences with grammar that makes them ambiguous, can be very amusing. For example, the sign at a pharmacist's counter may send an unintended message: "We dispense with accuracy". This mistake in written form is rarely used to deliberately deceive. However, the mistaken impression that results from placing incorrect stress on a word or words sometimes *is* used as a tool of deception. Here's how it works:

Slow men
Working

definitely reads differently from

Slow
Men Working

The example above is called *amphiboly*, a term which refers to statements that can have more than one meaning. It may be caused by careless sentence structure, a need to use as few words as possible, an unclear pronoun reference, or the use of a pronoun without a reference. The sentence is clear to the speaker or writer, but it can be difficult for others to figure out the meaning.

On the Internet, where most communication is through the written word, one of the greatest difficulties in expression results from the lack of *tone of voice*. Since you can't hear the stress the other person gives to their words and can't hear if there's humor, irony, or sarcasm in that person's voice, misunderstandings easily occur. So simple a sentence as "I didn't do it" can be read in a number of ways depending on which word is stressed:

I didn't do it. (It wasn't me that did it, but Jack.)
I *didn't* do it. (I may have thought about doing it, I may have considered doing it, but in the end I chose not to do it.)
I didn't *do* it. (I may have talked Jack into doing it, but it wasn't I who did it.)

I didn't do *it*. (I may have done any number of other things, but I did not do this particular one.)

Lack of a clear indication of accent frequently makes humor in written communication dangerous (not that it can't be dangerous in spoken communication!). As a reader or listener, it's important to be sensitive to statements that strike you as shocking or maddening — they may simply have been intended as a joke. If the context doesn't clarify this question, ask. I've found it less stressful, all in all, to avoid humor in situations where it's difficult to clearly indicate that a joke is being made. The *Keep Wicca Traditional* Web site was created as a *joke*! However, every day there is someone who sees it and throws a fit.

A quote deprived of its context is frequently used to deceive. I once became the resident "Red" of a small community by commenting that "Democracy is the least efficient form of government known to man." Obviously this remark doesn't actually imply that I'm against democracy unless I've also said that I value efficiency in government above any other consideration — which, of course, I did not! In the context of the full conversation, my meaning should have been obvious. It wasn't.

Unfortunately, quoting out of context is common in books. Some authors will edit a quotation from some authority so it appears to support their thesis when, in fact, an examination of the full passage will show that it does no such thing. This is one reason why page numbers should accompany quotations and why an author should indicate where words have been left out of a quotation. Obviously every author selects quotations that support the idea they are attempting to convey — this is an entirely legitimate practice. There are many places in this book where I have quoted from another's work hoping to show you that what I am saying is supported by others. However, careful writers select only quotations that *legitimately* support their idea; they don't butcher material to create the *appearance* of support.

In the form of a *slogan*, mere words can develop enormous power. Take the word *country*, as in "my country." Technically, I suppose, it applies to the geography between some arbitrary lines on a globe. But when John F. Kennedy said, "Ask not what your country can do for you . . ." he obviously was talking about something other than landscape. In that context, *country* can be imagined as a composition of all its citizens; a humanization of a vague, abstract concept; and/or a representation of this particular bit of real estate's government which, of course, consists of a number of (mostly) men who hold the actual power to do things in the name of the United States. Unfortunately, once you've analyzed the word, the statement itself is pretty much rendered meaningless, a consequence that is the very essence of a slogan. Surely no one is going to tell me that the slogan "It's the Real Thing" actually has any meaning; however, for many years it's made good dividends for investors in the company that uses it. Slogans are very dangerous constructions and more than once many people have died because of them.

Attributing a real identity to a concept or allowing it to assume a quality that only a person can possess is called *hypostatization* and it's a very useful figure of speech. However, it can also be dangerous because we tend to forget that *country* isn't actually something one can love (which is not to say that one can't love a particular part of the countryside). Because we accept the practice of adding personality to ideas, we talk about abstracts like *family, country,* or *the Craft* as if they were things with an objective reality and with which we can interact. I'm not suggesting that it's wrong or bad to speak of, say, doing something "for the good of the Craft," but when we allow an abstraction to become real in our minds, we can lose our ability to think clearly about it and we can create unreasonable expectations about *family values* or *traditional Wicca*.

For all too many people, the word *family* conjures a picture of Beaver Cleaver's household rather than the actual — sometimes good, sometimes bad, sometimes two-parent, sometimes one-parent — families that exist in reality. When the idealized, generalized, and self-imagined family comes into our mind rather than our own actual families, we are allowing our perceptions to be manipulated. Through this same process, *environment* becomes untouched wilderness rather than "this place where I am" and *natural* comes to mean "untouched by human hands." By this definition, a Pagan using a computer would be participating in an *unnatural* act.

Actually, I think it's a good idea to explore this idea just a bit more. When we call Paganism a *nature religion,* just what do we mean? Do we mean that all Pagans should "go back to the land" and live in homes they build themselves with logs from their own land? Sure, some of us live way out in the country in houses we've built ourselves — I'm one of them. And there are some of us who manage to raise the majority of our own food. But I doubt that those of us who've survived the first few years living this kind of lifestyle feel it means we're better than other Pagans. It's true that many Pagans find it easier to commune with deity in "the great outdoors" but I've done it looking up Fifth Avenue in New York City — easier for me, perhaps, since I've spent the majority of my life living away from cities.

Can you be a good Pagan if you live in a city and earn your living with a computer? Considering that the two top occupations of Pagans are health care and computer related, it's obvious that most of us think so. (By the way, Pagans employed in health care are generally ICU nurses, not herbalists.) A friend recently did a search on the Internet and found the word *pagan* turned up 869,000 references and *wicca* 240,000. While these numbers do not indicate precisely the number of different Web sites, they still indicate a high level of interest in both creating and visiting Neopagan Web pages, which requires using a computer and phone lines. Unnatural? No more than an athame.

Obviously, few Pagans define *natural* in such a way that computers are considered unnatural. Even genetic manipulation cannot absolutely be defined as unnatural — it may well be unwise, but humans have "meddled" with genetics since the first dog adopted a human to help it hunt. In general, humans and the results of their imaginations and inventions are accepted by Pagans to be as natural as hybrid tea roses. It's very important, especially when insubstantials are the topic, to determine that everyone's definitions have enough in common so that they can actually be talking about the same thing. If a word catches your attention by its lack of "hard" definition, you should take the time to track its definition and even its origin. You will quite likely need to find another word to substitute for it.

"What's black and white and red [read] all over?" is a well-known (spoken) riddle and it demonstrates another trap in our language. The women's movement has frequently been belittled for being so picky about language. However, the ease by which the word *man* can be used to refer to all human beings and then shift to mean only *male* human beings really is of sufficient importance to make the question worthwhile. This fallacy, whereby an item subject to two or more interpretations is used to mislead, is called *equivocation*. It is the foundation of most puns, whether they are good or bad. Used with some subtlety, it allows politicians and others to put extremely dubious logic past us without our noticing. "If you believe in the miracles of science, why can't you believe in the miracles of the Bible?" sounds like a rational question, but it is not. Miracles of science aren't at all the same sort of thing as miracles of religion, which is a fact that for most of us is automatically defined by context.

The Amazing Randy gets paid tons of money to appear on television to "prove" that psychic powers, magic and such are fraudulent. He accomplishes this by duplicating the claimed result through trickery, which he explains. He then insists that we must believe all instances of psychic power are fraudulent since he is able to fake them. However, it's impossible to prove anything in this way: one occurrence of a particular phenomenon (or nonphenomenon) proves nothing about another single occurrence. Today when I woke up it was cloudy and shortly thereafter it began raining. So tomorrow it will be cloudy and will rain? That it rained this morning obviously doesn't actually tell me anything about what the weather will be like tomorrow in this part of the world. I *do* expect the sun to rise tomorrow morning; I have observed the phenomena of sunrise for over sixty-one years, during which time the sun has come up every morning without fail. I therefore feel justified in assuming that it will repeat this action tomorrow.

The opposite of the error described above — attempting to use a single or few instances to make generalization — is to take something that is true of the whole and apply it to all of its parts. That the vast majority of Witches particularly like the color purple is probably quite true but it does not mean that I, as an individual Witch, am required to prefer that color. That "everybody's doing it" in no way requires any specific individual to copy them. A group frequently has many qualities that are not possessed by each — or even any — of its individual members. Musicians who have not achieved enormous stature on their own may make up the best orchestra in the world, as an orchestra is more than just its players. An orchestra made up of the world's greatest soloists probably isn't going to become as great a group.

As I mentioned at the beginning of this section, words are magic and we must learn to use them correctly and with care. We're all familiar with the story of the apprentice mage who mispronounces or misuses one word in an incantation and conjures up something he didn't expect or want. As Pagans, we rarely work with "abracadabra" spells; however, our words — all our words — may become magical even when we aren't doing traditional spell-working.

The human ability to formulate abstract thought depends upon words. Generally, a child deprived of language for too long will never really develop the ability to handle abstract concepts. We should, therefore, use words carefully if we are to think truly. If, for example, we believe that *anger* and *rage* are exactly the same type and degree of emotion, then we will fail to give appropriate attention to an often dangerous emotional state. A man recently said to me that the word *bible* applies to the writings of many religions. I suspect that the liberty he takes with the word reflects his inability to appreciate that Christianity is merely one of a number of religions.

I use the example of this person who thinks either that all religions are Christian or that the three book religions all call their book the Bible because we have all dealt with someone who has this kind of language disability. Obviously the man I described above also misuses the word *religion*, confusing the abstract word referring to many spiritual paths with his own specific belief. In other words, if he believes in it, then it's a religion; if he doesn't believe in it, then it's not a religion.

It should be obvious that each individual's degree of honesty and accuracy in defining and using words can either open their mind or help it be closed, unimaginative, and fallow. Amazingly, updating our understanding of the words we use is one of the few easy ways we can expand our mental horizons. A very small, free application called Word Web puts a very fast, accurate, and thorough dictionary on your computer desktop.[7] It makes checking to be sure you really do know what a word means very quick and easy. It's those chases through the *Oxford Unabridged Dictionary of the English Language* (Compact Edition) that turn into real work![8]

In our world, words have been debased, torn from their context, and hidden behind smoke screens in order to sell us new ideas or products. We have cooperated in these deceptions by not treating words with the care and respect they deserve and by not seeking to hear truth rather than things that make us feel good. We tend to listen and read lazily and if we are told that X proves Y, we don't even think about it, much less question the underlying facts (or lack of them) or whether the words involved are being used correctly. Nor are we good at separating the emotional content of words from their use in a specific instance.

If I say "Don't manipulate," everyone is going to agree that I've given good advice. But in addition to "changing another's behavior by indirect means," *manipulate* has another meaning: "using the hand to move objects." If immediately before a ritual I told a priest/ess, "Don't manipulate the objects on the altar," I'd be making absolutely no sense at all. But I know of an instance when a group of students very nearly walked out on a teacher when he made a comment about how one would move and handle objects on an altar and used the word "manipulate." The students reacted emotionally to a word that has been designated "a bad thing" by a portion of our population. They didn't stop to realize that in no way was this usage related to what their teacher meant.

Many words carry this kind of emotional loading. Words have attitudes and evaluations built right in! The study of words along these lines is called *general semantics* and it can be quite fascinating. The old and supposedly protective rhyme our mothers taught most of us, "Sticks and stones will break my bones but words can never hurt me," happens to be dead wrong. Words can completely change us. Words like *backward, culturally deprived, half-breed* and others such as *clumsy* or *stupid* not only give others the impression that we are inadequate, they have a habit of gluing themselves to us so that we believe we embody their message. The moniker "old wives tales" covers a good many of the things we actually do believe in, so Neopagans are often aware of this problem. Any community that lets itself in for dealing with all the baggage accompanying the word *witch* has to be aware of the power of "mere words."

On the other hand, if you've always been told that you are attractive, you probably believe it and because you therefore act like an attractive person, in most cases people will perceive you as attractive! Beginning perhaps even with our names, words shape who we are. If you are "John Jr." you can just about bet that your family hoped you'd follow in your dad's footprints. If you're Jane, your mother probably hoped you'd be practical and dependable. I've never quite figured out the motive behind a mother's naming her daughter "Pebbles"!

Analogies, which compare one thing or event to another, are important to communication. However, we must check them out and make sure they are appropriate and really apply, and determine whether or not they are used as a way of proving a point. Analogies between emerging

Neopaganism and early Christianity may either be appropriate or inappropriate, depending upon exactly which facets of the two religious movements are being compared. Overall, the two religions are based in different things and thus they will produce many false analogies. The use of analogy in discussion probably should be avoided — even though apples and pears can be compared by analogy, you have to use different recipes to make jam out of each. Always sort out just how far an analogy can actually hold true before you accept it as a basis for belief.

Engel says that intelligence is "nothing more than the ability, which may be learned and which certainly can be greatly improved, to make distinctions — that is, to distinguish between things that seem similar and to discover the similarities in things that seem different."[9] If someone says to you that "the exception proves the rule," you'll probably accept that this statement has meaning without much thought, even though a closer look shows that the exception *attacks* the rule, if anything. However, a less frequently used meaning of the word *proof* relates to testing — like *proofing* yeast — and, indeed, the exception does *test* the rules.

When it comes to generalizations, there is the *rule* and the *specific case*. It's important first to establish whether or not the rule in question applies to the specific case and then to examine why the specific case may not, with good reason, conform to the rule. Our constitution says that "All men have the right to property," but it's important to realize that the word "all" may not apply in a specific case where, for instance, the man in question is unconscious or unable to function in society and is thus committed to an institution or is in some way separated from the majority of men through some individual peculiarity.

It's just as bad to take a specific but single case and from it make *rules* or *generalizations*. "I met a woman who makes no sense and doesn't seem very clear on what she believes. Although she calls herself Wiccan, she doesn't seem to know very much about the religion so I've decided that all Wiccans are uninformed." This kind of reasoning is common. Certainly there are people who call themselves Wiccans and have very little knowledge about the religion, just as there are people who call themselves Christians and appear to have no real knowledge about that religion. Neither case should be taken as *proof* about the religions themselves or the people who practice them.

When we come to complex situations like, say, deciding which political party and candidate can best serve our country, it is far too complicated to address all the facts that go into the formation of a valid generalization. If, say, most of the citizens of the United States believe that schools are failing to perform as well as they could, enumerating the general collection of facts upon which such an opinion may be based would far outstrip the attention span of even the most serious among us. Out of this enormous pile of facts, each candidate has to sort the few they wish us to feel are the most important. Additionally, each candidate will attempt to show us why the solution they recommend will have results that we, as individual parents, want for our children. As a result, our two hypothetical candidates will each present us with statements that show X and Y are wrong with the school, and therefore we must do Z. Even though the specifics in each candidate's statement are true, their selection and treatment of those facts will be quite different. And although their conclusions — that we, the voters, will be happy with the result — are the same, their methods of achieving that good result will probably be quite different.

So how do we as individuals find our way through this teeming rain forest of words that are all twined together and hanging off trees we can't see or identify? Back in the olden days when I was young, many people were convinced that the answers to complex, large questions should be easy: we should desegregate, stop discriminating against women, get out of the war in Vietnam. In the course of accomplishing many of these goals, we discovered that such questions tend to be a whole lot more complicated than was thought at the time. Sometimes I sit and watch television and wonder what has become of us. What happened to a million of us standing out in the rain singing "We Shall Overcome"? What happened to our energy, our commitment, our dreams? Turning off my emotional reaction to this question, I can observe that a part of why "we" aren't dreaming those dreams today is because we have learned: we have learned it's just not that easy. For instance, we discovered that there was a huge number of people locked up in "insane asylums" who, if they took one or two pills a day, could function more or less as ordinary folks. So we let them out and closed the asylums that had horrid living conditions, abusive "caregivers," and antediluvian ideas about treatment. The result? A large proportion of the homeless on our streets are those same improperly incarcerated mental patients who either can't get or won't take their medications, which don't necessarily work as well as we were told at the time and don't have side effects as "minor" as originally advertised.

The problem with civilization is that when it has problems, the problems are likely to be as complicated as the civilization itself. Worse, the solutions are generally even more complicated than the problems. Certainly there is nothing a politician can sell in a two-minute sound bite that will measurably improve any current problem you care to name. Unfortunately, the solution to civilization's problems seems to depend on individual action, not governmental decree. The actions of politicians and governments can have an affect on problems but anyone promising to *solve* this or that problem in four years without pain to us, ordinary citizens, either doesn't understand the situation or is lying. National politics aside, TANSTAAFL (there ain't no such thing as a free lunch) remains a good thought to keep right up front.[10] As far as advertising goes, if it *sounds* too good to be true, it probably *is* too good to be true!

Once a situation is oversimplified and facts about it are selected for discussion primarily because they support the position of the speaker or writer, we can only determine the usefulness of the idea or product by being reasonably well informed about the general subject and by effing *thinking* about what is being said and comparing it to what we know. As far as our society goes, laziness — that is, lack of thinking about things — and invariably picking the simplest sounding and least painful of available solutions has gotten us to where we are. Somehow, I think those same methods are unlikely to get us out of the mess.

An effective way of forcing people to accept your thesis is to persuade them that there are only two choices: yours and one that nobody in their right mind would choose. It's actually pretty rare that there are just two possibilities in any given situation but because humans like being lazy and think having only two choices is easier, we let people get away with this ploy. "I'd rather be Red than dead" was once a catchword along with its alternate, "I'd rather be dead than Red." In fact, there are plenty of other choices available and furthermore, the population of Reds sure has fallen lately without noticeably affecting the death rate.

Sometimes the two choices offered are merely alternatives — and quite frequently not the only alternatives. You can only choose one, dead or alive, but most of the choices we have to make fall in between these alternatives, are not contradictory, and may only be different in degree. In the above example, "Reds" includes just about every possibility to which the word *capitalism* can't be applied (economic theory is at the base of this question, not form of government — representational or otherwise). The world is not composed of heroes and villains, just people.

It's always necessary to examine the premise of an argument. First, is it true: do you personally know it to be true? does your general knowledge support the likelihood that it is true? do you have sufficient confidence in the individual making the argument or in the authority cited by this person to believe what they say is true? Further, did the authority cited actually say what the individual making the argument claims they did? Sort through complicated language to be sure of what is being said. What kinds of words are being used: words that are free from heavy emotional loading? words that make judgments? words that imply intelligent people agree? words that refer to great immaterial concepts? words that are open to more than one definition? Does the premise actually apply to and prove the conclusion, or is the conclusion merely a restatement of the premise? Be wary of conclusions like "The Bible proves that God exists because the Bible is the word of God."

The phrase "When did you stop beating your wife" is the well-known warning against answering a question before you think about it. If someone asks you why Witches like chocolate best, wouldn't it be worthwhile to first inquire as to whether or not they actually do? Any time you encounter a complex question, first separate out the parts, then consider whether or not there's any reason to provide an answer. We tend to allow ourselves to be stampeded by a question, as car salespeople know as they rush you toward closing the deal: "Shall I write up the convertible or the ATV?"

Like the rooster who believes that the sun can't come up unless he crows, we are continually being urged to believe in false causes. The Lauren Hutton commercial I mentioned earlier, which attempts to persuade women to use hormone therapy, says that 20 percent of all bone loss in women occurs after menopause. Well, menopause occurs in women who are roughly between the ages of forty-five and fifty-five — which is just over half their current life expectancy! Obviously a 20 percent bone loss after menopause is less critical a problem than the 80 percent of total bone loss we, by implication, experience *before* menopause![11] It also appears that menopause can't be the *cause* of bone loss as purported in the past. Of course, there's always the chance that the figure is incorrect.

It's common in current politics to blame welfare payments for a lot of crime, drug use, child abuse and so on. Even though there is absolutely no serious proof of a connection between the two, many people think eliminating welfare will solve the problems of crime and abuse. We've heard that guns cause murders and black raincoats make kids shoot up their high schools. Well, murders are caused by people who evidently think their life will be better without the existence of someone else and kids wear black raincoats because they are in style, because they are different — or just because. Neither the gun nor the raincoat actually *cause* anything.

There is one very useful fallacy I call "The Red Herring." It goes like this: "I refuse to ever have anything to do with Wiccans; they always seem to be fighting." This statement actually doesn't apply to the topic, as "fighting" isn't nearly so frequent as implied. But by bringing in an explosive and distracting outside issue, many useful discussions about the role of Wicca in our religious movement have been stopped. Also irrelevant is any accusation that people only want to be Wiccan in order to gain initiation or status in the community. Such a narrowly defined outcome isn't relevant to whether or not Wicca is a worthy path; every religion or denomination has those who either help or hinder it — there are contentious and pacifistic police officers, nurses, or computer repair people.

Well, I've got to confess that I'm getting bored with trying to write about all the ways that we can be deceived into thinking that someone has proved their point when in fact they've done nothing of the sort. There are many more things I could describe but perhaps I've made my basic point, which is that much of what you read and hear purports to prove an idea or theory, but consciously or unconsciously, it has included a fallacy that negates the proof. If I were really smart, I'd have made this the book's last chapter rather than the second — that way I'd know you wouldn't be reading my work with the advantage of having been informed about all the possible ways to deceive a reader!

There's a lot more to be learned about analytical thinking and the use and misuse of words and language. If you've found what I've presented useful, you may want to study more about it. At least I hope you will. I'm going to end this chapter with some general points that I taught my daughter and teach my students. I've also included a list of books and Web sites which can help you look further into this subject.

POINTS TO PONDER

- Not everything that you read (in a book, newspaper, magazine, or online) or hear is true.
- People do poor research.
- People mislead — and even lie — to prove their point or take your money.
- Our society doesn't easily recognize implied untruths.
- Some people seem to have trouble telling the difference between what is news and what is fiction. (This includes the people who create those made-for-television biography movies in which the name of the primary character is the only accurate thing.)
- The news — and even documentaries like the ones aired on the History and Discovery Channels — has time and space constraints. As a result, the peripheral information presented about a subject may be very badly distorted.
- Everyone has a point of view that affects the way they treat the available facts.
- If a statement conflicts with what you thought you knew, check it further.
- Do not attribute to conspiracy what can adequately be explained by stupidity.

BOOKS

Engel, S. Morris. *Fallacies and Pitfalls of Language: The Language Trap*. Mineola: Dover Publications, Inc., 1994. Excellent coverage of the ways language itself is used to deceive.

Hayakawa, S. I. and A.R. Hayakawa. *Language and Thought in Action*, 5th ed. New York: Harcourt Brace & Company, 1990. I give this book my very highest recommendation. It's well-written, occasionally amusing, and the information is crucial to becoming aware of the misuse of language.

Infante, Dominic A. *Arguing Constructively*. Prospect Heights: Waveland Press, 1998. There is a difference between *discussion, argument, confrontation,* and *fight*. Only the latter should be avoided at all costs.

WEB SITES

The Atheism Web: Logic and Fallacies. www.infidels.org/news/atheism/logic.html. A discussion of logic, particularly as it may be properly applied to religious questions.

Conversational Cheap Shots. www.vandruff.com/art_converse.html. A real-world examination of fallacies.

The Nizkor Project. www.veritas.nizkor.org/features/fallacies/. An alphabetical list of fallacies and some links to other sites.

The Philosophy Pages Links to Logic. www.philosophypages.com/lg/. A lot of links to sites concerned with logical analyses.

Stephen's Guide to the Logical Fallacies. www.intrepidsoftware/fallacy/welcome.htm. An excellent discussion of logic by a professor at the University of Alberta.

NOTES

[1] This is my retelling. It contains some inaccuracies compared to the traditional myths (i.e., most say that Odin spent nine days on the tree) and is influenced by fictional treatments, primarily *The Fionavar Trilogy* by Guy Gavriel Kay (*The Summer Tree* [New York: Arbor House, 1984]; *The Wandering Fire* [New York: Arbor House, 1986]; and *The Darkest Road* [New York: Arbor House, 1986]).

[2] Robert Graves, *The White Goddess* (1947; reprint, New York: Farrar, Straus and Giroux, 1948).

[3] Ronald Hutton, *The Triumph of the Moon* (Oxford: Oxford University Press, 2000), 188.

[4] The Norns, Furies, and Graces were triads but were not major deity figures. Nor were they commonly divided into "maiden, mother, crone" aspects at that time.

[5] Those interested in exploring logic further are encouraged to visit the Web site www.deepeningwitchcraft.com where you will find more information on informal and deductive logic and links to other sites.

[6] S. Morris Engel, *Fallacies and Pitfalls of Language: The Language Trap* (Mineola: Dover Publications, Inc., 1994), 7.

[7] www.wordweb.co.uk/.

[8] The two-volume Compact Edition contains all the information in the twenty-six-volume edition; it's printed with four pages from the full-size edition on each page, in a type size of about minus 2-point.

[9] Engel, *Fallacies and Pitfalls*, 71.

[10] The phrase and acronym coined by Robert Heinlein, sci-fi writer, is found in a number of his books.

[11] In tiny print at the bottom of the screen is a note that this 20 percent bone loss occurs in the first five or six years after menopause. How many people are going to — or are able to — read this?

CHAPTER THREE

Mythology: *the body of a primitive people's beliefs, concerning its origin, early history, heroes, deities and so forth, as distinguished from the true accounts which it invents later.*

AMBROSE BIERCE

IN DAYS OF OLD, WHEN KNIGHTHOOD WAS IN FLOWER

History: Creation to Reformation

The myth told about the sources of modern Witchcraft and the ancient paganism from which it grew is a very attractive one. With it, we participate in the rituals at Niniveh and Tyre, Babylon and Thebes as we walk into our own Circles. Our bonfires on the hilltops resonate with history as our mind's eye sees kings and peasants from long ago gathered there with us. While this picture is not one of scientific reality, there's an underlying truth that need not be discarded because of the findings of modern researchers.

I do not personally know of more than a couple of religions that have a totally, objectively verifiable history. Certainly neither Judaism nor Christianity are among them. While we could argue about this, any exceptions do not disprove the following statement: The *history* — scientifically verifiable or not — of a religion has nothing to do with the *truth* of that religion. As I said in the chapter on analytical thinking, it is inappropriate to apply logic to most matters of faith.

Why, then, am I devoting a lot of space to a discussion of the history and myths of the Witches? Because many of us have had to deal with individuals who attempt to exploit the questionable historicity of the myth as a method of proving that Witchcraft (and/or Paganism) is a false religion. Knowing the best approximation of not only our history's truth, but why Gerald Gardner and other early writers probably believed what they wrote to be true, is important for our skills as spokespersons and for our ability to provide a really good education to our students. Witchcraft, because it is the largest subgroup of Neopaganism, is frequently the focus of discussions with representatives of the majority society. Attacks against the Craft may have an effect on all Neopagan paths, making it important that we all be able to answer charges made against it.

It seems strange to me, but a general interest in history is actually pretty recent. A nineteenth-century German philosopher named Georg Wilhelm Hegel is given credit for making history a legitimate study for philosophers, politicians, and other "thinkers" and later, part of the school curriculum.[1] Hegel had some (to us) rather odd views of what history is: he felt the key to history is the notion that we are all part of some grand design, that the processes of history follow some rule and logic and are aimed at the goal of an *Absolute Ideal*.[2]

This idea that history is some sort of sacred machine leading humankind to something better (with or without a deity's involvement) has been of great comfort to many individuals and is part of the basic philosophy of some political systems functioning today. My only reason for bringing it up, however, is to say that one must guard against accepting versions of history written under the sway of this idea as being somehow more correct than other histories. The implications of the "deification through progress" school of thought include believing that the *state* is more important than the *individual* and that the end justifies whatever the means may be.

The disciplines of history, archeology, cultural anthropology, and sociology are practiced by individuals who each have a worldview, a philosophy of life and deity, and an idea of what the past does or should mean. When it comes to religion, these individuals are usually venturing outside their areas of expertise. I've found little to admire in the work of cultural anthropologists and a great deal of sociological work is done with extensive agendas that are not necessarily openly acknowledged to the reader. Additionally, there tends to be a number of contradictory philosophies dominating the ways in which individuals connected with a college and university may acceptably approach writing within these disciplines. These worldviews and philosophies, both personal and institutional, change with time. In 1850, a time when much of the work on history and on the lives, beliefs, and activities of persons living in the distant past was being done, there were several highly contradictory attitudes toward the past. I'll discuss these in somewhat more detail in the next chapter. My point here is that, at the time, there was no absolute way of knowing if one attitude was more correct than the others. From our view at the turn of the millennium, all of them strike us as being less than optimal. In twenty years, the future will judge us and I doubt its verdict will be any kinder.

Fairly early in my own study of Paganism I decided that archeologists, when presented with an object whose utility they couldn't easily guess, threw it into a box marked "Religious Items" and forgot about it. A very amusing book, *Motel of the Mysteries*,[3] recounts a (fictional) dig that uncovered a 1960s chain motel complete with a temple filled with porcelain votive.

Quite possibly the most toxic and longest-lived result of this tendency to make unfounded assumptions is that an arrogant, smugly self-satisfied filter can fall across the eyes of even the most modern researcher. While all humans must see the "Other" through the filter of their own socialization, the conviction of most Westerners remains that the ways of the West are superior to any others. Ronald Hutton admits that he came under social and academic pressure because of his sympathetic treatment of Pagans.[4] All of these considerations make it necessary that we approach everything we read about paganism, ancient or modern, with an attempt at understanding the prejudices held by the author(s) and any constraints which may have been placed on them.

Much of what was written about both ancient and living Pagan religions during the eighteenth century was actually disguised criticism of Christianity and all religion. These atheist authors, prevented from publishing their opposition to all religion openly for fear of prosecution, wrote about how horrible pagan religion was with the hope that readers would make the jump and realize that Christianity was open to the same sorts of criticisms. These writers had decided that religion was either the product of brutish, ignorant, and primitive savages or the result of psychological disturbance. Either way, it was no proper practice for an intelligent person. These texts were, in fact, propaganda pieces written by individuals who'd probably never personally laid eyes on a real pagan.[5]

The myths about Witchcraft's history may have begun with Margaret Murray's writings about the witch cult in Europe and Charles Leland's *Aradia*, although there are some hints of an earlier genesis. The basic outline of this myth says that the beliefs and practices of Witchcraft have been handed down, essentially unchanged from mother to daughter, since before Christianity:

> According to our legends, Witchcraft began more than 35 thousand years ago, when the temperature of Europe began to drop and the great sheets of ice crept slowly south in their last advance.[6]

Attacks, some of them by other Witches, are really just so much noise. Many appear to simply be looking for any excuse to criticize Pagans. Gardner, Doreen Valiente, and others who wrote in the 1950s and 1960s were dependent on the sources and philosophies of history current at that time; a time when historical research painted a very different picture from the one we presently see. Their conclusions, accepted and supported then, now seem fallacious. Paganism, while one of the newest of new religions, has strong ties to the oldest of the old religions. However, the truth is that both the attackers and the defenders tend to be pretty careless with their sources and highly selective of what and whom they quote. I, too, have made careful selections of what and whom I quote, but at least I support a conclusion of "not proven yet." The myth about Witchcraft's history, in all its various forms, affirms our feeling of connection with the ancients, with the river that is human life and history. Perhaps it is self-deception to sit at our computer keyboards and experience a feeling of oneness with humans who sat on the ground and chipped flint. But science tells us that within our skulls, we are essentially unchanged from those innovative toolmakers who, by chipping a cutting edge out of stone, took control of their environment for the first time. To me, the athame is the symbol of that event — when we first began to act upon our surroundings instead of being acted upon by them.

In our imaginations, we move with the panorama of history: we ride with the eastern marauders, fight with the Greek armies, light the hearth-fires of Rome, paint ourselves blue to the terror of the civilized lands. Are we therefore romantics? Why isn't it socially acceptable to be a romantic? Perhaps the fact that romantics are less likely to see progress as the ultimate goal for human effort has something to do with the disdain usually exhibited when the word is pronounced. Without at all betraying my enjoyment of all our modern miracles like computers, I don't necessarily feel that progress has generally increased our happiness or has bettered human life on the spiritual level.

While ease of travel, lightning-fast communication, and all the other things we enjoy have made some aspects of our lives *better*, we probably don't often enough think on the things we've given up. Of course, if you buy into the attitude that a less civilized life is "the life of man solitary, poor, nasty, brutish, and short" (v. Thomas Hobbes), you'll consider any identification with earlier times as foolish and irrational. Nonetheless, there's good reason to believe that many people have led happy, satisfying lives under a great variety of conditions and I've yet to force myself to believe that civilization has increased our happiness overall. However, a complete revision of the Western European picture of primitive man is required before you can agree with my statement. So much of today's human lifestyle consists of things only. Much of the Western world's nineteenth-century philosophy was consumed with self-satisfaction and propagandized the idea that civilization, specifically the national lifestyle of the author, was the epitome of human accomplishment and all examinations of other lifestyles were presented in such a way to prove that point.

Into the twenty-first century, our attitudes toward *primitive, savage,* and *native* times and peoples are still colored by these long-outdated and never-accurate ideas. But the lifestyle of a hunter-gather during good times offers many improvements upon our own. For example, the workday was much shorter and less effortful than ours, certainly allowing for more personal time than any of us have ever seen. The richness of some of these people is obvious when you realize that they had the time and vision to create something like Stonehenge! (Evidently the Pyramids were not built by downtrodden slaves; there are graffiti hidden on blocks of stone bragging that team whatsis beat out all others, showing a "football team spirit" was felt by the workers.) As for all that adventurous, hairy-chested mammoth hunting, a recent report on digs at Paleolithic kitchen middens indicates that most of those mammoth steaks were actually rabbit stew.7 While stress is undoubtedly a cost of our peculiar human intellect, the degree of stress in the modern, civilized lifestyle is so high that it is *our* survival which is fantastic, not the survival of the naked savage.

*In the beginning were hunting and gathering, craftsmanship and children. The People found magic to aid the chase and to ease birth. And the family valued those who made the magic as they valued those who made the arrowheads and those who bore children. And the earth was populated with spirits as it was becoming populated with the People.*8

It seems to me that there's practically an instinct in humans to seek a divinity. Whether we need god/desses to explain why the rains come or why are we here (or to offer us some means to control these questions), we show a consistent need or desire for such a presence. Or perhaps the instinct is based in genetic memories of when we could see the god/desses and converse with them. Most current research seems to agree that both sorcery and some type of religious concept rose early in the history of humankind and that perceived deities tended to be connected with the life events individuals could not control.9 It has been said that a large percentage of all prayer is the plea that two and two not equal four — I suspect this has been true over time. Although there are a considerable number of thinkers who see all religions as essentially anti-intellectual and an impediment to progress, recent work by sociologists indicates that religious choices are made rationally and almost entirely by sane individuals.10

And the gatherers learned to leave the seeds of the plants in the places where they had gathered them as the mothers discovered the fathers and the spirits revealed the gods. And the goddess grew the crops and blessed the babies and the god ruled the hunt and made the arrows fly straight.

We don't really have much knowledge about beliefs and practices in the earliest prehistory.11 Things we once thought we knew were, to a great extent, drawn from early anthropological studies of isolated tribes done in the first half of the twentieth century and both their approaches and conclusions are now viewed with many reservations:

> For the truth is that Durkheim and the other early social scientists mentioned thus far were not really all that interested in primitive religion. Their real agenda was to link all religion to primitive irrationality and thus to bring contemporary religion into intellectual disrepute.12

Today's scholars place less trust in the accuracy of these earlier observations and acknowledge that for the most part, they just really don't know. There is so great a variety of belief and practice by isolated peoples around the world that few generalizations are possible. Applying anthropologists' descriptions of select existing (or until recently existing) tribes to people and groups of the past may give us valuable insights, but such a process cannot be confused with fact. This leaves us with very little we may assume to know about practices in any other time or place.

The gods became numinous[13] and numerous: gods of mountains and thunder; gods of sunlight and moonshine; gods of the hunt, and of husbandry and war.

Because Greek and Latin were essentially the first archaic pagan languages known to modern historians (Hebrew, Aramaic, etc., are from nonpagan cultures), we get an incorrect impression about the nature of pre-Christian deities because they were filtered through the attitudes, beliefs, and prejudices of the particular Greek or Roman doing the writing — not to mention the attitudes, beliefs, and prejudices of the Christian translators. A statement like "Curnunnos is Mercury [or Pan]" shows that it's possible to generalize about deity figure and in so doing, the real-time worshiper's perception of that deity is severely distorted. In fact, although most historians writing earlier in this century considered the Greeks the first *civilized* culture, Edith Hamilton makes the observation:

> Of course the Greeks too had their roots in the primeval slime. Of course they too once lived a savage life, ugly and brutal. But what the myths show is how high they had risen above the ancient filth and fierceness by the time we have any knowledge of them.[14]

We continue to see this prejudice today and it tends to color what is written about any other society or religion. On the other hand, if the translations are at all valid, the Greeks' deities show some signs of comprising a seriously dysfunctional family.

With them and before them came goddesses of childbirth and motherhood, of adolescent courage and caretakers of the dead; goddesses of wind and water, air and fire, sea and land.

The fight for the Equal Rights Amendment and the women's movement in general have sparked a good deal of reexamination of history as related by (usually) male historians. One of the most damaging myths popularized during this time was that of the *ancient matriarchy*. Obviously every society must have gone through a matrilineal stage, as there are intrinsic problems when lineage depends on the father.

While all of Europe and the Mediterranean countries could have figured lineage through the mother and since all — like any other group that wishes to survive — were required to devote a sufficient portion of the culture's resources to ensure the survival of mothers and their children, we are able to identify very few ruling queens and so far we have failed to discover any hard historical evidence for prolonged feminine (i.e., matriarchal) rule.

Throughout the lands there was the image of the Great Goddess, Mother of All: fecund, loving, wrathful against those who deserved Her ire.

There is some archeological evidence, in the form of thirty-five clay or stone female figures found from the Pyrenees to Siberia dated between 25,000 and 23,000 B.C.E., to allow theorizing that there could have been a cult of a Great Mother Goddess.[15] Of course, these figures might simply be pregnancy charms that were used superstitiously by ordinary people who weren't particularly religious, or children's Barbie dolls. We tend not to think of commerce as being widespread in prehistoric times, but it was.

Archeologists called this type of figure a *Venus* long before any theory that it had religious significance was propounded. This probably prejudiced us all to believe that these figures were indeed religious artifacts and until the 1970s, virtually everyone just accepted that they showed a widespread worship of some sort of Earth Mother. Actually, we didn't merely accept it, we got pretty enthusiastic about it. Interpreting many things in terms of the Great Goddess — including dots that *might* be nipples (or eyes) and spirals, triangles, and paired wavy lines that *might* be a woman's hips (or possibly a map of the local trout stream) — is all very well, but it doesn't prove the existence of widespread worship of a particular Great Goddess. However, a certain amount of evidence does support this idea.

The People worshiped and celebrated on the hills and in the deep caves of the earth with offerings and sacrifice, balefires and dancing in the night. The gods brought the good times and the bad; in the good times we gave thanks to them and in the bad times we offered them things precious to us so they might know that we valued them and that we asked them to fix things.

Most of us are aware that the deity of the peoples of Judea (now called Jews) was the deity of a single, tribal culture and wasn't interested in becoming the only god of the whole fertile crescent, much less the world. He was specifically the God of the Jews. In fact, the gods of other ethnic and/or tribal groups were also ethnically, tribally, and geographically centered deities. However, just as similar niches in nature hold similar animals, people in similar lifestyles have similar needs and look toward similar gods. When one group extended its secular reach or rule, the recognition of its deities might have become spread over a wider area. Nonetheless, most ancient god/desses were perceived to rule over a specific people and location. When someone moved to a new land, they frequently adopted the god/desses of their new home.

In time, the peacefulness of the land and the life of the People were broken as the barbarians came from the North bearing their bitter weapons, new gods, and new ways.

It's difficult to figure out just which barbarians are being singled out in this portion of the myth. Athenians saw Alexander (later "the Great") as an "invader from the North." Then there were the Indo-Europeans or Celts — the folks who attacked while naked and scared even the legionaries of Rome! At any rate, according to the myth some nasties came down out of the north and messed up all the lovely mother stuff that had been going on.

Women were no longer valued for themselves, but only for the sons they might bear. Men were valued for their strength in battle, in the fields, and in forges and mines, and there were other men who ruled over all.

There isn't much evidence that the position of women was any worse under the invaders than it was in Greece and Rome. While there is still some discussion about the precise status of women in both of these places and a lot of questions about the status of women in the invaders' (whoever they were) culture, the fact remains that it sure wasn't anything resembling equality. Not to mention that kings and emperors and pharaohs had been around for quite a while.

Always, though, in quiet and secrecy, the old times were remembered — the old ways in which people and their gods joined together to help the seeds to sprout and the harvest to be fair and the deer of the forest to fall to the hunters' arrows. These ways were protected and practiced by those few chosen to preserve this knowledge. And through good times and bad, as the religions of the People changed for good or ill, the chosen few remembered . . . remembered.

I spent my childhood in the Appalachians back in the dark ages before television and the standardization of most of the United States. I can testify personally that numerous bits of the things practiced through the 1950s had been handed down in families for at least a couple hundred years.[16] Because I know that knowledge passed down orally can persist over many years, I don't find it difficult to believe that some information may have been kept in England, Italy, or other parts of Europe. We've let many of the people who could clarify these matters die on us before we asked the right questions.

What we do know is that other sorts of information have been preserved in this way — herbalism, most clearly. However, there is no reason to believe that any of this knowledge was the least bit static. Herding and hunting had (and continue to have) their own collections of lore, from doctoring a horse's feet to calling a deer to your bowsights. The knowledge frequently bordered on sorcery — that is, magic — whether or not the sorcery in question might once have been part of religious magic.

What probably didn't survive are details about elaborate group rituals of worship or magic. Like stones in a swift-running creek, over time things get worn down and round-edged, with all the softer parts removed. What survived were the things which seemed immediately useful in a world with a cosmology that had shrunk to hold no more than a single deity. Even during the witchcraft persecutions, when witches were called the followers of Diana, they were accused of worshiping the Devil — the mirror image of the Christian God — because there was no room in people's minds for another deity and certainly no room to even consider the possibility of a female one.

On the other hand, Hutton appears to dismisses J.G. Frazer's *The Golden Bough* completely and evidently expects us to believe that all the seasonal country celebrations were begun no earlier than the Middle Ages, although he offers us neither actual proof of this nor any alternative explanation. That the celebrations might be holdovers from much earlier actions taken to ensure the fertility of crops and herds and to rejoice when this was the case is a possibility he seems to dismiss, although this dismissal is slightly modified (as you'll read later). It seems to me that if England and/or Europe were fully Christianized, they'd have the priests out there flinging holy water around. Fertility of the fields and flocks is obviously a concern into which a community's religion must be brought; certainly prayers for rain are not unknown in farming areas today. (The fact that a Christian priest or minister might go to the fields and pray for rain, by the way, doesn't make

Christianity a *fertility religion*, nor do Neopagan seasonal rites limit those religions to such a designation.)

I have personally met a number of Witches who claim to have received information through family tradition and I have to say that I do believe many of their stories. I've recently inquired of a large number of people and am even more convinced that some family-based practices of magic and/or ritual existed before Gardner published *Witchcraft Today* in 1956. However, that's a subject for another book and I am *not* contending that these practices necessarily date back to ancient times.

Later, the white god of the vengeful mountains and his dead son overpowered all the religions that had swept across the fields and forests. Black-clad priests brought their solitary deity to every hamlet and village. Still those few preserved the knowledge of the old religions.

Once Constantine selected Christianity, not only as his own religion but as the only state religion, the old patterns began — but only began — to change. General change was very slow because Constantine evidently decided that converting just the local rulers would be sufficient. Therefore, although it's claimed that England was converted to Christianity by the fourth or fifth century, the Romans actually had only managed to get the kings to say they had converted. Conversion of people below the level of the kings and their courts lagged a long time behind. Indeed, until the Reformation, very little was done to convert people outside the towns and the conversion of Europe has never been completed:

As for the ordinary people, during the Middle Ages and the Renaissance, they rarely heard mass *anywhere*, most entering a church only for weddings, funerals, and christenings (if then), and their private worship was directed toward an array of spirits and supernatural agencies, only some of them recognizably Christian.[17] (Stark and Finke's emphasis)

Very few authorities deny that one of the techniques used in this conversion effort was to absorb the local pagan practices and/or holidays into the rituals of the new religion. However, it's pretty clear from contemporary writings that many of the so-called common people weren't particularly enthusiastic about the Church. Over and over we've seen quotations from letters written by bishops of the Church directing the clergy to stop people from holding markets in the sanctuary, dancing in the churchyard, and participating in other possibly innocent amusements.

Even when the full power of the Church was brought against them in the tortures and burnings of the Inquisition, still they remembered and preserved and passed down to the future — mother to daughter and father to son. Despite the dying, knowledge lived on; the smoke of their fires raised a stench to choke that heaven the priests spoke of, yet there were those who did not die.

In defense of earlier Witchcraft writers, the figure of six to nine million victims they quote when they get to the period in history we call "The Burning Times" wasn't theirs. Nor were they the first to assume that there really were groups of "witches" meeting in the woods, generally doing things the Church wouldn't have approved. This information had already appeared in print in what were, in some cases, supposedly scholarly sources.

It was in an atmosphere of social chaos that the Church created the Inquisition to control — at first — heresy. However, in the spirit of most bureaucratic entities, when heretics ran short or were too powerful to attack, other enemies were found or created. We don't have room to go deeply into this subject and my point is that, whatever the inquisitors claimed and whatever their victims confessed to, very few of the persecuted were in any sense "witches," nor were they practitioners of a pagan religion or worshipers of the Devil. There is no reason to assume any link, other than the use of the word *witch*, between the imagination-based covens of the Inquisition and modern Witches. Jeffrey Russell concludes that it's very doubtful that any such groups existed. He theorizes that "the witch-craze was one particular form of a flaw in human nature, the desire of human beings to project evil on others, define them as outsiders, and then punish them horribly."[18]

A new book on the origins of Wicca[19] (more widely, the background of the pre-Christian religions of Europe and the Mediterranean) examines the extensive prehistoric civilization of the Indus valley and puts forth a persuasive argument that this was the basic starting point of almost all European religious development. The first half of this book in particular raises a lot of very interesting questions about what's been previously accepted about European history. But this isn't the time or place to discuss these questions, and I don't have the depth of knowledge required to explore them much further. I'd just like to suggest that we all attempt to maintain open and curious minds about the subject and continue our reading.

POINTS TO PONDER

- History is rewritten every ten or twenty years, making everything you thought you knew suddenly wrong. In order to obtain some knowledge that is as close to truth as possible, the worldview and philosophical persuasion of a book's author, as well as the establishment's prejudices *at the time of writing*, must be considered by the careful reader. Historians all have their own preconceptions and axes to grind and their treatment of the source material, selection, emphasis, and interpretation will tend to promote those prejudices.

- Thirty or forty years ago, we knew a whole lot more about prehistoric Europe than we do now. Today most historians, archeologists, social anthropologists, and sociologists will have a lot less to say about what objects were used for and what sort of rituals took place inside the temple structure — they're even less sure the structure in question was in fact a temple. In other activities many of us have found that figuring out exactly what we *didn't* know was the beginning of real progress. We can only hope that this will turn out to be true of history.

- Deities originally were local and specific to a tribe, clan or other ethnic group, and piece of geography.

- Deities that do similar jobs or represent similar ideas or natural forces or features (e.g., water, mountains, death, the moon) tend to resemble each other.

- If it in fact existed, ancient matriarchy was not widespread. Worldwide, division of labor between the sexes followed no logic whatsoever.

- Worship of the Great Goddess may have existed, but probably for a relatively short time.

- The Witch Hunts didn't have anything to do with pre-Christian religion or with the practices of any normal human beings. Nor does the word *witch*, as used by the inquisitors, have anything to do with modern Witches and Wiccans.

- Most grandmothers are just grandmothers (and new grandmothers are generally between the ages of 35 and 40, *not* 60 and 100 as is usually depicted in the media).

- The rituals of modern Neopagans, while they may reflect the inner spirit of ancient pagan religions, rarely reproduce any actual practices of those religions.

NOTES

[1] S. Morris Engel, *Fallacies and Pitfalls of Language: The Language Trap* (Mineola: Dover Publications, Inc., 1994), 33–4.

[2] Ibid., 33.

[3] David Macaulay, *Motel of the Mysteries* (Boston: Houghton Mifflin Company, 1979).

[4] Ronald Hutton, *The Triumph of the Moon* (Oxford: Oxford University Press, 2000), xii.

[5] Rodney Stark and Roger Finke, *Acts of Faith: Explaining the Human Side of Religion* (Berkeley: University of California Press, 2000), 4–5.

[6] Starhawk, *The Spiral Dance: A Rebirth of the Ancient Religion of the Great Goddess*, (New York: Harper & Row, 1979), 3.

[7] Discovery Channel, June 2001.

[8] All passages appearing in italic like this one are my own retelling of the myth of Witchcraft.

[9] Jeffrey Russell, *A History of Witchcraft: Sorcerers, Heretics and Pagans* (London: Thames & Hudson Ltd., 1980), 18.

[10] Roger Finke and Rodney Stark, *The Churching of America, 1776–1990: Winners and Losers in Our Religious Economy* (New Brunswick: Rutgers University Press, 1992), 252 and Stark and Finke, *Acts of Faith*, 85–6.

[11] See Ronald Hutton, *The Pagan Religions of the Ancient British Isles: Their Nature and Legacy* (Oxford: Blackwell Publishers Inc., 2000).

[12] Stark and Finke, *Acts of Faith*, 7.

[13] The word *numinous* refers to the perception that some beings and concepts are essentially lighted from within. The haloes on pictures of Catholic saints are a depiction of this quality.

[14] Edith Hamilton, *Mythology* (New York: Mentor Books, 1940), 14.

[15] Hutton, *The Triumph of the Moon*, 278–82.

[16] See the records of the Council of the Southern Mountains, found in the archives at Berea College in Kentucky (www.berea.edu/ApCenter/Default.html). Alternately, look through some of the Foxfire Books.

[17] Stark and Finke, *Acts of Faith*, 63.
[18] Russell, *A History of Witchcraft*, 172.
[19] Ann Moura, *Origins of Modern Witchcraft: The Evolution of a World Religion* (St. Paul: Llewellyn Publications, 2000).

CHAPTER FOUR

In the north-east of Scotland the Beltane fires were still kindled in the latter half of the eighteenth century; the herdsmen of several farms used to gather dry wood, kindle it, and dance three times "southways" about the burning pile. But in this region, according to a later authority, the Beltane fires were lit not on the first but on the second of May, Old Style. They were called bone-fires. The people believed that on that evening and night the witches were abroad and busy casting spells on cattle and stealing cows' milk. To counteract their machinations, pieces of rowan-tree and woodbine, but especially of rowan-tree, were placed over the doors of the cow-houses, and fires were kindled by every farmer and cottar. Old thatch, straw, furze, or broom was piled in a heap and set on fire a little after sunset. While some of the bystanders kept tossing the blazing mass, others hoisted portions of it on pitchforks or poles and ran hither and thither, holding them as high as they could. Meantime the young people danced

round the fire or ran through the smoke shouting, "Fire! blaze and burn the witches; fire! fire! burn the witches." In some districts a large round cake of oat or barley meal was rolled through the ashes. When all the fuel was consumed, the people scattered the ashes far and wide, and till the night grew quite dark they continued to run through them, crying, "Fire! burn the witches."

J.G. FRAZER[1]

DANCING ON THE HILLTOPS

History: Reformation to Gardner

The Middle Ages ended with the emergence of a free middle class of merchants and craftsmen strongly connected with the growth of towns and with the Church's loss of its monopoly on the teaching of literacy. The Renaissance reminded people that they could actually think for themselves and the Reformation was one of the results. The changes it brought affected ordinary life as dramatically as changes in the twentieth century, although the process moved a bit more slowly.

Even into the age when the god of science possessed the lands and belief was centered on that cold spirit and on the dead son on the tree, in the hidden places still they came to dance beneath the moon and remember the gods of times old beyond imagining.[2]

To simplify a complicated social system, the medieval pattern of life centered on the castle and its ruler. In addition to owning and ruling all the land, the king was also judge and jury. Each castle was essentially self-sufficient with its own blacksmith and other craftsmen as well as its own food production, storage, and distribution systems. To each castle was attached its own clergy and church organization. The Church owed its ultimate loyalty to Rome; the castle's loyalty lay with the king. While the division of authority and services between church and castellan was from time to time a matter of debate (if not conflict), between them they did hold all the power, bureaucracy, land, and knowledge. The people who did all the shit-work were all, in one way or another, permanently connected to the land, the castle or the church. People stayed, even when conditions were bad, because there was no place to go — except into the woods to be outlaws who could be killed on sight.

The Crusades had reminded the rulers of Western Europe that they didn't actually comprise the entire world. As travel and (ultimately) exploration increased, the Reformation opened peoples' minds to the concept of knowledge beyond what the priests taught, and people like Newton and Dr. Dee studied gravity, gunpowder, and magic.

All these factors combined to change everyone's worldview tremendously. Because more and more people were learning to read and because of the Roman Catholic Church's reactions to the Reformation and the reformed sects themselves, a greater proportion of the total population had the freedom and leisure to question the old explanations of "the way things really are." For the first time some attention was paid to the Christianization of the common people (as opposed to just kings and their courts), mostly by the reformed sects.[3] During these centuries, a spectrum of philosophical attitudes toward reality was developing. We'll deal with a number of these attitudes, which existed concurrently, as we continue to examine the myth of Witchcraft. The development of towns, where people could meet and talk about a wide variety of subjects, was crucial to developing the way of life we now experience.

The sun and planets danced their patterns in the heavens and the dour black friars of the Roman and Most Holy Catholic Church were replaced by the dour black ministers of the Reformation, and joy left the lands.

Between the end of the Witch Trials and the mid-eighteenth century, a number of near contradictory philosophical attitudes developed; each of these spread among people of the growing middle and upper classes in England. The first of these worldviews is still familiar. It combined highly devoted, protestant, Christian beliefs with a mechanistic/imperialistic view of the universe. These people applied to native pagans, as well as to ancient paganism, a view which attributed every possible cruelty and perversion their imaginations could encompass. For them, pagans worshiped idols,4 sacrificed humans/babies, and in general were guilty of every crime previously known or newly invented. (That cruelty of this sort is termed "animalistic" and that the perpetrators are termed "beasts" seems to me to ignore completely that it was man — not cats — who invented the tortures of the Inquisition and Nazi death camps.) Eventually this worldview extended to consider that even the civilized, Oriental religions the imperialists discovered were dedicated to evil and must not be allowed to contaminate proper European Christianity. A subset of this view could be found among self-conscious intellectuals who decided that no intelligent human could believe in religion. Since open atheism could be dangerous, many disguised their hostility toward Christianity by writing diatribes against pagan religions, ancient or still existing, with the hope that their readers would make the connection that Christianity was just as irrational and unattractive to a thinking man.5

But the Old Gods could not be banished permanently from the green lanes of England, the dark forests of Germany, and the rolling fields of France.

A second worldview was associated with the highly respected art and letters of Rome and later, of Greece. This worldview accepted that these religions, as muses, could stimulate great art and they were interpreted as being sufficiently like Christianity as to deserve limited respect. Darwin's theories encouraged the tendency to think of history as a process leading from the original beast to the highest ideal and proponents of this philosophy saw themselves as modern, enlightened Christian men — clearly superior to anything that came before them. According to this view, the basic religions of Rome and Athens were worthy precursors of Christianity in that they pursued creditable ethics and goals until the real thing came along. Religion itself was seen as developing and progressing from animism to polytheism to monotheism in its own sort of evolution, a theory which still underlies much of what is written about it.

In this group of thinkers, respect for the Roman and Greek pagan religions was far more acceptable than, for example, praise for the Roman Church. As a result, personal perceptions of Jesus and preferred parts of the Bible reflected a tolerant God, a kind and benevolent teacher of ethics and civilization. This image is still found among certain denominations and contrasts with the jealous and vengeful God retained by followers of the first worldview explored above. Later, as information about the Oriental religions filtered through to England, Eastern ideas were blamed for the downfall of the nice, healthy European paganism of Rome and Greece. From this point of view, the worthy and laudable religions of Rome were debased by the introduction of the evil cults of Osiris and Cybele.[6] While these worldviews were conservative, aimed at preserving Christianity and the interests of the followers' society, a couple of far more radical worldviews grew during the nineteenth century and self-consciously challenged those ideals. One postulated that there once had been a single, great, world-encompassing religion based on direct revelation, traces of which could be discerned in Roman, Greek, and/or Egyptian paganism. (Hmm . . . sounds familiar. Yes, Atlantis did make it into this worldview.)

However, it took Helena Petrovna Blavatsky's charismatic personality to bring this notion to the attention of a bigger audience. She combined Spiritualism (a movement founded by the Fox sisters in Hydesville, NY in 1848)[7] with Oriental philosophies and religions, and added the concept of the Ancient Masters (an idea similar to the one found in early men's initiatory groups such as the Masons). Her religion, Theosophy, had a good deal of influence in both the East and the West and brought many of the concepts of Oriental religions to the attention of Western nonscholars for the first time. To some extent, Theosophy removed the accusations of horrid behavior from both current and ancient pagan religions, though at the cost of some dilution.

Those of the Old Religions found again their circles on the hills and in the silent forests.

The fourth worldview that was developing during these times has frequently been characterized as a devotion to nature. The word *nature*, however, is generally interpreted differently by those who live in the Americas compared to those in Europe. In the US, for example, nature is usually a synonym for *wilderness* (i.e., areas like the Grand Canyon) while in England nature is *pastoral* (i.e., the tamed, cultivated lands, fields, pastures, and gardens of the inhabited countryside). This school of thought idealized country life and accepted the pagan gods as joyous, liberated, and life-affirming and ancient times as having been happy and peaceful. In Germany, this movement eventually prompted an interest in Northern European paganism rather than the classical paganism popular in England.

Awareness of the nature movement is particularly important to understanding the roots of modern Witchcraft. The poets involved in it wrote with such beautiful imagery that their books remain in print. At various times members of the movement went so far as to place statues of pagan deities in their gardens and spoke as if they accorded these deities their worship. The poet Robert Graves created a wonderful and lasting picture of the Goddess as muse, combining some highly inaccurate history and a lot of poetic imagination to create *The White Goddess*, a book which has outlived much of his poetry.[8] Once again there were Druids at Stonehenge,[9] magicians in rented halls in London, and herbalists and cunning men producing medicines and love charms in the small towns and villages of England.

Magic returned to the world; the secrets of the ancient ages were known again and the wise once more could feel that there might be a place for them in the world.

Along with the growth of the worldviews I recount above, a tradition of ceremonial magicians grew from a combination of clues from some Greek authors and Kabalism (a complicated divinatory and spiritual awakening system based on the Hebrew alphabet) on one hand and alchemy (the precursor of chemistry which sought life, healing, and knowledge) and Gnosticism on the other.

> Now the term "Gnostic" is slightly misleading because historians and Christian theologians have used it as a grab bag for a variety of heretical Christian (and possibly some Jewish) cults that were kicking around in the Mediterranean world in the late Roman Empire C.E. The only thing that all these cults had in common was a belief that the universe was created in a series of divine *emanations*, a belief that these emanations started with *pure* sprit and ended up furthest down with *gross* matter, a belief that spirit was good and matter was evil, and a belief that one could experience enlightenment directly through *gnosis* — or divine knowledge.[10] (Gonce's emphasis)

Another source that must be mentioned is the work of Arabic scholars and intellectuals in the fields of mathematics, medicine, etc. The Arabic world had managed to miss the Dark Ages and continued doing much good work and philosophizing while all of Europe was at a near intellectual standstill. What little of this work escaped the Crusades must surely be given a place in the history of ceremonial magic as indeed it has in mathematics. Taking much of their organization from secret societies such as the Masons, mages researched the past and assisted by science and invention, experimented with the new techniques to create several magical systems.

I haven't really studied the rise of the Ceremonial Magician in modern Western Europe and won't go into it deeply here. However, we must have at least a shallow understanding of it, as its story touches on ours. In addition to the roots mentioned, the Knights Templar get into the story along with Dr. Dee — and even Merlin turns up in the mix. Authorities also cite certain Greeks (Pythagoras, Herodotus,[11] and particularly Plato show up prominently in the way that the Ceremonial Magicians organized their knowledge), as well as native shamans of various sorts in combination with selected writings of the Essenes and later Christian minority cults, and some work of archeologists and folklorists. Translations of antique literary works (and supposed antique works) such as the *Eddas* and the *Mabigonian* provided inspiration, as did such works as Frazer's *The Golden Bough*.

These modern mages developed a magical system which actually took advantage of a mechanistic picture of the universe. The methods of this magic follow the rules that such a universe must have (allowing for necessary adjustments, considering that "science hasn't explained everything yet"). The development of the ceremonial magical schools has importance to us not in the least because so much of Gardnerian Wiccan practice obviously stems from them. This interest in the occult helped create an ambience which would nurture the birth of Witchcraft and all Paganism.

Currently the magickal community is going through twin phases of scientific futurism and historical revisionism — it is simultaneously reaching forward into the technological future and back into the scientific past. In the Middle Ages and the Renaissance men like Roger Bacon, Agrippa, Paracelsus, and Dr. John Dee could be both scientists and magickians. But the rationalism of the nineteenth century (the so-called Age of Reason) created a split between science and magick. Even so, some occultists tried to reclaim the mantle of science.[12]

The popularity of ritual magic waxed and waned until toward the end of the nineteenth century when Romanticism, Spiritualism, anthropology, and poetry seemed to combine to create a strong interest in the occult as well as in folklore, ancient paganism, and nature devotion. Interest in the occult flourished particularly in Britain and France with contributions from German philosophers and occultists, and clearly formed part of the basic atmosphere in which Gardner came to his discovery and/or creation of modern Witchcraft.

Many Witchcraft *traditions*[13] or denominations include ritual elements that come from ceremonial magic rituals. This does not *prove* that modern Witchcraft didn't exist before these rituals became available, as Witches always seem to have been willing to use "anything that doesn't run too fast" so long as it worked. Portions of ritual magic could have easily found their way into existing groups as ceremonial magic itself may well have been, in part, founded upon the framework of paganism or some form of witchcraft. Again, it doesn't seem that we're ever going to be completely sure.

Today we are so many that on the holy days we meet openly to celebrate the precious knowledge passed down to us by our ancestors in the Craft, long preserved in folklore and in the misunderstood customs and stolen rituals of the Romish Church.

The interest in antiquities and folklore that arose in England in the latter half of the nineteenth century and continued on into the twentieth sent song, story, and spell collectors roaming both England and the Eastern US seeking to gather and then assemble into a coherent story the tunes and maundering of the "oldest inhabitant." This activity was regarded as a hobby by academia and much interesting information lost a part of its value due to lack of scholarly documentation. They recorded the country healers and herbalists who were still in practice, found those identified as witches who had the evil eye and could cause a murrain on the cows, and located the cunning men who sold uncrossing spells and identified witches for people who thought they'd been hexed. One problem is that most of these folklorists firmly believed that the information they collected had to be truly ancient and most would refuse to accept that any of it was of recent invention, even if their sources told them that it was so.

While many of these folk customs doubtless were of recent invention as Hutton says[14] (and I have absolutely no opposition to the idea that they probably have changed in every generation) and as was sometimes admitted by the oldest inhabitant, it seems to me that at least *some* of them must have been built on elements already in existence. Isaac Bonewits says, "People writing rituals almost always start by reworking ceremonial material with which they are already familiar."[15] Hutton does not say that there is *no* basis for a belief that folk customs may have evolved from pagan beginnings, but most readers of his books seem to believe he does.[16] What he does say is that, because the collectors and writers desired to believe in the antiquity of folk-lore, it's important to read their works with care.

It seems to me that many of Hutton's readers want us to replace any conviction that the slightest old pagan belief or custom might have persisted in rounded-off form in the folkways of those living far from modernity with a belief that these same isolated peoples in many geographically distant places invented highly similar, faked customs which they then related to folklorists. I'm perfectly willing to take the middle ground here and believe that much of the information included in reports of folkways is of more recent date than believed by the folklorists or Frazer and his like. In the specific case of Frazer, we are asked to believe that farm workers in dozens of widely separate locations *all* made up tales of carrying leaves and flowers home to hang on their doors on May Day; or *all* of Frazer's correspondents and other sources made up these stories; or, at least more probable, that Frazer himself made all of it up — that the geographic attributions and the citations of books and letters are all falsified. You'll please pardon me if I feel that this is like swallowing an elephant while straining at a gnat. While I do not necessarily endorse all or any of the conclusions drawn by Frazer, Briffault and the like, to imply that the totality of their body of evidence was fabricated exceeds my credulity.

It is not my contention that Margaret Murray's[17] theory — that a complete pagan religion was preserved by some of the aristocracy, essentially unchanged, and passed down through the ages without a break in the line — is true. I don't know many Pagans who *do* believe this. Neither do I believe that it's impossible that any pagan beliefs could have survived due to the Christianization of Europe. In fact, the conversion of Europe was never completely accomplished. A visit by church officials to "30 parishes in Oxfordshire drew a combined total of 911 communicants in 1738. . . . This turnout amounted to less than 5 percent of the total population . . ."[18] While folklore in the countryside surely changed as society changed, Christianity couldn't have been the major or only force for such change.

Until it happened that a man who feared not for himself was given the mysteries, and he told of them to the world. Not a few there were who found in them that for which their life's searching had been aimed, although they knew it not.

Gerald Gardner wrote that he was initiated into a coven of witches sometime in 1939. What are the chances he was telling the truth? We cannot actually prove that his statement is either true or false. Philosophical, religious, and social changes in England over the preceding century had opened the door to all sorts of movements and organizations which prepared the ground for such a development. A number of mildly popular movements celebrating the health, beauty, and spiritual possibilities of the outdoors existed at that time, including the one that remains to this day and is known in the US as the Boy Scouts.[19] While scouting projects a very real-world image these days, it did — and still does — involve some of its members in a mysticism similar to that of the Masons, complete with initiations, rituals, and secret passwords.[20] Other similar groups existed; several of them actually met in the vicinity of New Forest and assembled there at least until World War II (1939). Many varieties of occultism were being practiced all over England and the New Forest area had its share, including organizations that grew from the woodcraft movement.

Theosophy, Spiritualism, and Ceremonial Magic were known to have active groups of adherents in the area and, whatever claim to antiquity the group Gardner says he found had, all of these groups — as well as Rosecrucianism, modern Druidism, Masonism, and varieties of Steinerism[21] — claimed ancient roots. Obviously there may well have been a number of groups anywhere in England getting together to either talk about or practice some form of ritual, magic, folklore, and/or religion.

Regarding Gardner's claim of initiation, there is a range of logical possibilities I would like to very briefly review:

I. Gardner made it all up
    a. alone; or
    b. with others
        i. from the Rosecrucian Theater,
        ii. from the woodcraft movement,
        iii. from some other group,
        iv. like Aleister Crowley, for example (Crowley kept detailed diaries and there's no evidence in any of them of a connection with Witchcraft, Wica, or Wicca), or
        v. from more than one of the above choices.
II. A long-established coven existed and did initiate Gardner
    a. as an initiatory magical group which had existed for some years;
    b. as a group descended from one of George Pickengill's nine covens; or
    c. as a coven founded in some other, unknown manner.
III. Gardner was initiated by a relatively new occult group and was or was not told of its relative newness as a group
    a. founded by someone initiated in a recently invented "witchy" group of unknown origin;

b. founded by Crowley after his initiation by Pickengill (for which there is no evidence at all);

c. founded by people from the Rosecrucian Theater, a wood-craft group, an initiate of some group in the Western Mystery Tradition, a Theosophist, or a Spiritualist; or

d. founded by some nut as a joke.

We can say pretty confidently that whatever such a group may have had when they initiated Gardner, he changed it a lot.[22] In an attempt to analyze this question, let's ask Old Gerry a couple of questions (GC = Grey Cat; GG = Gerry Gardner):

GC: Mr. Gardner, realizing that you were a participant in the early twentieth century occult movement in England, could you tell us why you chose to link your magical group with the witch concept?
GG: Well, um, er . . . it seemed like a good idea at the time.
GC: Granting that Mr. Gardner, why did you pass off rituals as ancient when you'd cribbed them from Crowley and others in the occult movement?
GG: Well, um, er . . . you know, it seemed like a good idea at the time.
GC: In other words, Mr. Gardner, you passed off as ancient a religion you'd invented in total or at least in part yourself?
GG: Well, um, er, you know . . . well, I guess so . . . it seemed like a good idea at the time.

Did Gardner publicize the new religion he called Wica or Witchcraft because he sought notoriety and publicity or because he wished to share a happy religion he had found with others of like mind? Just how serious was he about Wica?[23] If he, with or without the help of others, invented the whole thing, could he have remained quiet about that for the rest of his life?

The objective story of Gardner appears in many other books, most recently Ronald Hutton's *The Triumph of the Moon*, which I recommend to those of you interested in pursuing the matter further.[24] It's clear that Gardner enjoyed publicity — as did many who called themselves Witches in those years — but this does not necessarily indicate that his Wica was fictional. He appears to have practiced Wica for the rest of his life and initiated a number of people (although probably fewer than claim his initiation).

The fruit of Gardner's books, publicity, and initiations is the modern, nonconventional religion of Wicca or Witchcraft, and judging on the basis of "by its fruits you shall know it," Witchcraft can stand alone as a religion. It's my personal conviction that it doesn't matter how our religion began; what matters is what it is becoming. Some religions have a divine founder to whom its adherents look for legitimacy. Other religions look to ancient traditions for their mainspring (and there's even truth to the claim of ancient roots in some cases). Still others have a human or merely sainted or semidivine founder, but seem to have no particular problem feeling *real* (Buddhism comes to mind). Witchcraft, I believe, was a religion whose time had come at the exact moment it found a voice and pen.

What if Witchcraft was essentially founded by a nudist, occultist, British, eccentric civil servant who made plenty of mistakes and was a bit of a publicity hound? Over the nearly fifty years since his ideas reached print, we have built a "real" religion on his foundation. Living religions change.[25] "We need both heritage and innovation in creative interaction. We need not, and should not, choose between them."[26]

We who praise the names of the Goddesses and Gods nearly forgotten by scholars and work the magic of the ages lost beyond discovery or recall carry the knowledge of the hidden people into the future.

A notable difference between the Wica taught by Gardner and what might easily be picked up from the records of pre-Christian practice or ceremonial magic was the celebration of eight holy days. Records show celebration of the solar holidays (not always all four) and other records clearly mention the cross-quarter days of May 1 and November 1.[27] Documentation is also pretty clear for a Celtic festival held around August 1 although there seems to be less basis for a holiday on February 1. Eight sabbats or holy days, however, very conveniently divide up a sacred year and together with one or more lunar celebrations each month, create a convenient meeting schedule. By this arrangement, these days contribute to our religion.

The word *eclectic* applied to a Witchcraft group has recently been used as a derogatory term. However, Gardner was certainly eclectic and the New Forest Coven, if it existed, probably was so; most active groups these days share that quality. In actual fact, all religions which have existed more than a couple of years have added to and subtracted from their root materials. This is nothing new and to use *eclectic* as a derogatory term is to ignore facts. Obviously Gardner hit on something special since it has attracted so many of us to the movement he began.

Into the future, we of the Wicca carry forward the hidden secrets of the long past, bringing the Gods and Goddesses of our long-fathers to the People of today.

There are a few questions which haven't been covered in my examination of the myth of Witchcraft and I'd like to spend a very short time examining them. The first of these questions is why the myth, in many places, bears so little resemblance to the history I've set out above. I've gone into the fact that styles of historical research and writing change. While Margaret Murray's earliest ideas about the survival of ancient paganism and pagan practices met with a certain amount of criticism at the time they were published, there also was no lack of academics who were willing to agree that there might be something to them — otherwise how would she have been chosen to write the entry in *Brittanica*? The belief that many practices of isolated villages in England preserved activities from the very far distant past and that the *Mabigonian* and other tales from Celtic areas had survived from ancient times was generally accepted.

Serious academicians didn't find the idea of a world-covering ancient religion laughable and Murray was not by any means the first person to propose it. The Venus of Wilendorf was accepted not merely a goddess figure, but perhaps as an indicator of a general worship of a particular goddess over most of Europe. The Druids had something to do with Stonehenge, England was covered with old and new sacred buildings pointing the way to lines of energy and mundane travel, and the stone circles were built to tell the time of astronomical events.

As I point out in the chapter on early history, archeologists now admit that they know practically nothing about prehistoric religious activity,[28] although the possibility of a widespread goddess cult cannot be completely ruled out. Early Britons clearly were practicing some variety of a "cult of the dead," evidenced by the great number of visibly prominent (at the time) tombs which contained only a small percentage of the bodies produced by the population.[29] Additionally, many of the tombs were provided with a small auditorium area at or near the entrance. These tombs must be considered as something other than a methodology for disposing of dead bodies but there's very little indication of what they were. When styles eventually changed and Britons began building circular sites without formal burials, we have no evidence to indicate what they did in them.

The Masons, the ceremonial magic lodges, the horse whisperers and other craft brotherhoods, the Rosecrucians, and Mme Blavatsky's Theosophists all claimed to have direct roots in the far distant past and the great god Pan was sufficiently tamed as to fit in a flowery English garden or to find a lost otter baby in Kenneth Graeme's *The Wind in the Willows*. Gardner's story of the ancient roots of Witchcraft may not have been a conscious falsehood and until recently, many of the points made in it were generally considered accurate.

Unfortunately, the myth continues to be presented as factual by many writers in the field, particularly those producing the "Witchcraft 101" books. It seems sometimes that more writers than Witches believe the myth to be history. These writers have failed to complete their research by not being in touch with more modern interpretations of archeology and written evidence of the past. Further, their repetition of the myth as fact does Witchcraft no particular favors. Many people somehow feel that the myth needs to be true in order to justify Witchcraft as a religion. I disagree with this attitude. I do feel that continuing to present this mythical history as truth undermines our attempts to receive tolerance from leaders of other religions. Christianity, Judaism, and Islam are religions of *event*. They each base their beliefs on events which occurred in history (or, of course, are *said* to have occurred in history) and in many ways these religions are so focused on those events, that many participants in them might abandon them if the events were absolutely proved to be fictional. Witchcraft is not an event-based religion but perhaps some people feel that Neopaganism is as vulnerable as some other religions in these areas.

All religions depend on their particular myth to act as a teaching tool and one of the few ways to communicate their luminance. That, clearly, is the true role of the mythical history of Witchcraft. We do feel a connection to whoever built the stone circles of Europe and the temples in Athens and along the Nile. Whether or not this connection is factual or emotional and spiritual doesn't affect the reality of the connection itself, as such a connection is not a matter of fact or logic.

Another question frequently raised involves who might have been involved in Witchcraft's creation if Gardner didn't invent it out of whole cloth. Aleister Crowley is often mentioned since early forms of Gardner's ritual contained many quotes from Crowley's works. Gardner definitely had met Crowley and had received from him a signed charter to form a magical lodge. However, there is no evidence among Crowley's papers and very detailed journals that there was any close connection between the two men or between Crowley and any activities resembling Wicca or Witchcraft.

Another question is what role, if any, was played by a Cunning Man named Old George Pickengill.[30] Pickengill was dead by the time Gardner returned to England in the late 1930s. It has been claimed that Old George initiated Crowley and/or various other people associated with the occult movement in the early twentieth century. There is no documentary evidence either way. It should be noted, however, that in general, the cunning people were identified as the opponents of those rural sorcerers (frequently called witches) who practiced the evil eye and other spells intended to harm their perceived enemies — or heal their friends. A cunning man would sell uncrossing spells and in earlier times had assisted the witch hunters to identify suspects in the community.

The entire question of the pre-Gardnerian coven is a difficult one for all Witches. Once upon a time, the leader of darn near every Witchcraft tradition had been initiated at a tender age by his (or occasionally her) grandmother. Alexander Sanders, Leo Martello, and countless others told such (remarkably similar) stories and frequently got quite detailed about it. Now I'm definitely *not* saying that no Witch ever had a grandmother who was a Witch; after all, there's a fifteen-year-old boy in my hometown who definitely has a granny who is a Witch! My own grandmother happened to consider herself a "good Cath'lic lady" and didn't find her psychic abilities at all contrary to that religion.

The whole question of the family tradition Wiccan or Witch (or *famtrad*) is so difficult for many in the Craft that people have admitted to me only in private that they have received lore from a family member (or family). They refuse to acknowledge this publicly for fear of becoming a victim of doubt, ridicule, and sarcasm. Obviously a new initiatory religion is going to attract a certain number of charlatans hoping to profit from claiming some sort of special legitimacy, as well as a few merely insecure people seeking to give themselves a more authoritative background.

I am personally convinced, through free discussions with over a dozen such family tradition Witches, that such groups do exist and that there is a certain amount of objective evidence of their existence prior to 1939 (the year Gardner says he was initiated by the New Forest Coven). There is no room in this book for an extended discussion about such family traditions but I'd like to suggest that you give any person claiming one a serious hearing and make up your mind on an individual basis.

The last of the major misunderstandings about Witchcraft promulgated by Gardner is the idea that Witchcraft is *Celtic*. Examination of the Celtic worldview by modern historians makes it clear that there are many contradictions between it and Witchcraft and it's very doubtful that many Witchcraft groups reproduce any significant amount of actual Celtic lore.

We know quite a lot about the body of rules the Celts living in the British Isles followed. We know something about the nature of their society but very little about the actual stories they told, the songs they sang, and the deities they recognized. A lot of what we *thought* we knew about the Celts has turned out to be incorrect. For example, Celtic knotwork was elaborated from the art of the Norsemen; the stories from the *Mabigonian* cannot be attributed to pre-Christian times and some of them seem to have been rewritten from Oriental stories; and the stories of Robin Hood and King Arthur cannot be dated earlier than the late Middle Ages, the time of the traveling minstrels and the flowering of the knighthood.

However, in Gardner's time these facts were unknown, at least generally. Ceremonial magic, in England, had already by some been connected with the Celts,[31] as it was associated with the Aesir and Venir in Germany. Most British tend to consider themselves merely *English*, by which they mean that they have Anglo-Saxon and Norman ancestors. It's common to ignore any Celtic blood, though through the maternal line most English must be Celts (since the Saxons and the Normans were invading armies and as such were unlikely to have brought their wives with them). Likewise, most Celts must be British through an identical process. However, in part due to the prejudice against all things Celtic perceptible throughout British society, there is an air of "romance" about the Celts and Druids. Celts are also connected with the second sight (the psychic power of seeing the future), providing another reason for both Ceremonial Magic and Witchcraft wanting to share in the Celtic aura. That some mages and Witches linked their activities to the Celts seems to me due to these associations. While a lot of the groups descended from Gardner call themselves *Celtic*, in most cases I suspect it's because that's what Gardner called it.

In our hearts are hidden ancient secrets, in our brains is the knowledge long lost to civilized humanity, and in our spirits we hold the geis of the Gods to make these secrets and this knowledge available to those seek it. In us the Ancient Ones, the Great Masters, and the Priests and Priestesses long turned to dust live again and grow in fertile ground.

It's rather amazing to note how quickly Wica began to grow (even allowing for the help it got from the publicity). Gerald Gardner was not averse to appearing prominently in the newspapers as a Witch and a number of his competitors shared his enjoyment of publicity. Alexander Sanders billed himself as "King of the Witches" and at one time worked as technical advisor on a truly awful movie supposedly about Witches. Of course, Aleister Crowley, the Great Beast, could generally "out-publicity" all of them put together.

The Hippies, Freaks, Flower Children, and the New Age of the latter 1960s prepared a lot of people for the idea of leaving the established religions of their childhoods. A number of experiments in religious invention were made and a few have lasted till the present day, like the Church of All Worlds, Stephen Gaskin's The Farm (although much reduced in numbers as of this writing), Esalin, Hare Krishna, and I'm sure there are others of which I'm less aware. Many of the current leaders in the Pagan world were wearing flowers at the end of that time.

Witchcraft and Paganism, however, rarely truly qualify as *New Age* religions. In fact, there are several ways in which Paganism contradicts some of the original New Age philosophy's favorite ideas: almost all Witch groups recognize, at the least, the intrinsic hierarchy of teacher/student; Craft ritual, whether done by the book or performed as a *happening*, has a specific structure which is almost always respected; and cultivation of the concept of personal responsibility is an important aim of most groups.

No, the women's movement is not the reason — certainly not the sole reason — for the popularity of Witchcraft either, but an awareness of the narrowing effect that the preeminence of father gods has on women's lives (men's as well, for that matter) undoubtedly contributed to the fast spread of the Craft and Paganism. The important point is that the time had come for us to widen our view of women and when that happened, Witchcraft was ready to take the shape we needed. If Witchcraft hadn't been there I'm sure we'd have thought of something, but personally I'm glad that it was the Craft. Clearly, at least in the US, the women's movement has greatly increased an interest in religions that openly feature a female deity and accept female priests as at least the equals of male priests.

Ultimately, the errors in the myth and the unknowns in the true history have very little to do with Witchcraft as a religion. Whether we started last week, in 1939 by Gerald Gardner and some bored friends, or whether we have existed underground for 30,000 years, our spiritual paths receive legitimacy from us and from what we do with them. If Witchcraft leads you to be a deeper, better, more balanced person, then it's a good and totally legitimate *real* religion.

I think it is bad practice and bad teaching if we share with our students only the myth *or* only the objective history of Witchcraft. They need the myth for its spiritual message and they need the history so that they can interact with others as educated people. Witchcraft combines both fantasy and hard truth — both are part of the dynamic balance which is our idea of the best way to order our lives.

If you want to keep up with new interpretations of history and new archeological finds, you have a couple of options. There's a quarterly magazine called *The Pomegranate: A New Journal of Neopagan Thought,* which tries to give us notice of these issues.[32] Additionally, there are a number of Web sites that can help you keep up-to-date. Search for them under archeology and history — they are likely to be attached to a university.

The History Channel frequently airs shows on new discoveries in archeology but you must be careful about how much confidence you place in the presentations. A lot of the shows the channel runs are seriously dated, many of them whiz by fairly important facts, and a number make rather offhand comments, leaving out such words as *many, most, some* and *a few,* which can greatly distort what is being said. Additionally, I don't think many of the shows are checked to temper bias; in one about superstition a college professor gave a definition that took in all religions except science.

POINTS TO PONDER

• We can say that while many details regarding the story of Witchcraft's antiquity are inaccurate, its deeper meaning, which speaks to the connection we feel between peoples and times, is perfectly true and legitimate. Whether or not Gerald Gardner invented it, Witchcraft is growing into quite a nice religion with beauty, unmatched openness, and an extraordinary amount of participation by all its adherents.

NOTES

[1] Sir James Frazer, *The Golden Bough* (Chapter 62: The Fire-Festivals of Europe; Section 4: The Beltane Fires), www.sacred-texts.com/pag/frazer/ gbo6204.htm.

[2] As in Chapter 3, portions of this chapter in italic are my own retelling of the myth.

[3] Rodney Stark and Roger Finke, *Acts of Faith: Explaining the Human Side of Religion* (Berkeley: University of California Press, 2000), 68.

[4] There's little or no evidence that any pagans actually worshiped the stone or wood of an idol rather than seeing it as a symbol of deity. Statements alleging this direct worship of the physical depiction generally stem from Christian criticisms.

[5] Stark and Finke, *Acts of Faith*, 4–9.

[6] In *Origins of Modern Witchcraft: The Evolution of a World Religion* (St. Paul: Llewellyn Publications, 2000), Ann Moura traces the Oriental influence on European paganism quite extensively. I mention her theories at the end of Chapter 3.

[7] *Spiritualism*: the belief that spirits of the dead can communicate with the living, especially through a "medium"; a system of doctrines or practices founded on this concept.

[8] Robert Graves, *The White Goddess* (1947; reprint, New York: Farrar, Straus and Giroux, 1948).

[9] No, the original Druids had nothing to do with building Stonehenge and there's certainly no proof that they ever did any sort of ceremony there. However, in the latter half of the nineteenth century there was no way to date the archeological site or the Druids with any certainty. Mistaken or not, just invite me to summer solstice ritual at Stonehenge and see how little I care about historical accuracy!

[10] John Wisdom Gonce III, personal correspondence with author, 7 May 2001.

[11] Colin Wilson, *The Occult* (New York: Random House, 1971), 186.

[12] John Wisdom Gonce III, "The Evolution of Sorcery: A Brief History of Modern Magick," in *The Necronomicon Files* by Daniel Harms and John Wisdom Gonce III (1998; reprint, Mountain View: Night Shade Books, 2001).

13 In Wicca, a *tradition* is the initiatory downline of a single group or individual.

14 See Ronald Hutton, "Chapter 7: Finding a Folklore," in *The Triumph of the Moon* (Oxford: Oxford University Press, 2000).

15 Isaac Bonewits, *Witchcraft: A Concise History* (PocketPCpress [e-book, www.pocketpcpress.com], 2001), 96. Bonewits postulates that if Gardner's initiatory coven had any written rituals, this fact would be evident in his writings (Bonewits's theory applies in reverse, too.)

16 Hutton, *The Triumph of the Moon*, 131. "Two aspects of the phenomenon need to be restated in conclusion, as they cannot be sufficiently emphasized. The first is that all parts of it [the interest in and collection of folklore] were to some extent anchored in real, proven data, even though it ran beyond this to a very significant extent. The second is that this was no simple matter of an intellectual elite imposing its ideas upon the rest of society. The scholars concerned have those ideas, and made such a favorable impression, because they were so much part of the spirit of their age, and related to so many of its deepest concerns."

17 A leading and respected Egyptologist and archeologist working throughout the Middle East, Ms Murray wrote the sympathetic definition of Witchcraft that long appeared in *The Encyclopedia Brittanica* and authored several books postulating that pagan practices were preserved by certain members of the European aristocracy up until the present day.

18 Stark and Finke, *Acts of Faith*, 67.

19 Hutton, *The Triumph of the Moon*, 162–63.

20 The Order of the Arrow is a secret society open to Eagle Scouts. Ask a really good friend who was a Scout about it.

21 Austrian philosopher Rudolph Steiner founded a philosophico-religious movement called Anthroposophy with the basic assumption that one can, through thought, discover the reality of the spirit. See www.elib.com/Steiner.

22 See Aidan Kelly, *Crafting the Art of Magic* (St. Paul: Llewellyn Publications, 1990). This volume goes into the sources and rewritings of Gardner's Book of Shadows in reasonable detail for those interested in pursuing this thought farther. Kelly's attitude has been widely criticized, particularly due to his seeming obsession with Gardner's possible sexual deviance. In *The Rebirth of Witchcraft* (Blaine: Phoenix Publishing Inc., 1989), Doreen Valiente recounts her memories of the early days of Gardner's New Forest Coven as his High Priestess in counterpoint to Kelly's theses.

23 Gardner originally used the spelling *Wica* and later changed it to *Wicca*.

24 See note 14 for full publication details. As any author addressing this subject, Hutton comes to it with a point of view; everything written about Gardner must be read with a filtering mind. My point of view is that it's just as possible that Gardner found a working coven as it is that he made it all up himself.

25 Grey Cat.

26 Judy Harrow, *Wicca Covens: How to Start and Organize Your Own* (Secaucus: Citadel, 1999), 11.

27 The solar holidays — two solstices and two equinoxes — divide the solar year neatly into four parts or quarters and therefore have come to be called the quarter days, leaving the other four holidays to be cross-quarter days. Other sources make

the solar days the cross-quarter days, as in Gus diZerega, *Pagans and Christians: The Personal Spiritual Experience* (St. Paul: Llewellyn Publications, 2001), 65.

[28] Ronald Hutton, *The Pagan Religions of the Ancient British Isles: Their Nature and Legacy* (Oxford: Blackwell Publishers Inc., 2000), 34.

[29] Ibid.

[30] Much of the material relating to Old George can be found at www.fortunecity.com/roswell/angelic/361/page1.htm.

[31] Wilson, *The Occult*, 65. (Wilson quotes Robert Graves in a lecture on *The White Goddess*.)

[32] *The Pomegranate*, 501 NE Thompson Mill Rd., Corbett, OR, 97019. Web: www.interchg.ubs.ca/fmuntean, E-mail: fmuntean@unixg.ubc.ca, Subscriptions: antech@teleport.com.

CHAPTER FIVE

And thou who thinkest to seek for me, know thy seeking and yearning shall avail thee not, unless thou know the mystery: that if that which thou seekest thou findest not within thee, thou wilt never find it without thee.

For behold, I have been with thee from the beginning, and I am that which is attained at the end of desire.

FROM THE CHARGE OF THE GODDESS[1]

WHEELS, SPIRALS, HAMMERS, AND TREES

Neopagan Religious Philosophy

Since words are magic and one should use them with respect, let's examine the collection of words we apply to our religions, beginning with *religion* itself.

> *Religion*: An organized body of people following similar practices based on the belief in a supernatural or otherwise not ordinarily perceptible power(s) with whom adherents of the religion have or can develop a relationship. The nature of that relationship and the methodology used to achieve and/or celebrate it are prescribed by the religion.

I say *organized body of people* because this is a necessary part of the legal recognition of a religion. I qualify the term *supernatural* because not all spiritual beliefs accept that such powers are super-natural. I mention *nature* and *methodology* because agreement about the divine relationship is essential to making religion *organized*. Pagans are sufficiently organized as to have regular meetings of adherents to practice generally agreed upon rituals which express our relationship with deity. While we do not treat these matters stringently since we don't have scriptures, there is general agreement on these points. Neopaganism is a real religion.

The usual umbrella terms, *Pagan* and *Neopagan*, are frequently defined as a follower of a polytheist path.[2] Pagans don't believe in an all-powerful deity, a need for salvation, or the reality of sin; they do believe in the importance of the individual. It's probably this emphasis on individuality and an individual relationship with deity, individual inner growth, individual inspiration, individual power, and individual responsibility which joins the many differing paths that make up Paganism.

Witches, Wiccans, and Witchen[3] make up the most numerous subgroup of Paganism and most Witches practice Paganism as a mystery religion, meaning that they believe there is a special sort of knowledge available to those who truly seek it, which cannot be expressed or taught in words. In the introduction to her book *Wicca Covens*, Judy Harrow say she has come to believe that the religion of Wiccans and Witches is Neopaganism and the Craft is essentially a religious order within the Pagan religion.[4] I must agree because while our forms of worship may differ — although not in essence — the time and dedication those of the Craft focus on spiritual/religious matters, both personally and for the benefit of the whole community, is what most differentiates them. This is not to imply that there aren't similar small group activities and individual dedication found within the other subdivisions of Paganism.

There is a near infinitude of named and unnamed paths which fall under the umbrella term *Paganism*. Some currently prominent ones include: neo-Celtic paths; Asatru; reconstructionist groups (including Celtic, Egyptian, Greek, Norse, and prehistoric Judaic); Wicca and Witchcraft; unclassifiables like the Church of all Worlds; and hundreds of individual groups which cannot be briefly summarized, as well as large numbers of just "plain" Pagans. The main link between these groups is that their beliefs resemble each other's more than they do those of mainstream Western religions.

However, the Pagan paths can't really be said to have a theology in common. What Pagans share is a cosmology different from that of the mainstream.[5] Being a Pagan means that you have radically changed your understanding of the rules of the universe, the nature of the universe itself, the things found in it, and the proper role of humankind in it.

Pagans do not see the universe as a piece of string with knots to indicate the beginning (creation by the deity) and end (when, evidently, God terminates the experiment and cleans out the lab). Instead we see a circle, a spiral, a double helix with beginnings and endings connected to each other, so that out of every ending there is a new beginning: from the universal egg (the monoblock which explodes to create the galaxies) to the heat death (when all chaos is sucked into a new monoblock, ready to begin all over again); from the death of a person and the rebirth of their essence into a new individual to the repetitive and never-boring experience of spring following winter. The cosmos ever moves on, ever repeats, ever new.

The lack of absolutes intrinsic to a worldview in which there is no definitive answer to the question "Which came first, the chicken or the egg?" induces a feeling of insecurity in many, particularly in this scientific age.

> Just as the paradigm shift of the Enlightenment challenged the credibility and even the intelligibility of the prevailing theology of its time, so today the implications of the holistic/ecological systems theory challenge the credibility and intelligibility of contemporary conventional wisdom: scientific, political, and theological. If theology is to make any serious claim on the attention of the educated non-believer, it must interpret religious tradition in terms that are meaningful in the emerging holistic world.[6]

What is the holistic world we are now expected to perceive? A world of the poets where the wind, rain, and sun, as well as the flower and the seed create spring while being themselves a result of it. A cosmos where a tree falling alone in the forest not only makes a sound — whether heard or not — but shakes the world, which is intrinsically changed by it. A world where one can never explore all the consequences of stepping on an ant, but where that step is a natural and necessary component in the dance. A cosmos so delicately balanced can paralyze you: how do you know that a thoughtless action won't be felt by an intelligence so far away that you can never know the result of your action?

Some individuals have reacted to this holistic concept by strictly circumscribing any action perceived as affecting the *natural* world. But by what principal do they classify themselves as *unnatural*, and therefore unfit to affect the environment? Obviously they classify humankind as something *other* — something extraneous to the environment. Indeed, this is the teaching of the Christian church — that man is the result of a special creation, both separate and different from the rest of creation.

Monotheistic philosophy classes mankind *above* the environment, but these folks seem to have almost reversed that rank and see themselves as *less* than environment. To Pagans, humankind is inseparable from nature and the environment. The environment is everywhere: Times Square is just as much a part of the environment as Yellowstone Park. While obviously those of us alive now must accept the responsibility of attempting to fix the damages caused in the past (and present) it is ridiculous for us to shoulder all the guilt. If humankind is a legitimate part of the natural world, everything each of us does is important and potentially earthshaking; at the same time, everything each of us does is also a part of nature.

If this cosmology sees humans as a part of nature, then all human activities are natural — even those that take place in cities and with computers. As each individual builds this new cosmology for themself, the most difficult task is to place humans in their appropriate place. In the Pagan universe, the death of a single butterfly in the Jurassic age may be what determined that I would be like myself rather than like you. Pagans live connected to all that is without either being in charge of it (other than being in charge of themselves) or being secured within the charge and control of any other (human, deity, or impersonal force). While ecology is a major concern for almost all Pagans (some groups based on pre-Christian ethnic religions may have a different emphasis with respect to these concerns), there is often disagreement about extent and methodology. This is probably due more to the complexity of the issues involved than it is to having different goals and/or commitments.

For most Pagans, their cosmology contains the possibility of *magic*. Many actually define magic as causing change through the utilization of natural laws that science hasn't yet accepted or discovered. If the universe is interconnected, then every single action will have a "ripple effect," like a stone being thrown into a pool. Magic takes advantage of this effect by using a variety of techniques to "aim" the ripple in order to cause a desired change. Not all Pagans believe in magic or work magic, but most of them do.

In a very real sense, magic is a part of many religions. Certainly it's difficult to consider the Roman Catholic sacrament of communion, wherein the bread and wine becomes (although not visibly) changed into the body and blood of a component of their deity, as anything *but* magic (since the definition of *miracle* is essentially the same as the definition of magic). According to the Church of England's theology, the *transubstantiation*, in which the "inner essence" of the bread and wine is similarly changed, also fits this definition. Even the Protestant consumption of unchanged crackers and grape juice "in remembrance" partakes of magic as expressed in the definition given above.

To my understanding, the primary differences between a *prayer* and a *spell* is that the spell is usually more work and most of us were taught that spells won't work unless we also go out and actually *do* something in pursuit of our desired end. It is not only a truism but in fact true that the "God/dess helps those who help themselves." Both prayers and spells are acts of theurgy: magic accomplished by, or in some way connected to, the powers of deity. So how *does* Wiccan or Pagan magic differ from others' magic? In common with many non-monotheistic religions, we openly and knowingly practice that art. Unlike prayer in some religions, the practice of magic is not required by our religious beliefs; however, magic may be the way in which our not all-powerful Deities can lend us, their children, aid in our purposes. Prayer is usually seen as *asking* for what you want or need; magic is a method of *working* for what you want or need.

For most Pagans, the universe also allows the essence of a human (we'll call it the *spirit*) to survive physical death.[7] This spirit then incarnates[8] as a new person and experiences another life. Many believe that there is a time of rest when one life is finished; in Summerland the spirit can consider its life just completed and perhaps make some decisions about the next one. While a general belief in reincarnation is common among Pagans, details differ by group as well as by individual. Of course, not all Pagans or Wiccans realize that they are building a new cosmology and many people who name themselves Pagans and/or Wiccans haven't yet explored these paths and cosmologies in depth.

We must be able to compare our cosmology with that of the majority culture so we can understand how to talk with those belonging to it about religion and belief. More than that, we must bring our students to the understanding that they haven't just changed deities, they have changed the way they see the world. I believe this to be one of the lesser mysteries entrusted to us and a better understanding of this mystery can contribute to the strength of our community.

Most of us realize that although the majority of people in North America identify themselves with the monotheistic religions of Christianity, Judaism or Islam, even within any one of these three divisions there is more than one cosmology. Additionally, within any general cosmology, each individual modifies it for themself. We therefore have Christians who consult astrologers, not to mention scientists who see their methodology as if it were a set of commandments proclaimed by a burning bush. All details of a cosmology may not be logical and, indeed, may be contradictory. Since belief is not generally a suitable subject for logic, illogic and contradiction may not devalue an individual cosmology although for most people, examining one's cosmology and extending each belief to its logical conclusion will almost always be beneficial. For both personal growth and enhanced communication with those who hold different beliefs, the understanding that if a butterfly's death can change the universe then one's own actions are imbued with great power, is a crucial extension of a Neopagan's belief system.

There are some basic general statements we may make about the modern Pagan religion, though, and we should review this material briefly because it's important to have the main beliefs of our religion set out clearly in our minds. As clergy we are frequently called upon to discuss our beliefs with those considering assaying a Pagan path and with leaders from other religions. In both situations it is imperative that we be coherent. I am indebted to Isaac Bonewits for the basic organization of the following material, published on his Web site.9

Modern Pagans usually believe in more than a single deity. Moreover, we believe in deity both immanent and transcendent; that is, a deity which is both within us and outside of us.

> Deities can manifest at any point in space or time which They might choose, whether externally (through apparent "visitations") or internally (through the processes known as "inspiration," "conversation," "channeling," and "possession"). This belief often develops among Neopagans into pantheism ("the physical world is divine"), panentheism ("the Gods are everywhere"), animism ("everything is alive"), or monism ("everything that exists is one being") all of which are concepts accepted by some Neopagans.10

Pagans do *not* believe that we were born evil or with *original sin* and therefore, we do not believe that we must somehow be "saved." Further, Pagans do not regard the body and soul as representations of evil and good. We see the body, soul, and spirit all as essential parts of the individual and none is more good or evil than any other part. It is probably in large part due to this belief that Pagans have a nonjudgmental attitude about sexuality. Safety considerations aside, most Pagans make up their own minds about the morality of any relationship, whether it is sexual or not. Ideally, an individual's sexual choices should only come under comment by our clergy when the honorable treatment of a committed partner(s) is a consideration.

While many critics of the Pagan beliefs concentrate on the polytheistic nature of our religions — or on their interpretation of the worship of any god other than their own as "Satanism" — the biggest gulf between their cosmology and ours probably lies in our belief that we are not special in terms of creation. Because we are a legitimate part of the environment, we cannot sell ourselves on the concept that we have some right to do anything we want with it. Because we are essentially related to the animals, we do not have the permission of our deities to treat them as unimportant beings. We are not given dominion over all else in creation, nor do we rule by divine right. In fact, the idea that our God or Goddess would deliberately create us as imperfect beings, born with sin and apt to further sinning, is simply inconceivable to us.

Few Pagans believe in evil gods or gods of evil, although they generally have a healthy respect for tricksters and the few gods who don't seem to dependably be concerned that humans prosper. In general, Pagans are particularly inclined to worship deities connected to the world around us: Gaia, the world spirit; the Earth Mothers; gods and goddesses of field, herd, and hunter; and the spirits of the landscape. It is from this focus that most of the energy put into environmentalism originates. Although details vary a great deal, most Pagan paths connect their celebratory activities to the passage of the seasons, the phases of the moon, and/or the regular progression of passages of one's life. These celebrations are seen, in part, as a strengthening of our connection to and involvement with this earth. Although Gerald Gardner referred to Wica as a *fertility* religion (no doubt taking the idea from Frazer's *The Golden Bough*), I think this was primarily to explain the sexual content he hoped to include in it. Our actual beliefs and rituals really do not reflect the attributes of a fertility religion — assuming such a thing exists outside the imaginations of anthropologists.

Despite generally honoring gods connected with at least comparatively nontechnical civilizations, few Pagans have a problem with science and technology. In fact, following employment in the health care field, the second most common job held by Pagans is that of a computer worker or expert. On the other hand, many Pagans recognize that many scientists have a "One True Right and Only Path"[11] attitude, which practically amounts to a religious conviction that no one but they themselves can ever be truly right. As a result, most Pagans take the latest "great discovery" with a grain of salt.

Pagans believe that life is to be lived and enjoyed, not treated as an entrance test for some hereafter. Because most are concerned with living this life well and honorably, a positive ethic is evolving in the Pagan community. As with all new religions, this is an uneven process and, indeed, it can never actually reach completion. In general, the moral attitude is one focused toward growth, positive change, and a conviction that needlessly or heedlessly hurting others or one's self is to be avoided if at all possible. This outlook derives in part from the so-called Wiccan Rede: "An ye harm none; do what you will."[12]

In almost fifteen years of teaching Wicca I have read a couple of dozen student essays on the meaning of this phrase and no two of them were alike. The underlying ethical reality of the Pagan religion is that we hold each individual totally responsible for their own actions: the devil does *not* make anyone do anything. Since laws and creeds or other written instructions do not seem to have done a particularly good job of encouraging people to behave well, perhaps this one will work out better. We certainly think it's worth a try.

Joined to the belief that Pagans must take responsibility for the results of all their actions, the Pagan ethic includes an expectation that we all will contribute to the good of the community (to both our religious community and society at large), the earth, and each other. We attempt to honor the beliefs and spiritual paths of *all* others, not just other Pagans, and our ideal is a community which derives much of its strength from its diversity. Because many individuals and groups have experienced antagonism from the majority society based on their religious choices, Pagans tend to feel strongly that we must defend ourselves when we are threatened, and we must come to the aid of another so threatened. Pagans attempt to maintain a stance of tolerance for others' paths, as "Judge not the path of brother or sister for all paths are sacred" is a principle taught by many groups in addition to the one in which I was initiated.[13]

Most of all, the actual practice of Paganism — practice being the proving ground of all religions — can be observed to include thinking for one's self, accepting personal responsibility for all one's acts, displaying a certain dedication to the benefit and defense of the Pagan community, and showing a need to stand tall and look one's deities straight in the eye without shame or excuse.

It must always be kept firmly in mind that Pagans do not see a cosmos divided into pure black and pure white areas, nor do we have a mind-set which sees anything not pure white as evil. Pagans are aware that the universe just isn't that neat and tidy. We see possibilities of gradations, not just of black and white, but of all the colors you can imagine. You may hear someone speak of *shadow-walking* or you may find yourself dreaming, meditating, or traveling to realms away from the clear white light. This generally has nothing to do with ethics or morals; it is a metaphor, as is white light itself. As far as that goes, I don't believe most Pagans truly admit the existence of either the pure black or the pure white; for us the universe is in process and is therefore of mixed composition.

Christianity is often a sore point with Pagans for a number of reasons. Many of us were raised Christian and because we had problems finding our path within that religion, we may have been subjected to heavy-handed persuasions designed to return us to it. Additionally, if Christianity no longer practices forced conversion, many Christian sects certainly practice forceful proselytization. Historically there are many legitimate criticisms which can be directed against one or another Christian denomination with respect to their teachings about women and/or anyone practicing a religion different from that of the sect in question.

When speaking with many Christians, our first task is to communicate to the individuals that we are not a people of their book, and indeed we have no book. *The Charge of the Goddess*, part of which is quoted at the beginning of this chapter, is as close as we come to scripture. Many Christians have a cosmology which narrowly restricts the universe to an unshadowed black/white dichotomy. In it one may worship *the* God or one is automatically a follower of the Devil, meaning that the definition of religious freedom has no way of reaching any farther than Judaism or Islam — and it frequently barely reaches other sects of Christianity. I believe only time and the changing world can open up the universe to these folks. (As I edit this chapter, 9/11/01 is in my past. Those events and statements made since by a variety of clerics and politicians indicate that many people may have entered into a widening of their worldview, with a U.S. President of very conservative Christian beliefs at the forefront.) I suspect that our best possible tactic is to show them that we do not condone any who do active harm to themselves or others. Of course, most people who want to speak with us about our religion are not constrained by so narrow a cosmology and are genuinely interested in hearing about our beliefs and practices.

Many Christians react with more than just fear when faced with Pagans, whose most visible difference from the "Big Three"[14] religions is loyalty to a Goddess. In fact, you might notice that they seem to avoid denouncing Pagans for worshiping a Goddess, and accuse us of being "Satanists" instead. The concept of the Goddess is to some so ultimately frightening that many monotheists won't even admit what's really going on; like the Catholic Church's witch hunters in the fourteenth century and beyond, they can't believe that anything female could be running things — running *anything*. An understanding person shouldn't really blame them; after all, their God is awfully scary. You might say He has an attitude problem and has made it clear over the ages that the worship of Goddesses is something He truly doesn't like. I sometimes wonder if they wouldn't be less upset if we *were* Satanists! That way, they would be able to understand our deity much better and wouldn't be asked to deal with the intensely frightening concept of a female deity.

In rejecting the idea that there is something "dirty" and "evil" about a person's physical being, the Pagan cosmology has taken another extremely radical step away from more of the world's religions than just the Big Three. The idea that humans have a near godlike spirit trapped in an inherently vile physical prison has led to societies that find the mere sight of a naked human body obscene. The Pagan acceptance of one's body as an integral part of nature, as something which can commit good or evil actions but in itself is morally neutral, is probably a greater breach from the majority cosmology than is the worship of deity in female form. While many other paths picture life as the soul or spirit's fight against the body, Pagans attempt to fully integrate all the various real or analogical parts of a single self.

With this emphasis on the individual, can it be said that Pagans are selfish? Well, certainly some of us are; on the other hand, spiritual growth doesn't promote a self-involved attitude. In forging a personal relationship with the deities, the earth, the wheel of the year, the cycle of birth and death, and the spiral of our own lives, we who do grow find that our personal happiness and self-esteem depends in high measure upon our commitment to other humans. We are mystics, not just fully awake to all that's around us, but full participants in what is happening here and now. The collective number of unpaid hours Pagans devote to work which primarily benefits others in the movement is staggering.

Coming as we do from a society that almost universally believes in the existence of a One True Right and Only Path, some proportion of our newest members tend to be momentarily convinced that Paganism, Wicca, or whatever denomination of our general religion happens to be the one they've discovered, is the *right* religion. Usually people get over this notion pretty quickly, but a few manage to retain title to this conviction despite the reality that probably 95 percent (or more) of Pagans loudly and repeatedly deny the possibility.

I know that I reject any suggestion that I need to be somehow "saved"; that is, rescued from some originally evil state or "delivered" by the very deity who caused me to be possessed of this evil against which I, as a human, am helpless. The thought that some omnipotent, all-powerful entity first deliberately created evil intelligences and then chose to allow (or cause — Christian theology seems to me to be a bit undecided on this point) newborn infants to die even though this deity declares its capability of preventing such deaths is a frightening one. Further, that an infant would be sent to a place of everlasting life characterized by unending pain unless some simple charm be said or spell worked . . . well, such a theology is totally beyond my ability to perceive as a possible choice.

While I don't find the idea of being required to "pay" for one's ill-doing at a later date to be totally unreasonable (even so much later as to mean after death), I'm hardly able to connect the idea of persons who do less evil than a mass murderer being sentenced to eternal pain by the will of a "just and loving God." There's a favorite hand-painted sign here in the Bible belt: "The wages of sin is death." And the wages of virtue is . . . ?

Witchcraft differs from most other Pagan paths in that it teaches the idea that not all knowledge of its religion *can* be taught and that by undergoing a process known as *initiation,* an individual may be able to access this mystery. Let me stress that the ritual of initiation alone cannot bring the individual to the realization of this mystery, but it is an important factor that often leads to this knowledge.

Mystery religions are certainly nothing new and, frankly, the "mystery" in Witchcraft isn't new either. No one is going to be able to explain to you what this mystery is — that's why it's a mystery. There are mystery aspects to Christianity available to those believers willing to do a little research. The magical/esoteric aspects of Judaism are demonstrated by the Quabbalah and in Islam they are communicated by a concept based on the Qur'an's (Koran's) inner meanings. For most Witches, the mystery is one of the most important aspects of the religion — and the most frustrating. It's difficult for the teacher to assist the student in discovering it and it's difficult for the student to accept that it's a test for which they can't study. Not to mention that there's no sure way of telling that the student really has discovered it or that the newcomer hasn't learned it on their own.

The concept of initiation both within and without Wicca has accumulated a great deal of excess baggage. It's been used as a bludgeon to establish status and superiority, and as a trick to achieve sexual seduction. In truth, initiation cannot guarantee knowledge of the mystery and certainly the prominence of someone's initiatory line has no bearing on the worth of that person or the depth of their understanding of the mystery(ies). Initiation is a tool which frequently aids in assisting the student to the mysteries. Initiatory line is no more than the "name, rank, and serial number" of the Craft world; it can be useful as an introduction but is of little other extrinsic worth. If the person thus introduced has included a name known to another, it may well indicate a level of training — in the same way as two army majors understand each other's breadth of authority.

In literal form, initiation is a relatively simple ritual that follows the patterns Mircea Eliade describes in his books; that is, a *mystery play* which communicates the principles of death and rebirth on the spiritual level. In the deepest sense, knowledge of the mystery *is* initiation and in such a case, ritual is not an absolute requirement. For many people, however, the emotional support of having their achievement of the mystery acknowledged by others makes the ritual welcome.

Additionally, *elevation* — initiation to second and/or third degree in Wicca — is an equivalent to ordination as a way to identify *clergy*, who are those qualified to teach and initiate. This is a reasonable process considering that taking the role of teacher requires additional study of both Wicca and mundane skills. It's also handy in that most legal definitions of *clergy* call for such special training. Of course, many jurisdictions require that such additional education take place at some sort of special physical facility (i.e., a school) but luckily, the Craft isn't the only group that trains its clergy otherwise. (This isn't to say that you won't have trouble being recognized in your own county or state.)

"Why do bad things happen to good people?" Pain in itself isn't usually the real question. The real question always boils down to "It's not fair." Most grown-ups have managed to accept the reality that "it" just isn't fair — life isn't fair. However, we still seem to ask our deities *why* it isn't fair. The story of Job tells the Judaic religions that life isn't fair because that's the way God made it. Pagans believe that the appearance of unfairness is part of the balance of the universe. We also believe that in the long run, you get pretty much what you deserve.

As for pain, both physical and emotional, it basically lets you know that you're alive. Pain is part of life and into some people's lives comes more pain than into others'. It's not that these people have "lessons to learn," nor that they're being punished for sins or wrongdoings. It's just that pain, in all but a few cases, isn't that important to the universe. Even in today's world, if you've got food in the house for several days, a job or other income, and have someone to love (not necessarily as a significant other), you're a very lucky individual and you must have been a good person in this life or a previous one. We can get ourselves all tied up in anger because someone we perceive as not having behaved well is rich and happy; yet we don't really know that they are at all happy, nor do we know that there wasn't some mitigating circumstance behind their ill behavior.

In a perfect universe there wouldn't be pain, suffering, suicide, and early death. There wouldn't be any free choice, either, since the one thing I know for certain sure is that given a choice, some people will choose wrong. I'm sure there are people willing to give up the freedom to choose in exchange for a perfect universe, but I'm just not one of them. I'll make my own mistakes, thank you.

The *Wild Hunt* is a mythological explanation for the problem of pain. Once loosed, the hunt is outside of all controls. It chases and destroys the virtuous as well as the wrongdoer. It is this unplanned and uncontrolled ingredient in creation which undoes all the plans of the gods and of humans. The Hunt prevents all notions of a perfect universe and frees the gods and humankind to choose among the possibilities each perceives in their own way. The hunt doesn't judge those it kills, nor does it target according to any rule — the hunt just *is*. In other words, Shit Happens.

In addition to recognizing pain as a normal part of life instead of a consequence for having offended a god, it's important to take another look at the perception that things such as floods, earthquakes and hurricanes, which certainly cause much pain and loss, are somehow "evil." Most Pagans accept what scientists tell us: that earthquakes are caused by pressures deep within the earth, that hurricanes are caused by pressures within the atmosphere, and that no natural disaster is caused by the god/desses. If someone happens to survive such an event, it's not the result of personal virtue — that person simply came down on the right side of the knife-edge of chance. Can our God/desses intervene to save one of us from such a deadly situation? Beliefs differ; however, I don't think many Pagans believe that their God/desses can completely prevent such disasters from occurring.

By postulating the cyclic nature of the universe we have cut ourselves loose from many of the presumptions which the Judaic religions impose on believers. For one thing, the lack of an end point means no final judgment with its requirement that the identical personality, almost necessarily in the original body, be present both for judgment and for the punishment which follows. I realize that this doesn't fit in with the Christian belief that people go immediately to heaven or hell — I have no explanation for this circumstance. Our general belief in reincarnation of the spirit fits seamlessly with the circular picture of the universe and allows the "essence" of the person to find new life without all the complicated questions involved with judgment.

"What about karma?" you ask. Isn't a belief in karma a necessary part of a belief in reincarnation? How do things even out without karma — wouldn't its absence let undeserving people have fortunate lives and good, hard-working people have nothing but bad luck? Karma, as perceived in Hinduism, may be defined as follows:

> Karma could be both the activities of the body or the mind, irrespective of the consideration whether the performance brings fruition immediately or at a later stage. However, the involuntary or the reflex actions of the body cannot be called karma. Hindu philosophy, which believes in life after death, holds the doctrine that if the karma of an individual is good enough, the next birth will be rewarding, and if not, the person may actually devolve and degenerate into a lower life form. In order to achieve good karma it is important to live life according to dharma or what is right.[15]

Additionally, there are three types of karma: good karma, which is achieved as the result of selfless action (performed without any thought of obtaining good karma); a very human level of karma, which is achieved out of self-interest; and the karma, good or bad, which is obtained by someone who just doesn't give a shit. Pagans have a somewhat different approach to karma and in fact, it frequently sounds like cosmic bookkeeping.

When I say "what goes around comes around," I seem to have a way of satisfying a lot of the need for retributive karma. I'm pretty sure that few Pagans worry much about what kind of karma they are building. Either they are people who believe that they owe it to themselves to act honorably, or they give the subject no real consideration past wondering if they are going to get caught. I know the answer to that one: sooner or later, they will get caught.

The Witches with whom I have spoken about this seem to agree that neither karma nor the Threefold Law has anything to do with how they make decisions about their behavior. They agree that the principle of responsibility — to themselves, to others, to the universe — is what guides them and they doubt that very much of what one does or doesn't do in this life has any great effect on subsequent lives. At most, they theorize that if one fails to learn appropriate (spiritual) disciplines in one particular life, they might get another opportunity to learn them in a subsequent one.

Although rarely formally discussed, balance is a basic tenet of practically all Pagan paths. Beginning with the easy part, the reasonably simple balance engendered by the God and Goddess poises the Pagan deity not merely between the sexes, but between all the so-called active and passive powers and actions. I should mention here that a few groups honor a tripartite deity with the third representing a number of ideas, such as the melded quality of the God and Goddess merged and the "Community," which holds meanings that stretch from all of us to include ancestors and even the distant wise ones.

From these reasonably simple concepts of balance, we move on to far more complex and less static balances, such as the balancing of one's personal/spiritual self, which may have as few as five points (the four elements plus spirit) to as many as the mind in question can postulate. This type of balancing is based on the idea of improvement but does not throw in the impossibility of perfection. Ultimately, the principle of balance grows to include the universe as well. Because of balance, the universe necessarily contains good *and* evil as well as the many shades of the in-betweens. Under the principle of balance, many of the events which "just happen" are neither good nor evil, but are merely a part of the dynamic universe (including earthquakes, hurricanes, and other events which are a part of how our particular planet maintains its balance).

The Pagan cosmology is radically different from the cosmology of the Big Three in that we see ourselves as an ordinary part of general creation and the universe itself and all in it are a part of a dynamic multidimensional balance in which one cannot expect to find absolutes. This enables us, ideally, to meet adversity with a kind of "judo" wherein we can transmute clouds into silver linings by the way we look at them. We do not believe that we rule the earth and we do not believe that our Gods and Goddesses rule us — we are in balance with them as well.

Therefore let there be beauty and strength, power and compassion, honor and humility, mirth and reverence within you.[16]

POINTS TO PONDER

- Because "The Environment" includes every-place and because we ourselves are a part of "Nature," we can see ourselves neither in charge of the world around us nor somehow forbidden to affect it.
- Ideally, a religion is satisfying to the intellect, the spirit, and the emotions of its adherents.
- The "Problem of Pain" perceived in our culture is one which seems to lack a truly satisfying explanation from the monotheistic religions. In the Pagan cosmology, pain doesn't comprise a "problem"; rather, the idea that pain just *is* means it isn't treated as a thing that should necessarily be absent.
- A very good way to make yourself miserable is to see all pain, suffering, or economic setbacks as "evil." By accepting them as simply a component of a full life, a great deal of the time wasted in self-pity can be used for a better purpose.
- While each of us experiences reality through the filter of our own personal senses and intellect, and while, to some extent, what we experience in reality may be known by no other, this does not mean that we "create reality." What each individual perceives as reality may or may not actually exist.
- The role of humor in Neopagan religions should not be overlooked. Most Neopagans can be serious about their religion without being solemn. Our ability to laugh at ourselves is one of the most appealing qualities of modern Paganism.

NOTES

[1] Excerpt from *The Charge of the Goddess*. Traditional, first published in Charles Leland's *Aradia*; this version as rewritten by Doreen Valiente.

[2] A polytheist believes in many deities.

[3] *Witchen* is a term that was first used by Michael Finnegan Rhys.

[4] Judy Harrow, *Wicca Covens: How to Start and Organize Your Own* (Secaucus: Citadel, 1999), xiii.

[5] *Cosmology* — Cos•mol•o•gy, n. [Gr. kosmos the world + -logy: cf. F. cosmologie.] The science of the world or universe; or a treatise relating to the structure and parts of the system of creation, the elements of bodies, the modifications of material things, the laws of motion, and the order and course of nature. Source: *Webster's Revised Unabridged Dictionary*, www.dictionary.com/bookstore/.

[6] Fritjof Capra, *The Turning Point: Science, Society, and the Rising Culture* (New York: Bantam New Age Books, 1983), 266–67.

[7] This is a belief which has received its first scientific confirmation. "Scientists find evidence of human soul," Reuters, *Excite! News Service*, 28 June 2001.

[8] *Incarnate*: give true life to a physical body.

[9] Isaac Bonewits, *What Neopagans Believe* 5.6, www.neopagan.net/NeopagansBelieve.HTML.

[10] Ibid.

[11] The "One True Right and Only Path" is a phrase coined by Isaac Bonewits.

[12] The genesis of this saying is not at all clear. Most books credit it to Aleister Crowley who is quoted as saying, "Love is the Law." There are some other variants, none of which equate to the Rede. It has also been traced to a supposedly Christian saint or monastery; I've seen both of these sources cited but again, the quotation itself isn't very close. Since I have no further citations, for the moment we must credit the Rede in its present form to either Gardner, the coven into which he was initiated in 1939, or possibly to an early member of Gardner's coven.

[13] Michael Ragan, classes of the Temple of Danann, Irish Witta, Hanover, IN, circa 1983.

[14] That is, Judaism, Christianity, and Islam.

[15] In Sanskrit *karma* means "volitional action that is undertaken deliberately or knowingly." See *What is Karma?*, www.hinduism.about.com/religion/hinduism/library/weekly/aao40100a.htm?terms=karma.

[16] Excerpt from *The Charge of the Goddess*. (See note 1.)

CHAPTER SIX

I am the gracious Goddess who gives the gift of joy unto the heart of man: upon earth I give the knowledge of the spirit eternal; and beyond death I give peace and freedom, and reunion with those who have gone before. Nor do I demand sacrifice, for behold: I am the Mother of all living, and my love is poured out upon the earth.

. . . .

And therefore let there be beauty and strength, power and compassion, honor and humility, mirth and reverence within you.

FROM THE CHARGE OF THE GODDESS[1]

I SEE THE MOON,
THE MOON SEES ME

The Pagan Concept of Deity

Within the Pagan movement, many different deities are recognized on an individual basis; in fact, few Pagans would admit to *not* believing in any named deity whether or not that person has ever specifically worked with or honored the God/dess in question. It's impossible, therefore, to discuss individual deities in one chapter. However, there are some general things we can say about the attitudes and beliefs held in our community with regard to deity — with the reservation that there are groups that differ from these generalizations.

Pagans have taken a very courageous position when it comes to deity. In addition to rebelling against the Judeo-Christian God, we have taken upon ourselves responsibility not only for our own behavior, but also for choosing which god/desses to give our respect. Rather than shivering in our shoes at the thought of god judging us, we have assumed the job of judging god. And we have chosen deities who do not give us the kind of surety and well-marked road the God of the "Big Three"[2] provides for His followers.

We deliberately choose god/desses who are "imperfect." After all, what is perfect cannot alter for the better — only for worse — and without change there is no true life. Living religions must change and so must living god/desses. For if the universe and the god/desses are already prefect, what hope then is there for our own desire to be in some way better? The

Wiccan cosmology is actually a very hopeful one, which sees life as good in itself and in our opportunity for study, enjoyment, and happiness. Actually, we see death in much the same way: our universe is not a finished product, but is in the process of becoming — even as we ourselves and our god/desses are involved in the same process.

Of course, in a sense everyone chooses their own god/dess(es)[3] in that one can choose how one perceives the god(s)' attributes and abilities. However, the peoples of the Books are more stringently limited in how they are able to "personalize" their deity than is even a Pagan who happens first upon a group with a set pantheon. The monogod (if I may be allowed the word), being already perfect and possessed of all the powers and glories His followers have been able to define, is more "cast in stone" than any stone idol. He has everything and His human worshipers cannot hope to share in His powers and abilities, nor in any meaningful way be like Him.

In general, we believe that we hold our God/desses within us, although at the same time we believe that they also exist independent of us. In our view, the pervasive presence of deity makes the entire world numinous and all things are sacred, as we are ourselves. We frequently don't name specific deities in public ritual but use the generic *God* and *Goddess* instead, knowing that each participant will "see" a different face in response to these words. Most of these faces will be a version of the Earth/Moon Goddess and the Horned God, which we usually visualize as the basic identity of the deities that infuse all that is. The Moon Goddess and the Horned God are often the preferred faces of our gods because they symbolize for us the cyclic nature of the universe, as well as bring to our minds the beauties of the natural world.

What is the nature of these deities? Isaac Bonewits discusses Neopagan beliefs on his Web site and the following discussion owes a large debt to him despite the fact that we don't agree on everything.[4] Generally, we believe that all things are alive with presence of deity. This is not to imply that we worship stones or trees but that all the universe, including humanity, is part of deity or contains a part of it. This belief sees deity as imminent, existing within the world. Pagans also see deity as transcendent; that is, as existing outside of our objective world. We therefore may contact deity within, as well as outside, ourselves.

We see transcendent deity most often as a balanced pair. Groups may use a single pair of gods, male and female, while others may work with an entire pantheon from history. Groups may also address a god and goddess selected for the occasion. Whatever the names and personalities of the gods and goddesses addressed, few Pagans would be comfortable if no god/dess were invited to preside at the ritual.

Whatever the specific nature of the modern Pagan gods, the universe is not seen in terms of dualism. Most Pagans reject the good/evil, black/white vision of the cosmos in favor of a belief that doing evil is a deliberate choice available to humans. Because humans and the god/desses have free will, sometimes painful things happen. To quote Isaac Bonewits:

> Along with polytheism comes a logical tendency towards pluralism, leading thoughtful Pagans to reject dualistic or "binary" logic systems that paint the universe in terms of black vs. white, in favor of multivalued or "fuzzy" logic systems that accept the astonishing complexity and ambiguity of life, the universe, and everything.[5]

In other words, we see the cosmos in terms of many colors, shades of colors, hues, tones — a zillion diamonds in a net, each of which reflects all others. While *good* and *evil* are perfectly definable in such a cosmology, they are not the only possibilities. In the spectrum of actions between those ultimates lies a multitude of intermediate points.

Generally, Pagans do not see the deities as entities in total control of everything that happens in the objective world. While one is able to communicate with deity and, indeed, deity is able to speak to the individual, whether by agreement or by mere lack of the right kind of power, our deities are limited in the amount they may interfere. While deity may take action with regard to a single person, they are neither responsible for nor able to prevent such things as earthquakes and hurricanes. Pagans would never term these events "acts of God" — they merely happen. Whether the individual perceives the results as good, bad, or merely neutral is up to the individual's emotional response to these occurrences.

Pagans love and respect nature because she is a part of deity in her own right and because her health is part of our duty and responsibility. Pagans usually are ecologically aware and are attuned to these kinds of issues, whether it be picking up trash at the roadside or worrying about the hole in the ozone. However, they rarely are on the extreme of the environmental movement and often concentrate on the problems they can personally affect.

Pagans have no Book. Each individual knows deity in their own way, addresses deity in their own language, and requires no mediation between themself and the gods. From the Prime Mover of the universe to the least scampering shadow in the woods, each Pagan is responsible for their own belief and relationship with the supernatural powers.

It is difficult to make any general statement about just *how* Pagans believe in the god/desses. Obviously, many believe in the actual living existence of the ancient deities, adapted perhaps, but essentially unchanged from the days when whole nations recognized their presence. Others theorize that all deities spring from a singular *force*. In this case the deities may, in a sense, be creations of the force or they may be the recognizable and comprehensible faces which humans put on that force so they may more easily feel a connection with it.

A lot of Pagans have read Carl Jung and find truth in his theories about *archetypes*; that is, inheritable memories of powerful, generalized, anthropomorphized figures which are potentialities within each of us and which the ancients (and now modern Pagans) externalize as gods and goddesses. In other words, the gods have their only reality within us.

Now, the problem with a big nameless and genderless force is that it's, well, big and nameless and genderless and basically impossible to relate to, especially when you just crawled out of the ooze not a billion years ago and can't do algebra yet. So, humans in their wisdom started splitting the Force into manageable parts, creating individual deities to explain and simplify this creation energy and giving those parts names.[6]

Underlying all three of these philosophical explanations of deity lies the conviction — which is part of the mystery of the mystery religions — that the individual also shares in deity. We each recognize the true reality of the god/dess within ourselves as well as in the entire objective universe. Obviously, there probably will never be a neat and concise summary of what the Pagan deities really are. In some ways, Pagans have a very practical attitude toward their deities — what difference does it make exactly what they are so long as it works? Each Pagan has their own strictly personal relationship with deity. This relationship involves and concerns no one else — not the teacher, not the High Priest/ess, not the leaders or elders.

Because each Pagan oversees their own personal relationship with deity, the role of Pagan clergy does not include some tasks which are the lot of other clergy. No one tells us what we "have" to do for deity; no one dictates what deity expects of us; no one can dispute our individual perceptions of the universe — there are no Pagan heretics, not really. Neither can any other accuse us of "sin," as morality depends upon our individual perceptions. Which, of course, is the case for those of other religions; for Pagans, it's just made obvious. The Pagan movement does, however, have ethics which most expect of all who term themselves Pagans. These are explored elsewhere in this book (see Chapter 7) and are primarily concerned with respecting the rights of others and repaying the trust that the community extends to the individual.

In every religious philosophy, there is an unspoken "contract" between deity and worshiper, although few look at it in these terms. In the case of the Jews, this contract is set out in the *covenant* made with their deity. Most other religions do not examine this "deal" closely, but it generally is some form of "You'll worship me and I'll sometimes act to make life easier for you and/or I'll ensure that you have something to look forward to after death."

When it comes to the Pagan religions, it's impossible to generalize on the details of the "deal" although there's a general belief that deity receives strength from its worshipers and in return listens to our requests and, on occasion, grants these requests or at least lends a hand if an individual has been doing their share. However, running alongside this agreement lies the perception that there is energy available in the universe and techniques for utilizing it, which may or may not fall under the province of deity.

In practical terms, most Pagans feel it is appropriate to formally honor our deities at certain times of the year which have historically been dedicated to such activities. Many of us also honor the cycles of the Moon. In our homes it's common to find small shrines or altars dedicated to one or more deities, designed to keep individual consciousness of the deity immediate (and the other way around). Levels of devotion to one or several particularized deities differ greatly among Pagans. There is no general "rule" covering how or how much an individual should be devoted to deity — that's part of an individual's personal and private relationship with their deity(ies).

This seems like a good place to discuss some of the entities not of the ordinary world which many Pagans, as well as many other people, believe in. These entities may be spoken of as totems, fairies, little people, spirits, ghosts, brownies, demigods, and many other names. Even more than the *existence* of deities, modern scientific thinking strongly denies the *reality* of such intelligences.

At some point when you were a kid you probably came home to tell your mother about something you'd seen or almost seen in the woods. To this claim many — perhaps most — parents reply, "It's just your imagination. There aren't any fairies in the woods." How do they know? Think about it: they don't *know*. They just know what they were told when they were kids. A friend who taught pharmacy was doubtful for a long time about anything herbal. "It has not been scientifically tested," he'd say. I replied that 30,000 years of concerned grandmothering probably would arrive at as valid a conclusion as double-blind testing. *Science* is the magic word of the majority culture. Its followers tell us what we may or may not believe, what is or isn't possible. This despite the reality that the "facts" of science change as quickly as any other category of knowledge.

What evidence can really be better than the experience of your own senses? Scientists will inform you that only *they* can tell you the real truth. Sounds very much like what the priests used to say when someone like Copernicus or Galileo revealed their insights or discoveries. The reactions of most scientists to the supernatural reminds me a lot of the pre-Renaissance Catholic Church, which tried to keep all knowledge under its own control by limiting the people who were allowed to read or write and publish the conclusions of their own work and intelligence. Steven Hawking and others among the "new physicists" come in for criticism or sneering dismissal because they have disturbed the feeling of control that modern science desires. For some people, science is a religion and they are its fundamentalist members, with all the defensive reactions of any other fundamentalists.

But think how many of you reading this book have some disease with a long, uninformative name and no cure. Does naming something you don't understand give you real control over it? Of course not. Calling the diuretic fraction found in asparagus *asperigin* does nothing to explain why it makes you pee. Yet it enables scientists to act as if they knew. But, just like when they threatened Galileo with the fire, there's a lot more to the universe than is known by the establishment, whether that establishment is scientific or churchly.

There are other factors in our reactions against deity as presented by the majority culture, including the objection many of us have to the general status of women within the Christian philosophy. While many, if not most, Protestant Christian denominations now accept women for ordination, this does not remove the direct statements as well as the general tone of their Book with regard to the lesser position of females. Most of us of either sex are sufficiently familiar with this aspect of Christianity that I need not go deeply into it. It does strike some of us as rather silly considering sociologists have clearly shown that the success of a church depends not only on the participation of women, but on women making up a certain percentage of the total population; if this percentage is not achieved, "religious activity" — that is, a preacher and/or a church — is not likely to come to a community.7

Many Pagans have made the choice to add a goddess to their concept of deity — or to replace a god with a goddess. While there are Christian churches which have at least attempted to enlarge their concept of deity to include the female or to upgrade Mary to the position she has held from time to time for some within that religion, these actions seem to be more public relations-driven than substantive. The question is whether or not an adjustment to the concept of deity will lead to other reforms.

Rituals, done by groups in a circle, are not the heart of our religion but are an expression of it. The same holds true for the names by which the deities are called by one person or another. What matters is that we know the gods live within us as well as somewhere outside us; that the power is ours just because we are — it's there for all who recognize it and pay the price in study, concentration, and follow-up. We care for the earth because she is of us and we lift our spirits to the stars because they are the children of our bodies, just as we are composed of "star stuff." Religion never really lies in the words and forms or even in the beliefs and deities. Religion lies in the spirit of each human who, lifting their eyes to the world, sees something greater than mud and compost. (Although Pagans are among those who recognize the beauty in compost!)

Being human, we must elaborate on this basic recognition. And from the elaboration has come good as well as harm. While any one person looking at the mountains sees and experiences the emotional content of religion, those of us who teach know that more is required to bring the intellect into harmony with spirit. And without the involvement of the mind, nothing is human. Religion must be lived full time as well as believed to reach its full expression.

What are the differences in perceptions of deity among the various Pagan denominations? Clearly, groups strongly invested in following specific ethnic, national, and/or historical religions will expect all members to recognize the same pantheons. In some of these groups the gods are seen as ancestors; for some individuals this is a mystical truth and for others it's considered an objective fact. In many groups the goal is an accurate re-creation of both the religion and core worldview of the ancestors, be they of blood or of the heart. Not surprisingly, since these groups must base their activities on research in history, archeology, and social anthropology in tandem with attempts to work backwards through myths and folklore, different groups interested in the same culture, religion, and ethnicity can arrive at varying conclusions.

Within Witchcraft, many different deities are honored. Some groups having a permanent and specific pantheon while others have no prescribed pantheon and the deities to be honored in a specific ritual are selected by the appointed ritualist for the occasion. Since Gardner's published books refer to Celtic religion, we might infer that Gardnerian covens use Celtic deities.

It is my impression that there is very little "competition" among Pagans as to who has the "best" deity. While each individual or group thinks very highly of their chosen deities, the idea that others should also worship those same deities doesn't seem to exist.

In fact, most Pagans have no objection to attending a ritual dedicated to deities other than those they themselves commonly work with. Exceptions are occasionally made when the deity in question is one of the tricksters, such as coyote, or others whose myths are less easy to understand, such as Seth or Loki (the myths of Seth and Loki are more myths of history than myths of deity in any event). Neither of these deities is necessarily evil or dangerous, but working with them can be uncomfortable for many.

A problem arises from this free choice of deity, however. Some people don't know quite enough about an individual deity, which can result in invoking a deity in a ritual not particularly well suited to its interests and powers. Worse, sometimes deities from two completely different pantheons are paired to the confusion of all involved, including the deities. While I suspect this stems mostly from ignorance and thoughtlessness, it results in trivialized ritual (at best) and may cause those attending the ritual to lose respect for the ritualist(s).

In the case of deities taken from the more obscure corners of ancient history, little is known about them other than their names and possibly the Roman or Greek god that seemed to the Romans or Greeks to most resemble them. It's probable that those choosing such a deity designation build up a picture of the deity's attributes to suit themselves. In this case, does the name still forge a connection between the human and the old god? Are the attributes credited to the deity of old changed? I have absolutely no idea. I suspect that research should be the first step in adopting such a deity, no matter how much its name calls to you.

One of the characteristics of deity very commonly seen in Paganism is the idea of the Triple Goddess: the Maiden, Mother, and Crone. A few tripartite goddesses and demigoddesses were known in the ancient world. For example, Hecate of the crossroads had three heads/faces so she could look in several directions. (A few gods or demigods took tripartite form as well. Cerebus, the guardian of the doorway to the underworld, had three heads for the same reason as Hecate and Janus, god of doorways, was depicted with two or three heads.) The Greeks had a number of trios which were rather interesting, including the Graces, the Eneryes or Furies, and the three little pigs...oops, sorry, wrong mythology! In Norse mythology, the three Fates spun, wove, and cut the threads of life. Hecate herself was actually a fairly minor goddess in Greece, although she is popular with Wiccans. None of the other threefold goddesses were considered of great importance in the hierarchy of deities and the divisions were not analogous to maiden, mother, crone.

The Goddess as three seems to have first turned up in *The White Goddess* by Robert Graves.[8] As I stated in Chapter 2, Graves's book is neither history nor accurate mythology. It is, however, a very powerful evocation of the goddess of poets and Pagans and it's not surprising that this vision has gained depth and breadth and has transmuted into what is, in some ways, a new religion and a widespread image of the modern Goddess. The image of the Goddess as representing the three dominating periods of a woman's life speaks powerfully to modern women as they attempt to juggle all that is expected of them. In some cases, however, Goddesses taken from antiquity are shoehorned into these roles inappropriately, injecting unintended humor and/or chaos.

I do not intend to imply that men do not find difficult demands made of them or that they don't sometimes feel confused by all the different roles they are asked to play. I can't really speak to what may aid them in dealing with modern life, though I will take this opportunity to commend to them God the Plumber. (Yes, that's almost a joke — but not entirely.) I suspect that some god forms are in the process of developing and will speak more clearly to a man's life in the new century than does the horned god of the hunt (the god form men are most likely to hear about in Pagan ritual). Some experimentation with triple gods has been going on as so many lives are divided into the stages of young/single/carefree, adult/parental/responsible, and older/retired/wise. The biological divisions are obvious for women, but many of the same changes happen in a man's life.

Many of the ancient deities assumed roles which were familiar to their worshipers. The king, emperor, or chief had his counterpart in the pantheon, as did the hunter, the shepherd, the farmer and so on. Ordinary people probably spent most of their religious time on whichever deity they felt was most like them. Those who devoted more than an average amount of time to such matters might have used other methods of deciding which deity spoke most clearly to them. From a city apartment it may be difficult to appreciate fully the difference between the deity of shepherds and the deity of hunters, since neither employment means the difference between eating and starving in our lives. On the other hand, some of the old deities need only a simple linguistic update. Mercury still governs communications and is one of the patrons of the Internet, among many other things.

The Maiden, Mother, and Crone faces of the Goddess have been exhaustively discussed in many other places and I don't really have any new thoughts to add so I'm not going to explore these concepts here. As with religion as a whole, one's chosen deity must appeal to the total person: their intellect, inspiration, emotion, physicality, and spirit. One person may chose one or more deities which they always use regardless of what they are doing, while others will choose among a pantheon or even a number of different pantheons for a set of deities which they feel will be most open to the purpose for which the deities are invoked or evoked. I do recommend that, in general, you should not expect deities from different pantheons to work together well. Even within a single pantheon, choices should be made with care; Aphrodite and Hera cannot be expected to cooperate harmoniously.

Stories about deities, generally called myths (unless, of course, the story is about Christian deity, in which case it's called *holy writ*), are teaching tools. But they really are more than that because they add to an understanding of the deities and the nature of the Pagan deities. The favorite myth of Witches probably is concerned with the capture of the earth or harvest goddess's daughter by Hades, the lord of the underworld. In sorrow, Demeter allows the fertility of the earth to lapse (incidentally explaining the seasons) while she searches for her daughter, Persephone. Eventually she reaches the gate to the underworld and seeks entry. She is told that the price of entry is to give up all her clothes and jewelry (and in some versions she is flogged). She then is allowed to speak with Hades and ask him to return her daughter. However, during her captivity, Persephone has eaten of a fruit (that darn fruit keeps turning up in religious mythology in a negative role so far as females are concerned) and consequently, she can spend only part of the year in the world above.

I must admit I've never been very fond of this myth. Its theme of a goddess's capture with subsequent disrespectful treatment, possible rape, and denigration which culminates in her being forced to parade naked in front of a court full of males (to say nothing of the mistreatment of the captured goddess's daughter) seems to me rather poor imagery for today's women. The myth does have some slightly more positive interpretations, however. The primary one to my mind is that although everything is against Demeter — she is stripped and abused and made to beg without any of her power available — she still gets part of what she wants. Although we all hope such things are changing, there is some good to be taken from a story in which a woman survives all that can be done to her and, in the end, triumphs. Not to mention that the lord of the underworld has managed to fall in love with the captive daughter and must spend half his time without her at his beck and call. Not a complete victory, but then complete victories are few and far between in real life.

We seem to still be concerned with myths as a historical phenomenon, but I'm hoping that some new ones will grow out of the need to understand our deities in more modern situations. It's easy enough to imagine a modern day Hera deciding that enough is quite enough and chasing a suddenly undignified Jupiter out of his temple with an iron frying pan. How about Athena in a smartly tailored business suit carrying an attaché case . . .

Lord Cyprian's Creed

I believe in the Goddess and her consort, the God.
They have made my beautiful Earth and created me, its guardian;
I will not profane Their creation.
I am Their Custodian of all life and I gladly bear my duties.
The God and Goddess have given me Mind and Body and Spirit,
with these I worship Them;
not through fear but in Perfect Love and Perfect Trust.
And when this life is ended
I will return to the God and Goddess for rest and strength and wisdom.
When I am prepared,
They will return me to my beautiful Earth
to live again amongst those I love.
So Mote It Be![9]

POINTS TO PONDER

- The Goddess as *Mom* is very attractive to many Pagans; I find that God the Plumber is a great comfort to me and certainly wouldn't want to face modern life without God the Auto Mechanic.
- Are "invented" Gods or Goddesses as real as those passed down from antiquity? Does it matter?
- There's never a need to invoke Eris (Goddess of mishaps); She never misses a ritual.

NOTES

[1] Excerpts from *The Charge of the Goddess*. Traditional, first published in Charles Leland's *Aradia*; this version as rewritten by Doreen Valiente.

[2] That is, Judaism, Christianity, and Islam, so-called because they dominate the religious scene in the Western world. At the moment.

[3] For convenience, I am asking you to assume that the word *god* also takes in the word *goddess* and I will alternate in their use when using *god/dess* seems awkward.

[4] See www.neopagan.net.

[5] Isaac Bonewits, *What Neopagans Believe* 5.6, www.neopagan.net/ neopagansBelieve.HTML.

[6] Lisa, "Deity Concepts," posted Jan. 2000 at www.sibyllinewicca.org /lib_wicca101/lib_w 1_deity.htm.

[7] Roger Finke and Rodney Stark, *The Churching of America, 1776–1990: Winners and Losers in Our Religious Economy* (New Brunswick: Rutgers University Press, 1992), 35–9.

[8] Robert Graves, *The White Goddess* (1947; reprint, New York: Farrar, Straus and Giroux, 1948).

[9] The *Lord Cyprian's Creed* was written by Lord Cyprian, who taught many Witches. It is used here with the permission of Lady Elspeth, one of his last students. May his memory remain green within us.

CHAPTER SEVEN

Pagans are people who bow down to idols, offer up blood sacrifices, and represent the religious aspect of human savagery and ignorance. . . .

All of course ends happily, when the protagonists are saved from death in the nick of time by the appearance of a single genteel English missionary who converts the tribe which is holding them prisoner. The result is amazing; in one instant the natives are bloodthirsty, cruel, treacherous, and debauched, and in the next they have become peaceful, kind, honorable, and modest. The alteration is effected by the burning of the idols of their former deities, as if the latter were literally devils who had possessed them hitherto, and whose hold over them is broken by the cleansing fire.

RONALD HUTTON[1]

GO YE THEREFORE AND
SIN NO MORE

Morals and Ethics

And that, essentially, is what Witches and Pagans have done. Most dictionary definitions of *sin* refer to it as the act of rebelling against god. The Pagan cosmology just doesn't embrace this concept; our gods and goddesses don't give us orders about what we should or shouldn't do and do not generally have the sort of parental relationship with us against which we might rebel. Yet there is a stereotype of the pagan as the ultimate rebel against god, immovably steeped in the blackest of sins and guilty of every possible wrongdoing available to the wildest imaginations of good Christians (who, I might say, have proved to possess wild imaginations indeed).

There are plenty of people who argue that without orders from a god, there is no way that humans can know right from wrong. Witches and Pagans believe that most humans can differentiate between "good" and "bad" acts and that humans can chose to behave well without being terrified into following a set of rules through threats.

In order to continue this discussion, we need to agree upon what we are talking about. *Morals* are defined as "rules or habits of conduct, especially of sexual conduct, with reference to standards of right and wrong" while *ethics* are "principles of right conduct."[2] *Situational ethics* are based on the idea that "circumstances *alter* rules and principles" (my emphasis); the problem with situational ethics stems from the difficulty in making decisions when there is no firm criterion for any given course of action.

According to these definitions, the Bible's ten commandments constitute an outline of an ethic and an individual person's rules of behavior derived from this ethic are their morals. Theoretically, an ethic will in some way answer all questions regarding the goodness or badness of any proposed activity or action. One notes that historically, this approach has not been notably successful.

In Witchcraft, the only ethic we have is the First Law (also called the Wiccan Rede[3]): "An if ye harm none; do what you will." This isn't actually a bad or inadequate basis for an individual's moral behavior. However, before an ethic can turn into individual moral behavior, the individual in question must first decide that they have a good reason to seek good behavior — a wish to do good rather than evil.

In thinking over intergroup patterns of behavior within the Pagan world, I have noted that it seems like the people with the firmest principles of right action receive the most respect. They also garner a greater share of the nasty gossip. However, before you can consider the accuracy of this remark, you need to know my personal definition of *morality*. To keep it short and sweet, here are Grey Cat's Eight Commandments:

- Tell the truth because lying usually gets you into more trouble than truth will. If a lie is really necessary, make it a good one.
- Don't take or keep material objects that don't belong to you. If you need intellectual property belonging to someone else, make sure everyone knows where you got it and don't publish it without proper documentation and permission from the author.
- If you said you'd do something, do it. This is particularly important when you've told a deity you'd do something.
- If you said you wouldn't do something, don't do it.

- If you want to change the rules, inform any other(s) involved before you act on this change.
- Treat everyone — without exception — with the greatest degree of respect and politeness available to you at the moment.
- Keep your anger and irritation to yourself except when the time is appropriate to try to work something out.
- Don't be a pain in the ass.
- Think first.4

We have, in the few paragraphs above, uncovered a number of problems involved with a discussion about right behavior for Pagans:

1. Is there any reason for a Pagan to care about morality and ethics given that an individual's personal deity has imposed no requirements on them? Without the threat of hell, what can adequately inspire a human to seek right behavior?

2. How can we define right behavior from wrong, evil, or bad behavior?

3. How can we apply the First Law so as to evolve an ethical system and/or moral behavior?

4. Is there any reward for good behavior or penalty for evil behavior?

5. What are the attributes of a good person?

6. Pretending that we have the answers to all the above questions, how do we pass these principles on to our students in a world which practices so few of them?

Why *should* a person who doesn't fear being sent to hell, being denied afterlife in heaven, paradise, Valhalla, etc. be concerned about right behavior? This is a fair question, particularly since we live in a culture which doesn't generally seem to adhere to any code classifying deceit, cheating, lying, and general "me first" qualities to be wrong. Admittedly, this statement is based more on television — from the nightly news to *The Simpsons*, with particular attention paid to commercials — than may be applicable to the behavior of the individuals you interact with in person.

Many arguments have been advanced to justify a requirement that Pagans behave well: that evil behavior, specifically lying, can make your magic weak and ineffectual; that moral behavior is necessary for spiritual growth; and that evil behavior usually causes direct harm to someone. I'm not sure that any of these points are sufficient to encourage right behavior.

I'd like to present the thought that moral behavior is a necessary part of self-respect and that feeling respect for one's self is absolutely required of anyone hoping to find fulfillment — not just in a specific religious path, but in life itself. Humans are motivated by things that make them feel good in some sense. We're nice to our children because it makes us feel good to see them smile. We're nice to our children because it makes us feel good to think of ourselves as good parents. We're nice to our children because we can then hope that someday our grandchildren will be told that they had good grandparents. We're firm with our children, which causes us pain at the time, because we hope that our firmness will help them grow up to be fine men and women, and that will make us feel good.

Some things make us feel good in the short term: eating chocolate, making love, going shopping for new clothes, watching a ball game. Some things make us anticipate feeling really good later: studying to pass a test, working to get a college degree, doing a good job of training a student for first degree initiation, dieting to lose 50 lbs. Short-term pleasures tend to make us feel good; long-term pleasures tend to make us feel good *about ourselves*. Because humans can contemplate their own death, we can hope that by living an ethical life we can feel proud about that when it's our moment to die. But how much motivation can the thought of how we might feel about ourselves at some indeterminate moment in the future provide? I can assure you that every thoughtful person (given the time) does look back over their life and remembers wrongs done as well as those occasions when right was chosen despite the cost. The motivation provided by the anticipation of later personal pride seems to me at least as strong as the fear of an after-death hellfire, as described by someone who hasn't seen it personally.

Resolving to practice moral behavior is probably a lot like taking up a "healthy lifestyle": both are life-changing decisions. It requires a lot of sweaty effort and it involves a good deal of interim satisfaction when it's practiced faithfully. And after you've been doing it for a while it gets easier. In order to succeed at this task, a person does well to be sure they know what their motivation is and what other possible motivations they can find.

This age, sometimes termed *postmodern*,[5] lacks the type of societal pressures that tend to enforce moral behavior and encourage the individual to at least appear to conform to its rules. That sort of society did exist when I was young and I have to admit that I don't miss it much. Pagans, postmodern almost by definition, must then not only generate the rules of their morality themselves, but also provide the motivation to stick to them. For the "generic" Pagan, who does not adhere to any of the somewhat organized modern or reconstructionist groups, this no doubt presents quite a problem. While I'll be speaking of the First Law (a moral guideline specific to Witches and Wiccans) in some of the discussion following, such a Pagan may find the discussion useful despite not sharing any allegiance to the law.

It's been my experience in observing Witches that the First Law is inadequate to fully energize many individuals to create and adhere to a code of behavior which requires being truthful, dealing fairly, doing what is promised, and refraining from exploiting others. Are these the qualities that a Pagan should cultivate? Certainly. If we wish to form a community, we must have some accepted standard of behavior which supports cooperative endeavors and by which we may evaluate ourselves and others.

Can we agree that truthfulness is a desirable trait? On a personal level, it's crucial to one's inner work. Only by being absolutely truthful with ourselves about ourselves, to the best of our ability, can we fulfill the Witch's goal of personal growth (not to mention what lying does to one's magical work). Yes, there seems to be some Pagans who have no interest in personal growth. There will always be some people who make the noises of a group they would like to hang out with but who retain the idea that morality is "whatever I can get away with." However, it is extremely unlikely that the people who feel that way are reading this chapter.

The volume of criticisms made by Pagans about the clergy of other religions and how they have lied and manipulated their followers leads me to believe that most Pagans can identify a moral life and wish to lead one themselves. Because Pagans want to be able to trust others, many realize that they themselves must be trustworthy.

A community that accepts lying, cheating, undependability, exploitation, and abuse will never reach a state of cooperation, nor will outsiders see it as "worthy." Not that there aren't individuals in *all* communities who have no moral standards, but if the community doesn't *expect* behavior it defines as "good" from its members . . . well, it's not likely to get it.

We must, however, approach any discussion of these "rules" keeping in mind that free will is a concept which forms a large part of the foundation that Paganism as a whole is built upon. I cannot expect another person to be honest because *I* said they should be; I can only suggest that you make honesty a part of the personality you visualize for yourself. For us, moral behavior must come from inside, from the goals we set for ourselves as part of our inner spiritual growth.

Honor is a term often used when we are speaking about moral behavior. Unfortunately, some bells and whistles got attached to this concept and they cause bigger problems than the concept solves. Take, for instance, the idea of dueling because of some minor offence or slight, or getting into a fight in the parking lot with the rationale that someone "insulted my wife."

This sort of touchy, pissing-match honor is absolutely *not* what I want you to think about.

The *Oxford English Dictionary* says that *honor* is "a fine sense of and strict allegiance to what is due or right." I can see you cringing at the words *strict allegiance*. Didn't you get into Witchcraft in part because it offered great personal freedom? However, it's not mere semantics to say that control and discipline are necessary for you to experience real freedom. If you are constantly having to remember the exact details of many lies, apologize for failing to do what you said you'd do, and war with others who complain about how you treat your students, just how free are you?

A person with honor doesn't have to continually think about every action in order to avoid lying, cheating, stealing, or causing unnecessary hurt to others. While honor can lead to attaining respect from others, the motivation for its practice must arise from within the self. Honor is *not* the way to popularity, respect from the world, and coronation as Witch Queen of the Universe. I can actually guarantee that some people will hate you just for having it. If it's any consolation, the hatred is rooted in others knowing that they themselves aren't honorable. What honor does for you, in the long run, is allow you to feel proud of yourself. It gives real substance to a positive and confident self-image that just cannot be accomplished through lying, cheating, and showing off how smart you are.

While the word *honesty* will cover many of the traits which make up an honorable person, honesty alone can become a weapon when misused. Everyone knows someone who slashes emotions with personal attacks and then excuses themself from all responsibility, claiming they're "only being honest" about their feelings (or observations). "Harm none" is a useful concept in preventing the offhand hurt that a person with perhaps too rigid an interpretation of honesty frequently inflicts upon others.

Without getting into the concept of *unconditional love*,[6] an honorable person is concerned about other people. Not *all* other people, but those who actually do touch upon one's life. I feel sure that Mother Teresa (a person most of us can find to be both honorable and worthy of respect, regardless of specific religious affiliation and/or politics) didn't tell herself that she was going to abolish poverty or feed all humanity. She simply went to work to feed people physically within a foot of where she stood. As she obtained more resources, she expanded to people two feet away, maybe even ten feet away. She just fed them, nursed them, cared for and about them, one individual at a time.

One cannot develop honor without having first determined for themselves a working and workable definition of right and wrong. What is *good* and *evil*? Both these terms have "soft" meanings.7 The dictionary can't help us; it assumes we *know* what they mean. Well, for one thing, *good* doesn't mean the same thing as *positive, right-hand path,* or *white magic;* and *evil* doesn't mean the same thing as *negative, left-hand path,* or *black magic.* I tend to define *evil* as those actions of an individual so self-engrossed that they are completely blind and deaf to what they may be doing to others. Is good, then, only those actions of a person who does nothing for themself and only does things for others? No, I don't believe so — although those actions usually are good.

Good is a small collection of ideals discovered way back in prehistory, constituting a handed-down-through-the-ages tradition. But these ideals cannot become a part of your honor unless you choose to internalize them, accept them as part of your own definition of good. Such ideals include being honest; dealing with others in a fair, straight and trustworthy manner; keeping promises and oaths; respecting the needs and feelings of others; and showing a willingness to do your share, whether it's in saving the world or getting supper.

So *is* there any reward given to those who have a collection of good morals and who, all in all, live up to them? If peace of mind and a good self-image seem desirable to you, then these are among your rewards. Living honorably will result in some very worthwhile people respecting you, although there will always be loudmouths (particularly those who have failed to do likewise) ready to find fault. The product of honor isn't a smug sense of superiority, but a confident feeling that you don't have to be ashamed of your actions, that you don't have to alibi for yourself and, most importantly, that you don't have to explain your actions to your peers. There's an old truism: Virtue is its own reward. In one sense it had better be — you probably won't really get any other. In another sense, if you can avoid the superior smirk, being honorable can really make you feel pretty darn good about yourself.

So let's say that we've all figured out exactly what honorable behavior means to each of us. Now, how do we teach our students to be honorable people? Unfortunately, "by example" is the primary teaching technique for passing on ideals of honor. Another thing which can help is to have more than just one discussion with each student, on both a group and an individual basis, about what it is to become an honorable person and why it's desirable to attempt to do so. You can give the First Law some extra teaching time or maybe have some good discussions on how your own behavior affects your satisfaction in life.

We also need to *demand* honorable behavior from our students and coveners. We must not let lies, deceptions, exploitations, or failures to keep promises just go by. I find it's rare that someone can lie to me without, one way or another, my finding out. I'll hear from someone who happened to actually be there when "it" happened, someone who knows the liar's family — something will happen to let the lie out. I've learned that part of helping students become honorable is to show them how much lying can complicate their lives. If someone can't keep their promises, I stop accepting promises from them. Yes, sometimes they leave the group — that's OK. In the long run I wouldn't have been able to keep them in it or initiate them anyway. Yes, we are loving and caring individuals, but that must never be used as an excuse to avoid taking an uncomfortable stand on an important issue.

Before I go on to discuss the First Law, the Law of Three and karma, I'd like to suggest a list of concepts which might well be included in one's description of an honorable person. Be aware that I consider being honest, dealing with others in a trustworthy manner, keeping promises and oaths, respecting the needs and feelings of others, and showing willingness to do one's share as necessary components of *any* system of morals dedicated to the good. To those, however, many people may choose to add the following:

- Demonstrating compassion (without maudlin devotion to every poor soul who bends your ear).
- Showing respect to those who have earned it, but withholding respect from those whose development has been concentrated on large-quantity gas storage.
- Having tolerance for the paths, ideas, and preferences of others. You don't have to agree with their choices to honor their right to make them.
- Respecting all the entities in the universe, each of which has its place. Don't forget that it is the role of some objects in the universe to be kindling.
- Displaying politeness and good manners. This doesn't cost much and probably doesn't have a great deal to do with morals, but it certainly makes group interaction a lot easier.
- Developing self-discipline. Actually, it probably isn't possible to behave honorably without self-discipline. It doesn't appear to be a particularly attractive trait but you'll be surprised at how much easier life is with it.
- Recognizing duty. There are jobs you have taken on by implication rather than overt promise. If you have a baby you have, by implication, promised to spend eighteen years growing it up. Duty is important because it generally refers to work related to the well-being of others.

- Assuming responsibility. The biggie. Responsibility to one's self is the basis of Witchcraft. It's our responsibility to ourselves and to the mystery that we work on personal growth and the inner mysteries, and it's responsibility to ourselves which gives us the power to be honorable. It's responsibility to our religion which makes us teachers, coven leaders, clergy.

The First Law is one of two sets of words which could possibly be considered *scripture* by Witches (the other is, of course, *The Charge of the Goddess*). It provides a code of unparalleled freedom and self-direction — a heavy responsibility for humans. The Law is considered binding by most Witches, Wiccans, and Witchen,[8] but not necessarily on other Pagans. I'll continue this discussion as if all my readers take it seriously, whether or not they are bound to its command.

> The essential religious question is, "What does it mean to live by this?" *Code* means the behavioral guidance that all religions provide, both ethics and etiquette. The central purpose of religion is to sustain, amplify, and clarify the connection between our values and the way we live our lives, to actualize our conscious contact with the Sacred. Lacking a concern for ethics, ritual observance becomes at best a feel-good exercise, a cheap, safe, and legal high — or at worst an excuse for blasphemous hypocrisy.[9]

Most people have noticed that the Law has two halves: "harm none" and "do what you will." It's important to realize that these two portions must be kept in balance. By simply breathing one may be harming bacteria, algae, and microscopic entities of every sort. Must we then stop breathing and walk so as to avoid stepping on ants? Obviously such an interpretation freezes us solid with no ability to act — it's simply not workable.

It's necessary to define *harm* more specifically, since by merely living, taking up space, and eating we cannot guarantee that we aren't harming living things. Defining harm in a way useful for moral guidance brings me to the idea that it may be defined as (1) deliberate action taken despite the knowledge that it will cause probable pain or damage to a *particular* other or (2) deliberate, malicious, or thoughtless action taken without regard to what harm it may do to a particular other.

Accepting these definitions, we are free to obey the other half of the law: to actually do things. (I'll cover *will* in my discussion of magic in Chapter 8 so I don't need to go into it here.) In terms of moral behavior, the point to remember is that we are not required to stand motionless lest we somehow inadvertently cause harm. Gus diZerega raises the point that this isn't at all the same as minimizing harm, which is basically an impersonal directive and therefore hard to keep in mind or to judge.[10] In part, the effort we must expend in analyzing the potential for harm represented by each choice in a range of actions makes us far more sensitive to the interrelatedness of our world and our own place as very much a part of it.

> The ethic of respect is a deeply Pagan ethic. It is found among hunt-ing and gathering peoples in many places who recognize that they live in an inspirited world, that all beings in that world require respect, and that some beings in that world need to die so that others can live. This is not moral relativism, but neither can it be broken down into a series of do's and don'ts engraved upon a tablet.[11]

Most importantly, following this Law makes us more mindful people; people who think about everything we do and say, which results in our becoming more the people we want to become. When I defined harm you probably noticed that I used the words "a particular other" and wondered why I put it that way. Pretend that you want to get a new job. If you succeed in getting a desirable job, chances are that one or more other people also wanted it. Would it therefore be unethical to work magic to get the job? If it is unethical to work magic to get it, would it also be unethical to put in an application for it?

The second question probably clarifies the first question for you a good deal. If you want a specific job and someone you know and like also wants that same job, what's your position then? This is the sort of question I ask when someone comes to me requesting help in figuring out an ethical issue. What's the answer to the question? I don't know. I only know what the answer is when it's my actions that are in question. We are a religion of personal freedom and I definitely do not know what is ethical for you.

The Law of Three or Threefold Law is often used as a "stick" to make us behave ethically, particularly with regard to working magic. This law states that everything you do will return to you three times. Therefore, if you work magic to hurt another, you'll get three times the hurt back. I've never felt that this really fit in very well with the general Pagan cosmology, nor that it was particularly effective in terms of encouraging moral behavior.

I did a good bit of asking around but couldn't find anyone who knew how this "law" got into Witchcraft lore. Mention of this concept appears in the Initiation Ritual in Gardner's BOS:[12] "Thou hast obeyed the Law. But mark well, when thou receivest good, so equally art bound to return good threefold."[13] In its full context, the Gardner quote refers specifically to the initiate scourging the officiant with three times as many strokes as she received. I do not know when or how this law came to be applied to honorable behavior. Knowing the source may make it a little more impressive; I suspect that here again it probably came out of ceremonial magic.

Though there are many descriptions of how this law works, the following seems to me the best explanation of the way most Pagans interpret it:

When you act, that energy goes out from you, whether it be in the form of words, of a physical thing, whatever. The energy spreads like a ripple in a pond: it goes way past the original target of your action. It touches all of creation even if only ever so slightly, and those ripples rebound and multiply and eventually come back to you. Using another analogy, it's like pulling on one strand in the spider's web: the vibration spreads through the entire web and bounds back to you so you experience the aftershocks of the vibration.[14]

As Eva says, you put out a particular sort of energy, whether it's intended to heal or to cause harm to others. I tend to call my students' attention to the idea that if you have a particular emotion pervading your thoughts and coloring the magical or personal energy you put out, you open yourself to that particular sort of energy. If you are putting out hurt or angry thoughts, your mind will be that much more likely to concentrate on all sorts of hurt and anger and be more vulnerable to similar energies another might direct your way.

Actually, in the course of working over this thought to write the above paragraph, another explanation of the law occurred to me. The first return is the one mentioned above: opening yourself to the energy you put out, whether positive or negative, makes it easy for the same sort of energy to come into you. Second, whatever "spell" you cast, your personal energies are involved and there is a possibility that the spell will drain more and more energy from you through your emotional involvement. (And when you're upset enough to work harmful magic, your emotions are likely to be stronger and less controlled than when you work a healing or work for another positive outcome.) The third facet of the return is the backlash — particularly if you've sent an attack toward someone who has defended themself magically — and backlash can be stronger than the original blow.

Pagans' talk of karma often sneaks into our conversations about ethics (I assume because most believe in reincarnation [see Chapter 5], which is a part of Hindu and Buddhist religions[15]). However, reincarnation doesn't actually require karma and I suspect some people feel that it is a substitute for hell and purgatory. I'm not going to go into a long exploration of exactly what karma means to a Hindu or someone practicing one of the various forms of Buddhism. My point is that we often use the word without thinking, as if it were some sort of coinage made up of good and bad deeds.

The Oriental interpretations of karma are quite subtle and do not really add up to an idea that everyone pays for being bad. It certainly seems to us that there are people who "get away" with an awful lot of immoral stuff. Well, the Goddess didn't ever promise me that life would be fair so I guess I shouldn't complain. I have to confess that if I really think about what a stinking cesspool those people have to live inside (their minds), I find it hard to be too worried about just when what goes around is going to come around to them.

Although Pagans almost unanimously believe in reincarnation, there's a wide difference in their ideas about the ways one's current life can affect one's next life. Some believe that there's a record of all your good deeds and evil actions and the circumstances of your next life depend on how "good" you were in this one. Others think (and this is the version I prefer) that the sort of person you become in the course of your life affects your spirit and the "shape" of your spirit will have an effect on just who you are, probably not only in your next life, but henceforth. Many of us believe that before reincarnating, a person can decide on a general path they wish to take in a new life — or perhaps chose a new lesson to learn. But here we're getting into theology, which belongs in a different discussion (see Chapter 5).

In order for either the Law of Three or the concept of karma to affect our behavior,[16] we'd need to have a clear idea about how it works and a conviction that it would actually do what it says. I don't think that Pagans have the same kind of belief about the workings of these systems of thought that many Christians have about hell. I think the bottom line is this: If we want to have a religion of trustworthy people who are careful not to harm others when it's avoidable and who always do what they say they'll do, we need to encourage them to accept, bone-deep, that respect for self and others, dedication to truthfulness to self and others, and responsibility and self-discipline are the hallmarks of a worthwhile person and a "real" Witch.

POINTS TO PONDER

- Lying is *very* stressful and requires that you remember the full details of all your lies so you don't get caught later.
- In order to be successful in the practice of a religion, each person must do the inner work of spiritual growth and personal perfection, as well as the outer work of being a moral and responsible individual.
- Without an exchange of energy, neither giving nor taking completes the balance. Just as a teacher gives energy to a student or a gathering's workers give energy to all who attend, so must the student give energy back to the teacher in some way and the festival attendee make a reciprocal contribution to the community. TANSTAAFL.[17]
- You've probably have noticed that I've said nothing about morality with regard to sexual matters. Pagans believe that so long as honesty and fidelity (in its older meaning of "keeping one's word or oath") are preserved, sexual matters are private between the adults involved.
- In the long run, it is neither knowledge, nor initiation, nor magic, nor insight that is the clue by which you'll recognize a real HP/S or Elder. You recognize them by observing their ethics. They are responsible people. They take responsibility for their own actions. If they accept a student, they accept the responsibility to train them well. They answer to a responsibility, even to those to whom they speak briefly at a gathering. They become the kind of person who can behave in no other way.
- Ultimately, all discipline is Self-Discipline. Children develop self-discipline by learning to follow principles and rules set out by their parents.

NOTES

[1] Ronald Hutton, *The Triumph of the Moon* (Oxford: Oxford University Press, 2000), 5, 7.

[2] All definitions in this section are from www.dictionary.com/.

[3] *Rede* is an archaic word meaning to guide or to direct.

[4] Of course, each person must add any of their own rules of living, like my friend Nan who considers "Thou shalt not internalize the shit of others" a very important moral imperative (meaning that if your waiter is rude it doesn't mean there's something wrong with you!).

[5] *Modern*, to sociologists, means a world which is the product of evolution and will reach, more or less, a point of fulfillment. *Postmodernists* take the view that (1) society is *not* evolutionary; that is, ever progressing, improving, and eventually reaching the "best of all possible worlds" and (2) in fact, events, stages, and/or philosophies aren't necessarily connected or progressive. See www.hewett.norfolk.sch.uk/curric/soc/post1.htm.

[6] See Chapter 13.

[7] A "soft" meaning is one which depends on a comparison to another word, which in turn is defined in terms of the first word. In this case, *good* is that which is not evil and *evil* is that which is not good.

[8] *Witchen* means *Witch* or *Wiccan*. The term was first used by Michael Finnegan Rhys.

[9] Judy Harrow, *Wicca Covens: How to Start and Organize Your Own* (Secaucus: Citadel, 1999), 104.

[10] Gus diZerega, *Pagans and Christians: The Personal Spiritual Experience* (St. Paul: Llewellyn Publications, 2001), 152.

[11] Ibid.

[12] BOS: Book of Shadows. A blank book or notebook in which rituals, spells, specific information, or anything else you want can be written down.

[13] Gerald Gardner's Book of Shadows (n.p., n.d.).

[14] Eva, PagTen mail list, 5 Mar. 2001.

[15] Reincarnation is also found in the belief systems of many early Christian and coexisting esoteric Judaic groups.

[16] Obviously, if one or the other is a law of the universe, our belief has no effect on whether or not we are so affected.

[17] TANSTAAFL: there ain't no such thing as a free lunch. This phrase and acronym was coined by sci-fi writer Robert Heinlein.

CHAPTER EIGHT

Before you can practice magick successfully, it is necessary to prepare yourself thoroughly — indeed, most of the work of magick is in the preparation rather than in the ritual. This is important, because after all, you are the most important element in magick — the crucial tools are your mind, will, body and so on — not your athame and candles. Few magickians would enter the circle wearing a torn robe and carrying a dirty pentacle, yet how many people perform rituals every week with muddled minds. . . . Instead, train and prepare as though you were an Olympic athlete.

AMBER K[*1]

Double, double toil and trouble;
Fire burn, and cauldron bubble.

FROM SHAKESPEARE'S MACBETH

PLUCK YOUR MAGIC TWANGER, FROGGIE

Advanced Magic

I am not going to go into the basic theories of magic, the laws of magic, or other general discussions of magic; this information has been excellently presented in Isaac Bonewits's *Real Magic*.[2] If you don't have this book but have a continuing interest in understanding more about magic, I strongly suggest that you buy it.

Following my own advice in the chapter about analytical thinking, let's begin this discussion of magic by defining some words.

Magic is defined in a number of ways, including "causing [objective] change in accordance with will" without physical causation, which is a good enough definition to go with. However, it's as well to spend a moment on the magical definition of *will*. To any practitioner of magic, getting what one *wills* is not the same as getting what one *wants*. Will is a concentrated, clear distillation of the magic worker's intellectual mind. The will must be completely focused and the desired end must be clearly defined and clearly visualized in order for the magic to have any chance of working. In many ways, the development of this honed and concentrated will is the lifework of any serious magic worker.

The working of magic is not a necessary part of any of the Pagan paths. Many groups and individuals celebrate, worship, or otherwise honor their Gods and Goddesses but do not attempt to work magic in ritual (group or solitary) or in any other way. For those Pagans who do work magic, the magical workings are very much integrated into their religion. So far as I know, none of our deities punish people for not doing magic. Magic is merely one of the tools available to us.

In the beginning there was *sorcery*. Sorcery has been (and still is) practiced all around the world. A modern *hedge witch*[3] combining urine with old rusty nails and broken glass in a mustard jar[4] is a sorcerer, as is a jungle witch doctor mashing together berries and roots to tie into a charm for protection from evil spirits. Sorcery may or may not be connected to a religion. However, sorcery — and, indeed, all types of magic — must be connected with a philosophy and worldview which explain to the sorcerer how and why the magic works. A cosmology that allows for magic need not be nearly so conscious or elaborate as the ones I wrote about in Chapter 5. Most people aren't conscious that they have a cosmology anyway.

In the Pagan cosmology, magic is accepted as the utilization of forces which actually exist and which follow an organized table of methodologies and conditions (laws). We believe these forces and laws are just as "real" as those of gravity, radio, or magnetism, all of which are also invisible and one of which can be described but neither measured nor directly detected (gravity).

To explain what I mean by this, it will be useful if we define another word I'm sure you've heard before: *superstition*. On a History Channel show the other day a university professor said, "When the first human decided to believe in some sort of deity, superstition was born." This man evidently believes that anything he can't touch and measure is mere "superstition" and therefore a "bad thing." Many people's attitude toward practices like crossing fingers or knocking on wood is that they probably aren't true, but they can't hurt. Others tend to think that anything which doesn't agree with the most popular current worldview is a superstition. The facile definition of various sorts of beliefs — "It's my religion, your myth, and his superstition" — is quite true.

Jeffrey Russell defines *superstition* as any belief that is not backed by a coherent worldview in which it has a place.[5] Certainly there are any number of actions common to many people in our culture which I'm sure future generations will see as superstitious. Take those who demand a pill or a shot from their doctor when they have a cold, even though their doctor (and they themselves if they haven't been living under a toadstool for years) know perfectly well that there is no effective medicine for a cold.[6]

Sorcery isn't superstition when practiced by someone whose worldview provides an appropriate explanation as to why it is useful (although just because a cosmology accepts the possibility of magic, it doesn't necessarily mean that magic works). Most Pagans hold a cosmology wherein all components of the universe are interactive (a view shared by many at the forefront of scientific theory). Sorcery (magic) works because what affects one part of this interactive cosmos affects all other things.

(A funny thought: Many people will be happy to respond to this chapter by sending me e-mail instantly from everywhere in the world, explaining how magic just doesn't exist. They will be using a system of communication that could only have been perceived as magical by all but a very few adults the year I was born!)

A *shaman* is more a healer and diviner than a sorcerer, although it can be said that shamans use magic as part of their trance-working and shape-changing. In many societies a shaman will do magic, but assuming that "shaman" is a job description like "priest," such sorcery may be considered an additional service that shamans provide. Shamans, like sorcerers, may be found anywhere; they may or may not be considered a working part of a religion. Their practices and identifying qualities are very much the same no matter where they are found and unlike priests, their work is usually only peripherally defined by the culture.

There are several traits that identify shamans, which are as follows: they had a sickly youth and/or underwent the experience of almost dying; they have experienced one of a short list of fairly specific visions or dreams; they are in some way apart from the community; they do their work by sending their spirit to another plane to seek answers from incorporeal entities, including totem animals; and/or they shape-change into such animals. A shaman actually serves others in the community by utilizing these abilities to seek answers for others. Were the oracles at Delphi shamans? Probably not, although they did work in trance state and use drugs. However, the death experience, diagnostic dream, and shape-changing qualities don't seem to have been required of them. Some definitions of shaman insist that the use of hallucinogenic drugs is required. While this is often the case, there are plenty of exceptions. Such drug use in its original setting always required a great deal of physical, mental, and spiritual preparation — it wasn't just a drug trip.

The word *priest* or *priestess* identifies a religious *professional* with a specific selection of duties. You cannot be a priest without being a part of a religion; this is the important difference between priests and sorcerers or shamans. A priest may also be a shaman and/or a sorcerer, however. The work of a priest differs from religion to religion, from one time to another, and even according to the personality of the individual.

You won't be surprised to hear that we can't prove that magic works. So far as I know there has been no study done to even give us a clue. I'm hoping someone will soon undertake such a study. In reality, however, magic works on so many levels that it would be difficult to separate them out and determine whether the magic actually affected reality or the person involved. The following list gives you a hint at the number of levels on which magic works.

- Magic works on body chemistry, at least in ritual. For instance, actual testing has showed a significant drop in blood sugar levels after ritual.
- Magic works on the mind through the intensive visualization process that is a part of working.[7] Positive visualization is an example of a magical work on this level. (Even winning football teams use it.)

- Magic works on energy as you raise power and then direct it into the focus.
- Magic works on the emotions, as clearly expressing a desire and doing something about it makes you feel better about a situation.
- Magic works through the spirit, as it fosters full communication within you and communion with deity.

The items on this list, of course, don't answer the question about whether or not magic works to change the objective world. It's simply that experience has led many of us to consider magic sufficiently useful to invest time and effort into it.

Divisions in magic have been made in many ways: some are based on whether or not the magic is intended for good or for evil; others specify the magic's use, such as for healing, love, success, etc. Since the actual magic used is essentially the same I've never found the distinctions necessary, although many find them useful to help attune the power to the purpose.

There are countless types of magical workings with names such as high magic, low magic, left-hand path, ritual magic, earth magic, hedge magic, green magic, black magic, white magic, spells, cantrips, enchantments, conjuring, etc. Rather than getting into a long discussion of weighted words and a rainbow of colors which will be disputed by the first adept to read this, let's concentrate on the fewer "styles" of magic-workings.

- *Theurgy* refers to magic worked through or with deity. Magic that doesn't call upon deity is called *thaumaturgy*. Either may incorporate additional magical techniques.
- *Emotional magic* takes advantage of the power that can be raised by the deliberate increasing of emotion in an individual or group. Dancing, drumming, chanting, and sexual techniques are some of the ways in which human emotion may be focused on a magical goal.

- *Intellectual magic* involves the use of concentration, meditation, and focused will to accomplish its goals.
- *Circle* or *ritual magic* generally refers to a working by a group of people, all of whom have at least some training in both the ritual and the symbols used by the group. It may utilize the techniques of theurgy, emotionally fueled magic, or intellectual magic. Most often it attempts to utilize all of these.

Now I've finally gotten to the interesting part: spells, hexes, curses, and the evil eye! This is an advanced book and is not aimed at beginners so I'm going to assume that you already know the following: that magic is a tool neither good nor bad in itself; that it does work; and that there's a price to pay for any magic and the price for magic which will harm another being can be greater than most of us wish to pay. The Rede, "An ye harm none; do what you will" may or may not be all you need to live a good life, but it's definitely important to keep in mind when working magic. And *not* just the admonition to harm no other (so far as you are able); it's also OK to do magic for your own benefit, profit, or even amusement. I urge you not to take too much on yourself when defining *harm*. If you should do a spell to the end that you get a job instead of your friend who also wants that specific job *and* you are aware that they want it, then the spell is harmful. However, if you do a spell aimed at finding a suitable job, you cannot be held responsible for the "harm" done the unknown others who won't get it if you do.

I've observed a few people get their knickers in a twist over the issue of working magic which might not be completely free of any possibility of doing harm. Like a weapon, it's appropriate to use magic to protect yourself or another. My favorite protection is a big silver Mylar balloon, which creates a type of mirror. Since a mirror will reflect magic back on the spell-caster, there's a possibility that someone can be hurt by the backlash. While

I don't consider such a protection unethical, it is a decision each person must make for themselves. What if I get angry and yell, "Damn you!" at someone: have I cursed them? Not unless I took the time and effort to make it a magical working. While I do suggest that you try to think before you speak, I doubt that very many of us are so overwhelmingly good at magic that a couple of words are sufficient to cast a spell! Hexing, cursing, and casting an evil eye are activities which lead nowhere and have their strongest and worst effects on the perpetrator.

I'm not going to go into the extensive vocabulary of magical work; let's call everything a spell and leave cantrips, enchantments and such to a good dictionary. I'm defining *spell* as a distinct magical working aimed at achieving a specified end. Magic is a tool and you can improve your skill in using it. The physical details of a working — picking the perfect minute according to the complicated table of magical hours,[8] selecting ingredients according to the long lists of correspondences,[9] or following the complicated instructions in some old book — are not the most important things. The only really important element in a spell is you.

There are six parts to a spell-working:

1. Defining exactly what is to be done.
2. Determining the appropriate method for doing it.
3. Making all preparations, both mundane and spiritual.
4. Doing the actual spell-working.
5. Following up on the working.
6. Cleaning up afterward.

Before doing a working, you must figure out what exactly it is that you *really* want. I suspect more workings are screwed up here than at any other point in the process. While he was living at home with his parents, a student of mine did a spell to find a new home. Three days later his parents found out he was Wiccan and kicked him out of the house.

Undiscouraged, a few years later he worked to find a better job and living arrangement. Yep, he lost his live-in job the very next day.

Link this step in with the more romantic-sounding concept of *true naming*. If you don't know the true name of your desire, it's almost impossible to magic it up. My friend didn't just want to live somewhere else, he wanted to be able to move — in an orderly fashion — to a better living situation. On the other hand, don't attempt to constrain magic more than is necessary; if you don't *need* to find an apartment in the most expensive condo in town, don't ask for it — you could end up the janitor there! If you need dependable transportation, don't ask for a Vette — just ask for a dependable car that gets good gas mileage. Don't be stingy with the time needed to sort out your thoughts and make sure that you're seeking your exact desire. As everyone says, "Be careful what you ask of the Goddess — you might get it."

Do you need to get a group together and do a big ritual to accomplish your task? Would it be best to do a formal candle-burning, use a poppet, or create a talisman? The answers to these questions will depend on what you've decided to do. Which method will best focus your own will? Which will provide the magical power needed? What is possible? Some delay can make a spell-working more powerful but sometimes you need the result by next Wednesday. As you work more magic you'll learn what you do best, what sort of magical process you are the most comfortable with, and what gives you the best results.

It can be appropriate to invest time and money in a spell-working. Doing so will, if nothing else, convince *you* that the result is really important. On the other hand, merely spending a lot of money has never been known to be enough to make a spell work. Usually there's a happy medium that's just right for the work being done.

First you'll need to gather together all the material elements needed to create your magical object (if any are called for), which will be the focus of your spell. Whether it's handmaking a pure beeswax candle, gathering a dozen herbs with correspondences that perfectly emphasize your intention, or just finding a votive candle and holder that *feel* right, never begrudge the time needed to gather what you need. Don't forget to think ahead to all the tools you'll need in the course of the working. If you forget that you'll need a needle and thread and have to stop in the middle of your working, the least you'll have to do is start it all over again.

Obtaining rare or obscure objects for a working is necessary only to the extent that you believe they're necessary. The point is to have materials that are going to work for you. I occasionally do a spell-working that consists of placing a *visualized* burning candle just in front of my left ear and a couple inches away from my face. This imaginary candle is not, however, at all generic! I know, for instance, its size, color, and whether or not it's scented or has been touched with scented oil. It's a specific candle, magically prepared and lighted.[10] (The greatest benefit of this virtual candle spell is that I generally use it as a means of helping people over difficult life passages: as long as the candle remains burning, I know that they are still troubled.)

Again, don't hurry through this part of a spell-working. If you really feel that you need a particular ingredient, wait until you've obtained it or until you have figured out a really good substitution. Part of the function of a spell's ingredients is to help bring your nonverbal faculties into full participation. Slavishly following some printed laundry list of materials probably won't make your spell better. Approach your materials list as you would a Chinese menu: select a variety of specifics from a list of possibilities.

Don't forget to prepare yourself! Whether this preparation requires a ritual bath and a robe of cloth so fine that it can be drawn through your ring; time-consuming exercises designed to attune you to the elements; or merely being emotionally and mentally centered and focused, take the time and energy needed to do it right. With practice, you can be very thoroughly grounded, centered, and focused between one breath and the next — but no one starts there! There was a time when I thought that as people learned more and more about doing magic they did less and less of it; for one thing, you rarely saw them doing it. However, an additional ten years of observing myself and others has shown me that we probably do far *more* magic — it just doesn't show nearly so much. Preparation is very much a part of the magic. As you choose and prepare the ingredients, they become attuned to you and you probably begin charging them with power before you even begin the working.

What can I say about successful magic-working? Give it your best shot. Focus firmly but don't try to raise a sweat; just keep your thoughts strongly on your purpose. Encourage your emotions to be there too (one reason people are tempted to work harmful spells is it's easier to get hate going than other emotions). If you're attempting to find the perfect job, put yourself emotionally where you'll be when you have it — that lovely mixture of pride, disbelief, trepidation, and satisfaction.

Whether you're working in a circle or not, ground and center; be sure you know where you are in relation to the universe. Call in your helpers, elements, deities — whatever and whoever will help. Give a last look at the mundane environment just to make sure you won't be interrupted: turn off the phone ringer and turn on the answering machine, let the cat out (or in) — whatever is required to give you the time you expect to need.

When your working is complete, let all beings you've invited in to help know that you're through, then ground and center again to make sure you aren't carrying excess energies which may be harmful. This also makes a necessary "break" between you and the energies placed in the spell so there's no chance that you'll drain it for your own needs — and it won't drain further energy from you unless that is the intent (not recommended until you have a good bit of experience in energy work). Clean up all your tools and accessories and put everything away. The spell is done — it needs to *look* done.

The fact that you've completed the actual working doesn't mean your spell is complete. Does your spell object need to be buried at a crossroads at midnight? Does it need to be cast into running water? Take care of this as soon as possible; generally, you need to do this immediately after you've completed enchanting the object, or at least as soon as it's midnight.

This is probably not the only follow-up which will be needed, though. If you've done magic for a new job, you need to start applying immediately for jobs which seem to be the right sort; perhaps get your hair styled or buy a new suit. Do you need a new place to live? Stop and check out "For Rent" signs. And don't just check out apartments for rent in the part of town you think you want to live in. Check *all* the vacancies out: what's inside may not be apparent from outside. If you've done a spell for needed money, make sure you open all the mail and glance inside; look in your old purse, in your raincoat pocket. Try not to overlook any possibility. Magic can be sneaky and I'm convinced the Goddess has a strange sense of humor.

I do *not* want to visit your house and see on your shrine or altar a dust-covered collection of old spell bags, poppets, half-burned candles, and crystals holding ambiguous energies! Spells *should* run out after a certain length of time. When they run out, you need to properly dispose of the material objects involved in the spell. Many spells run out after a week (seven days is one of the magical numbers) or a month (when the moon returns to where it was at the time of the working). Others may have a variety of time limits either built into them at the time of the working or may have just used up all the energy raised in the spell-working.

If a spell for money has had no results in a week, it's probably a good idea to dispose of it and try again. A spell for a job should be redone after a month, if not sooner. Common sense and some other "sense," which you'll develop as you work, will tell you about how long to wait. But it's a mistake to assume that any spell will just go on and on until it produces the result you want. If you see no result after time has passed, the spell either produced a result you haven't recognized, or it didn't work — perhaps because you weren't properly focused and/or your visualization wasn't informative enough. Alternately, perhaps the universe thinks it's protecting you from getting something you're better off without. Regardless of whether it's come to be or not, there's a time to put the spell to rest.

There are several ways to properly dispose of the mundane objects used in a spell-working. If the spell worked, it's a good idea to dispose of all the ingredients completely. However, for a spell that didn't work (for whatever reason) so far as you can tell, it may be safe to cleanse and reuse some of the ingredients. Crystals, semiprecious stones, metallic objects and such can usually be completely cleansed of all the energies they absorbed during the working. Suggestions for such cleansing include submersion in running water, usually for several hours or days; soaking in clean water to which salt or another appropriate addition has been made; formal grounding; or even burial and later retrieval. Though most energies can be removed from reusable spell-working materials with these methods, it's important to check the objects out very carefully before reusing them or giving them away.

Material elements of a spell-working are usually disposed of (assuming they aren't already buried at a crossroads) either in running water or by burial. Charged (magically empowered) objects buried in your yard or anywhere else where they might be found should be retrieved, separated into their component parts, and disposed of unobtrusively after being cleansed of energies. Just as you shouldn't skimp on preparation time, you shouldn't skimp on the time and energy needed for proper cleanup, either. Magic, like genius, lies partly in the ability to take the pains to do it right.

And that's all you need to know about how to work good, effective personal magic. Oh, there are a lot of spell "cookbooks" that can give you excellent ideas for lots of different kinds of spells and provide good sources of correspondence information.[11] The real magic, however, is in you. It's in your ability to visualize, to focus, to create the appropriate emotional cues, to choose the right ingredients regardless of the lists in books. There really isn't any "advanced magic" in Witchcraft or Pagan practice — just advanced magic workers.

There are certain attributes and skills you can concentrate on if you want to become a better magic worker. Through thought and practice they can be cultivated to make your magical workings more successful. This cultivation and development is not easy. In fact, it is the life's work of the most serious Witches and the *great work* of ceremonial magicians. To succeed, you'll probably need a better reason than simply wanting to work better magic. Luckily, the skills and attributes that make up the following list are not only important for working magic, but contribute to spiritual growth and have significance far beyond the narrow field of magic:

- Grounding and Centering
- Concentration
- Focus
- Visualization
- True Naming (understanding what you really want)
- Energy Sensing (other sight)
- Emotional Control
- Discipline
- Knowledge
- Honor
- Silence

Since this is not a beginner's book, I really hope that you've already learned the basics of *Grounding and Centering*. Why these linked skills are always listed in this order I don't know, as it's best to learn centering before grounding. I believe that the teaching of these skills is described well by Mercedes Lackey in her novel, *Arrows Flight*, and recommend that you find the chapters that describe this process.[12] Although we are forced to do without the help of either companions or the forest inhabited by Vanyel's spirit, I've used the techniques Lackey describes for both group and individual instruction.

Finding one's center isn't nearly as easy as it sounds and is complicated by the fact that the center of a woman's body isn't in quite the same place as a man's. Most people can "feel" their third eye — that invisible spot on the forehead between the eyes which holds the source of *other sight* (see below). Get your students to work within the balance of their body until they can "feel" or "see" that spot to which their physical balance is attached.

Once the center is found, the practitioner must shift their mind sufficiently to visualize an attachment forming between that center and the earth. A brief guided meditation that shape-changes a person into a tree is one of the best, time-tested methods of accomplishing such a grounding.

Picture yourself standing with your bare feet on moist, warm ground. You are standing straight and tall with your arms raised over your head. Feel your feet sinking slowly into the earth; your toes are growing longer, digging downward deeply into the cool, dark earth. Your skin is darkening, thickening, becoming smooth, glowing, brown bark. Your arms are growing longer; your fingers are lengthening into branches and soft, pale green leaves are sprouting from your fingertips. Your roots are deep and firm in the earth, reaching deeply into the dark heart of the planet; your branches are lifted high in the air, reaching for the stars. You stand tall and green and brown, connecting the earth and the sky. You are at peace, perfectly balanced between above and below; the energies of all that is flow through you and are not impeded.

NOTE: Do not fail to do this meditation in reverse at the end of your practice session, working, or ritual because it spooks some people when your red nail polish turns green and leaves poke out your ears. Grounding and centering without using a progressive visualization of this sort does not necessarily need to be reversed.

My daughter, a massage therapist, says that visualizing a guy wire going from the back of her head to the ground behind her feet helps her pull upright so she makes the connection between earth and sky. Further, by being balanced on a tripod, she feels more securely grounded. You can also try visualizing a wire leading from the top of your head up into the infinity of the sky. Experiment until you find what works best for you.

When individuals are properly grounded and centered, they will feel different. If they seek to *feel* the flows of energy in their body, they should feel free and unconstrained, unrestricted. Their attention should be generalized rather than highly focused as it usually is. They may have a feeling of openness and balance. They may feel that they've become transparent to a certain kind of light, or that they actually glow softly with light.

With practice, most people can become so adept at this technique that it takes just a moment for them to become solidly grounded and centered. It's a really good idea to make it a habit to ground and center as often as possible. You can identify repetitive events in a normal day and set them to trigger the thought that "it's a good time to ground." This is an unparalleled technique for reducing the stress of modern life. Even those who happen to live a quiet country life find it doesn't hurt to reconnect several times a day. While it's hard to work in a garden and remain ungrounded, I have confidence that humans can become grounded anywhere. In the discussion of personal growth (see Chapter 13) there's a description of an elemental cleansing ritual which can help people prepare to ground and center well on a really bad day.

Moving on to the next item on the list, there are a number of types of *Concentration*. There's the sweaty concentration you manage when working to finish a complicated task under a deadline, the relaxed concentration you can experience playing solitaire or a video/computer game, the peaceful concentration of a good meditative state. For magic, ritual, and most everyday things, some sort of reasonably relaxed concentration is your goal. The Silva Mind Power meditation method is one of the quickest and easiest ways to learn both meditation and relaxed concentration.[13] The Silva method is taught in two-day workshops and through a book. The program used to be fairly reasonably priced but I find no mention of cost on the Web site. Please note that I am not making a recommendation of the Silva movement's total program. I have no reason to recommend against it; I will merely point out that it appears to be another full-time job and may not be beneficial to the aims of a Pagan or Witch. The Silva method, however, teaches very useful meditation techniques which are easy to learn and result in achieving the kind of meditation levels most useful to a Pagan.

The most common image of meditation is a person sitting in an uncomfortable position, staring at a candle flame, completely unaware of the physical world. Without denigrating this particular school of meditation, that state isn't necessary when working magic; it is aimed at the achievement of *satori* or *nirvana*, an idealized condition of rest, harmony, stability, and joy. In life, this is a momentary state in which the individual is not just *in touch* with the universe but *is* the universe. As such it's a fine thing, but it's not a state in which you can *do* anything. Obviously, anyone who has accomplished this state of meditation can enter the appropriate state for magical workings.

The meditative concentration we wish to cultivate combines openness and a *peripheral vision*[14] — an awareness of our surroundings which monitors, but does not distract us. In this state it's unnecessary to either call specific thoughts to mind or to get rid of whatever thoughts rise to the surface. The key is just to relax and let go of a concern for what happens in your mind. I believe that this is the state generally called a *light trance*, wherein you are aware of what's going on around you, but you feel no need to be a part of it or to affect it in any way.

This trance state is very useful for many things. It's a great way to relax for a few minutes and while it won't replace getting enough sleep, it can give you a second wind during a difficult day. If you trance lightly just before going to sleep, you can concentrate on a specific time in the morning and set a mental alarm which almost always works to wake you up at that hour. Light trance right before sleeping is also used to aid dream-working.

To learn meditation most students probably will work with a book or tape on the subject, or work with someone while they're developing the elementary techniques. These techniques are actually very simple — though not quite as simple to accomplish. First teach the student to ground and center carefully (making sure that they are in a comfortable position) and devote a couple minutes to relaxing their muscles. You can mention that it's helpful to select a specific visualization to be used every time one meditates. The visualization acquires the power to ease one very quickly into trance once the process has been repeated enough. Like grounding and centering, achieving trance state gets much easier fairly quickly.

When someone is in a light trance, their eyes aren't actually quite focused on anything, nor are they unfocused exactly. Nothing that person sees carries any emotional tone to their brain; everything is just what it is — a generic thing which neither matters nor doesn't matter to the person meditating. They may have a slight feeling of muscle tiredness in their temples, scalp, or jaw. This is because they have relaxed the normal tension of their brain used for purposeful thought. Most other bodily discomforts seem to fade when inventoried. (People often realize how much of an emotional load pain carries by how much less it bites when they are *experiencing* it rather than *feeling* it.) On the other hand, the student may find that something like a headache is worse because the mental muscles they'd been using to ward it off are now relaxed. The most important quality available to the appropriate level of meditation is a feeling of emotional distance and mental quiet.

Now I'm going to discuss how to *Focus*, even though I've just told you how to become completely unfocused! You may wonder what I'm trying to pull on you. But it does make sense: you can achieve a clearer focus — particularly on a nonmaterial object — if you start from a light trance. This is because you won't be layering one focus on top of others. The trance erases your RAM, the chalkboard in the front of your mind, and the new object of your focus won't be blurred by all the things you've thought about that day.

One must try not to work hard at achieving and retaining a focus. Like the meditative state, if you tighten up and work hard at it, the effort itself tends to become the focus. One of the reasons that many spells require incense, scented oils, lighted candles, herbs, colors, sounds and so on, is that each of these is an excellent method for helping retain focus without tensing up on it. By making everything you see, smell, hear, and touch a part of the spell-working, the focus is preserved without effort from your "boss-brain."

To practice focus, I suggest that you encourage your students to add an exercise to meditation once they've made progress at reaching light trance state. Rather than picking out something *magical* to focus on, have them pick out some sensory objects which should recall a pleasant past experience. For example, baking bread, vanilla flavoring, and lily of the valley are all scents which might well raise pleasant memories. Alternately, a fuzzy stuffed animal or a recording of Jerry Lee Lewis singing "Great Balls of Fire" may work. Specifics aren't really important; the point is to get used to being more aware of input that isn't direct and isn't visual.

Let the moment your accessories are recalling to you fill you. Let yourself experience the feelings they call to your mind. Let your mind bring back pictures of that moment: where you were, who was with you, the sunlight, or the moonlight. Let yourself experience the moment again with all your senses. Encourage it to become almost real.

When you have done this, work on creating a new experience. Gather some sensory cues to create a moment you can imagine but haven't particularly experienced — perhaps standing under a pine tree in the wind. With pine scent, an electric fan, and a windbreaker, you can produce the sensations of that moment. With your imagination, you can build up the rough surface of pine bark and the movement of the green needles against the light. These two exercises demonstrate how much power various sensory stimulants can produce.

Good magical focus should feel good. You should feel no anxiety and no pressure to succeed. The object, thought form, or visualization you are focusing on should be clear and sharp but not overwhelming. It doesn't need to be dominating your vision, hearing, and mind; it just needs to be nice, clear, real, and there.

Visualization is an important magical skill. It's not easy to figure out how to teach people to see clear mental pictures and I imagine each teacher will have to find their own way of conveying what's meant by visualization and how it's best learned. Unfortunately, many people who are very good at it seem to have been born with the ability or talent. You can find out if people visualize by asking them if they know exactly how the protagonist of a book looks.

It seems to me that there are several approaches to teaching visualization: you can have students look at an object and then attempt to "see" it again with their eyes closed; you can have them imagine that they are traveling a familiar route, "seeing" the roadside as they walk or drive along; or you can have them bring up a visual memory of their bedroom from when they were twelve. All of these approaches separate visualization from imagination, perhaps making the first steps easier. I suspect everyone can afford to work on their visualization skills from time to time. Personally, I can never clearly see the faces of people I'm emotionally close to. Visualization is definitely one of the important keys to most Neopagan styles of magic and spirituality — I certainly consider it a very important part of a good circle-casting and magic-working. Besides, it's a good excuse when you get caught reading fiction!

Now we've arrived at a really tough skill: *True Naming*, or understanding what you really want. Remember that one of the very few things just about all Pagans can agree upon is this: "Be careful what you ask of the Goddess — you might get it." Being too specific about what you want is just about as bad as being too general. In part, this skill falls into a "know yourself" category. What do you really want: just a new job or one that provides specific things? A "new job" could perfectly well turn out to be one at Taco Bell and I doubt that is what you'd have meant!

It's also good to remember that asking for *unreasonable* things generally doesn't work, probably because you can't make yourself believe you'll get them. Doing magic to get rich rarely produces results, but doing magic to pay bills or to buy enough gas to get home probably will. It's because of the "unreasonable" factor that the so-called love spell usually runs into trouble. For one thing, no outside magic can bring another person to love you; love is the result of some primal, internal magic humans have, which nothing can counterfeit or duplicate. Some of the other pitfalls of love spells include the fact that they are really *lust* spells and can all too easily turn into *obsession* spells, which are horrible for all involved.

The whole question involved in determining what you really want actually gets you solidly into the First Law (see Chapter 7, on morals and ethics). Remember how part of it says ". . .do what you will"? Well, *will* is what you focus on your true intention. Many people seem to think that this law says that you can do whatever you want to. Its true meaning is that you are *able* to do what you truly *will*. This is a much deeper truth than merely fulfilling one's transitory wishes and yens. Will is intrinsically involved in establishing one's true desire and, luckily I must say, it's difficult to properly focus will on whims. The greatest danger lies (as always) in using sloppy language. Practice the art of true naming, for in this way you have a far better chance of not doing all sorts of magical work just to get what you don't really want. The many jokes about the misuse of the genie's three wishes is a very important teaching story for magic workers. The devil isn't needed to ensure that the individual fails to get any profit from misguided wishes. Humans are completely able to screw up all on their own.

On another level, finding out what you *really* want brings up the question "What do I want to do with my life?" In fact, as you get a clearer idea of what you want the rest of your life to be like, the easier it should become to sort out what your short-term goals and needs are.

And here we've come to another tough skill. Folks, teaching yourself or another about *Sensing Energy* is no easy task. In the end, the only way one can know if they *really* sense energies is if they believe that they do. All I can do is try to give you some ways to teach your students to build this perception and some ideas of in what way they might sense energy. There comes a point where a student will have to cut loose from everything the majority has been trying to tell them: that there aren't any ghosts or spirits, that there are no "other planes," and that the only sorts of energy which really exist are those measured by engineers.

I've found it useful to ask my students to suspend their doubts and *pretend* that they sense the power. This way they seem to be a little more open to what's going on. Don't, however, attempt to encourage them to see the power in the same terms you do; I don't think any two people perceive it the same way. I actually see it as a touch on my skin, with none of the color and brightness details which others perceive. It doesn't matter, though, whether you hear it as a hum or tone, feel its touch on your hands, see blue or white lights, sense it as heat or cold, or even smell it as violets. What's important is to have some sense of whether or not it's there and an idea about whether it's growing or lessening.

Whether you are trying to teach a student to sense energies or are trying to make sure that you yourself are doing so, the most important thing is to believe in yourself. Whatever vague sense of power you manage, don't make fun of it or tell yourself that it's just imagination. What if it *is* imagination? Imagination is a tool of the will which is used to bring power to the focus.

Since emotions play such a large part in all we do, developing *Emotional Control* is a significant factor with regard to magic. There are a number of ways in which emotion is used as part of magic-working. Sometimes magic workers deliberately create high emotional levels within themselves in order to use the power generated by these emotions to give energy to the purpose of the working. Ecstatic magic, tantra, and other forms of sexual magic fall within this category. In other types of workings, sometimes there is need to prevent the interference of emotions which might have a bad effect on the strength of a working.

Shutting out doubt is the most common example of such a situation. Emotions such as fear, doubt, self-consciousness, anger, and hatred will do nothing to help most magical workings. In fact, they will usually get in the way of your focus and will. Obviously, if you are doing emotional magic to harm the object of your anger or hatred you would feed these emotional states. However, the personal cost in working harmful magical is likely to be rather high and I do hope you'll follow the First Law and avoid magic which is intended to harm another or to interfere with their freedom of choice.

In both emotional and willed magic-workings, it's important that the worker be able to control their emotions to keep them in line with the style of the specific working. A person under great emotional stress due to an event such as the death of someone close or the breakup of a relationship must carefully analyze whether or not they can successfully complete a magical working, and must choose a working that does not demand an emotional control they won't be able to accomplish under the circumstances.

Discipline. Now there's a nasty word for sure! It's been really out of style lately but I urge all Witches to get to know it, practice it, and learn to love it. Discipline is the only thing, ultimately, which will enable a person to do the right thing. Good intentions are just so much dream candy until you cultivate enough self-discipline to actually take action. Teaching discipline to your students is probably going to be your unspoken curriculum for the whole of first degree studies since our current social systems aren't giving this quality much good time.

Self-discipline is simple: just do what you said you were going to do — always. That's all there is to it. Without self-discipline very few people ever get through a magic-working. Somewhere between looking up the right materials and pulling everything together in preparation to work it all falls apart and nothing gets done except that a new mess that isn't going to be picked up anytime soon is created. Start small: only promise to do one thing this week and really do it. Next week you can promise to do a couple more things. As you get used to following through it generally gets easier and easier.

Why is discipline important for magic-working? In addition to preparation, it's necessary for focus and will, as well as for follow-through. Not much magic is possible without it; nor, of course, is a successful life. Part of self-discipline, you may be relieved to know, is *not* promising to do everything people ask of you. Keep your total commitments to things like family, self, and job in mind before you volunteer to take on more. No matter how great it would be if more were accomplished, saying you'll do it and having to neglect other things, or just not being able to do it won't make the situation any better. Maybe if you don't accept the responsibility someone new will step in and begin their journey into leadership.

If you didn't know that *Knowledge* would help you, you wouldn't have gotten this far through what is admittedly a pretty difficult book. Whether it's self-knowledge or general knowledge about things like history, art, music, anthropology, religion and the occult, there's no end to the things it can be useful to know about. Don't stop learning things and don't let your students do so. Build in them the hunger to know more just for the pleasure of knowing. You can never tell when some obscure fact may be just the thing you need to know.

Know yourself. How else are you going to figure out what you really want or find your true will? Why do you do what you do? Why do you do the things you know you shouldn't do? Don't just answer that you're self-destructive — that isn't a true naming. Sometimes it feels good to hurt if only because it reassures you that you are alive. I've always tried to really know why I did things — I went on and did them anyway, mind you, but at least I knew why!

We've arrived at *Honor*, which I talk about extensively in Chapter 7. But it's important to mention it again here in relation to magic-working. The concept of honor and honesty is actually rather simple: if you lie to other people, you know that you are lying. If you know that you are a liar, why would you believe yourself when you're doing magic? Honesty, like lying, is a habit, but unlike honesty, lying is a very bad habit.

The other way in which honor is important to magic has to do with the part of the First Law that says "harm none." An honorable person doesn't need to harm others in order to feel good about themself. While it certainly can cost you a lot when you work harmful magic against someone, an honorable person doesn't refrain from hurting others because it's costly. The point is that an honorable person just doesn't do that sort of thing.

And here we are at the final item on the list: *Silence*. Do you know someone who wants to be a writer and tells you all about their novel, over and over? Do they ever actually write any of it? Maybe not. Frequently, all the talk takes the place of actually doing the work. This can easily happen to a magic worker. Besides, I can't believe that the person who goes around bragging about all the wonderful magic they are doing doesn't see how the people who hear them think that they are a complete idiot. Not to mention that all the talking about magic can destroy the communication established within the self, which interferes with the working.

There are some exceptions to this "code of silence." If someone tells you that they have a problem and asks you to do magic to help, you should let them know that you mean to do so. However, the details won't matter to that person particularly. When a spell-working is completely finished and properly cleaned up, it's permissible to discuss what was done and why, as well as what happened, with another magic worker. Comparing notes, discussing strategy, and critiquing your decisions will probably result in a better working the next time. Just make sure you choose someone with skill, knowledge, and experience for this dissection and evaluation.

Don't expect to be able to fully communicate this skill to your students on the first try. It's difficult for people to understand that magic is not something to brag about, and that bragging can mess up the magic. It's probably a good idea to keep reminding them about it from time to time and they may eventually make the connection with the success rate of their spells and the amount of talking they've done.

In order to attain your maximum power when working magic, it's important to bring the various facets of consciousness into full cooperation and focus on your intent by developing *internal communication*. It's useful to use one of the conceptual systems which sees the human consciousness as having several "selves." The paradigm I use is that of the *speaking-self*, the *wordless-self* and the *spirit-self*. The speaking-self is you in your usual mode, using language as the main mode of communication and giving the senses of hearing and sight preeminence over touch, smell, taste, and any others. It's the part of you which is from Missouri; it must be shown. It's the person in you that can say, "I can't be hot, it's only seventy degrees." In no way do I want to imply that the speaking-self is somehow less worthy or worthwhile than the others; it's just that there are some human activities for which it isn't entirely well suited. When working with the power, it's necessary to bring the other selves into the work.

The wordless-self does not use spoken (or written) language. It communicates only through symbols of many sorts and through play (or what it perceives as play). We communicate with this self in many ways. In personal magic-workings, you will usually use scents, textures, music, and movement to communicate with this aspect of self. The wordless-self is important for several reasons. One is because it is through this self that intuition can reach you. Another is that one's spirit-self communicates best with the wordless-self (ever get the feeling that humans were designed by a committee?). The third self, the spirit, can be in direct communication with the Gods and is your tie with the universe — and the Goddess within.

Please understand that I do not mean to present this division of self as being objective reality — it's just a useful way to think about yourself in order to design better magic. In order to focus will and perceive power, you have to use some qualities of mind which you have been taught are not useful for "real" life. Specifically, you need to use that part of yourself that, as a child, saw brownies in the woods or *something* dashing down a dark hallway — things your parents told you weren't real. Well, the powers we work with in ritual and magic aren't "real" either, at least in terms of this year's science. To reach these powers, we must find a way to use the senses we had when we were kids. This system of seeing ourselves as a multiple can be one way to accomplish this.

If you look at descriptions of magical rituals and spells, particularly ones from the past, you'll note they frequently include things which speak to us in nonverbal ways. By temporarily looking at your wordless-self as something almost separate, it may be easier for you to think of good ways to help it understand your message. The wordless-self can communicate to your spirit-self, but your spirit-self is also aware of what the other two are doing and that they are in communication. This in itself communicates the importance of your actions to the spirit-self. The spirit-self, among other things, can actually touch the powers and communicate with the deities, which explains why we put so much effort into letting it know our intentions. And through the spirit-self, you can perceive what is going on outside of ordinary reality.

Most Witches seem to work less and less magic as their experience and knowledge of the Craft increases. This is very likely only an appearance since there is no advanced magic, just advanced mages. I suspect most Wiccans are natural *chaos magicians* in that many of us strip off all the extras so that we do only those things which really contribute to the working we have in mind. As we gain experience and teach ourselves the skills needed, we require fewer and fewer "props" in order to accomplish the same effect. Preparation of the self is the most important ingredient in any magic-working.

All magic works first on the magic worker and only after that can it be directed outward.

POINTS TO PONDER

- Magic isn't going to solve all your problems, particularly not personal and emotional ones. Can you figure out why this is?

NOTES

[1] This specific quote is from Amber K*'s prepublication notes, which grew to become *True Magick: A Beginner's Guide* (St. Paul: Llewellyn Publications, 1990).

[2] Isaac Bonewits, *Real Magic: An Introductory Treatise on the Basic Principles of Yellow Magic* (1971; reprint, Olympia: Capitol City Press, 1989).

[3] *Hedge witch* is one of several ways to refer to a person who knows folklore about working magic. This magic is generally not connected with any religion and does not use Christian saints, etc.

[4] This is generally buried in a safe spot on one's own land as a protection spell.

[5] See Jeffrey Russell, *A History of Witchcraft: Sorcerers, Heretics and Pagans* (London: Thames & Hudson Ltd., 1980).

[6] This statement was written in February 2001 and was true at that particular moment. As there's a shot which actually reduces flu symptoms being tried out this year, the statement may not be quite so true by the time you read this.

[7] Performing magic is commonly referred to as "working" by Pagans and most other magic workers.

[8] Magical hours divide the day into dark and light halves, which means that the halves generally are not composed of the same number of minutes. Midnight is defined as the centerpoint, in minutes, of the actual hours of darkness on a particular day (noon is defined likewise with the hours of light). Obviously, the hours thus determined will probably not be sixty minutes long. Each of these hours is identified with a particular planet, considered astrologically, so that one can do a love spell during the hour of Venus, for example.

[9] This includes traditional connections made among countless substances such as herbs, semiprecious stones, metals, etc. and the qualities of the planets from astrology.

[10] For much more information on candle magic I can recommend no one more thorough than Raymond Buckland. I believe that there's an edition of *Practical Candleburning Rituals* (St. Paul: Llewellyn Publications, 1982) still available. Scott Cunningham has written several good spell books (all from Llewellyn) and Amber K*'s *True Magick* (see Note 1) is also excellent.

[11] Scott Cunningham's many books (from Llewellyn Publications) on herbs, oils, minerals, etc. are good and inexpensive sources for many useful spells and correspondences of many common and uncommon spell ingredients.

[12] Mercedes Lackey, *Arrows Flight* (New York: Daw Books, 1987).

13 See www.silva2000.com/.

14 Starhawk calls this *starlight vision*, which is contrasted to the *flashlight vision* of ordinary consciousness. See Starhawk, *The Spiral Dance: A Rebirth of the Ancient Religion of the Great Goddess* (New York: Harper & Row, 1979), 18–20.

CHAPTER NINE

Groundmist rises to wreath the mossy grey stones as the sun disappears below the sea. Dark figures — hooded, robed — pace slowly through the grass as low voices take up a quiet chant.

Yea, yea, we all know how this goes on; mystic Witches making magic in the woods. What I want to know is, can we recreate this?

GREY CAT

STANDING ALONE IN THE CENTER

Designing and Leading Large Group Ritual

So the gathering is almost over; everyone had a good time and they are deciding who is going to do what next year. The subject of "The. Big. Ritual." comes up and somehow you find your hand in the air. Oops! Now you've done it — what *are* you going to do?

Creating and leading public ritual isn't really all that difficult, but you have to follow a few rules. The most important one is the KISS principle: Keep It Simple, Sweetie! You want a ritual which tells a story, but doesn't make the story too complex. Concentrate on one single point you want to get across to everyone and make everything in the ritual communicate that one subject. Get people in quickly, get the cakes and cup around quickly, and do everything else slowly in order to maximize understanding.

Don't forget that the primary purpose of ritual is to open up the participants to commune with deity. Communion with deity may happen to some participants even in poorly planned and poorly led public ritual. Ritualists should be aware of this possibility and all participants should be told in advance that it could happen, particularly since at most public rituals there are a number of newcomers with neither experience nor training to help them cope with such an occurrence.

Public ritual is different from home-group ritual in several important ways, the most important of which is that there is a level of love and trust in home-group ritual which cannot be present in an open or bigger group ritual. Public ritual is also larger — much larger. It must keep moving all the time; you'll want to simplify and shorten the usual casting sequence. Most public ritual is done with "generic" casting and invocations. Of course, some of the participants won't really know what is going on no matter how much you simplify things. (That's why I like to have a Ritual 101 workshop at gatherings.) Remember that different groups may use different vocabularies or have different definitions for familiar words. Further, it's generally unwise to attempt really powerful magical work when you can't know much about the people who will be attending. Large ritual, particularly when part of a festival weekend, can raise enormous amounts of energy — more than is convenient to deal with. The result can be a campground full of ungrounded beginners; in other words, real chaos. In general, you don't need to worry about raising power as much as you need to worry about handling it well after it's raised.

Gatherings, festivals, and stand-alone public rituals are important to Paganism on both a community and an individual basis. For the community, they help foster the feeling that we do have something special in common and that there is, actually, a community rather than just a miscellaneous collection of weird religious paths which happen to fit under one word. Even though Wiccans cast a Circle with fourfold imagery and many Druids use threefold imagery and Asatruar don't necessarily define sacred space at all, we have a lot more in common with each other than we do with anyone else. Effective ritual, even if not in the specific form we use at home, can do a great deal to draw people closer together.

On an individual level, group ritual addresses a number of needs which many people have and which they look to their religion to fulfill. First, of course, is the added dimension of ritual when it is performed in a large group. Though the rewards of coven or other small-group ritual are many, joining with a lot of others brings a particular joy which isn't just based on the realization that you're with lots of people who believe in the same strange God/desses that you do (because Christians also gain benefits from this kind of large group participation). Perhaps a psychologist could be more specific than I about the emotional and spiritual effects of doing ritual in a large group. Anyone who has participated in one has surely noticed the special feeling.

The primary purpose of Pagan ritual is to, in one way or another, foster the possibility of communion between the individual and deity. Because Pagans place so much emphasis on this personal communication, many of us value religious ritual more highly than members of many other religions value their rituals. It seems odd to me that the Christian denominations who place the least emphasis on this personal communion are the ones who have the most ritual. As a result, many Catholic, Church of England, Lutheran, and related church rituals, while generally done very well, seem to have no real meaning to the participants.

It's my belief that ritual becomes empty, not because it's repetitive (for there is a special power and effect of repeated ritual), nor because it's led by a professional, and not even because the priest does the ritual and everyone else just watches. Ritual becomes empty because nothing much is expected of it. I well remember the first Craft ritual I ever attended. There were, at most, eight people there, counting the HP who worked alone. I was, to say the least, a mature adult at the time and although the ritual hit me considerably harder than a ton of bricks, I don't think I showed the effects on the outside much. To a great extent, though, what happened to me was more due to the fact that I was at a Pagan ritual with people I'd never met before that weekend than it was due to what went on in the ritual itself. For me, at that moment, just being in ritual with others of like mind was enough to trigger one of the most intense experiences with Goddess I've ever had. I've wondered since what might have happened to me had the ritual been better adapted for a mixed-path group.

I've described this experience to attempt to communicate that when you put on a public ritual, there is a lot going for you. People want to have a good experience at the ritual. They are excited and reassured by the number of other people participating and they are very open to participating in it fully. In other words, you don't have very much resistance to overcome. Deep down, most of them really want the ritual to succeed.

It's my impression that people also get something special out of contributing their own physical movement to ritual. Many Christians leave dignified churches in order to participate in more charismatic groups, many of which encourage an assortment of physical actions as part of the *spirit*. My readings in *The Churching of America* seemed to me to indicate that part of these groups' pull may be a combination of the appealing aspects of large groups, the encouragement of a more direct experience of deity, and the release from being a member in a merely receptive congregation.[1] Since the unofficial motto of Witchcraft is "If it works, use it," let's keep these points in mind as I discuss ritual design.

I have a few general suggestions that my experience both attending and designing large group ritual has taught me:

- Don't keep the participants standing around. If complications have delayed ritual preparations, don't summon people to the ritual site until everything is ready.
- Don't keep the participants standing around. If you plan to anoint or smudge people as they enter or after they enter Circle, recruit a lot of people to do the anointing or smudging. This not only speeds up getting the ritual started, but allows this process to be more personal without rushing people through.
- Don't keep the participants standing around. If you plan to offer the cakes and cup, have four or eight or sixteen cups and plates and people to pass them around.
- Don't keep the participants standing around. (Have I gotten the point across?) Avoid rituals which consist of the celebrants doing all speeches and moving around while the rest of the participants are *congregation*. Build in an element which invites everyone's

participation: throw something into the fire, hand something on with a blessing, divide into "working groups" for a portion of the ritual, etc.

• Don't plan long processions that use the same chant throughout. Arrange to sing a selection of chants if a long procession is unavoidable.

• Avoid too much complexity, particularly complex movements. You won't be able to rehearse the ritual with all the participants (you'll be very lucky if you can rehearse it with the primary celebrants and aides), they won't be able to see lines drawn on the ground (in the dark) after a couple hundred people have scuffed through them, and half the people there won't have a clue about what's going on.

• Moving around holding hands, as in a spiral dance, has some dangerous drawbacks: small people are in danger of having their shoulders dislocated when being pulled around by large people; anyone who arrived at the ritual with a staff becomes a danger to all around them; "crack-the-whip" occasionally sneaks in, endangering everyone making up the tail; and children tend to be lifted off the ground. If the space is limited *and* you enforce a very slow speed, most of these drawbacks can be reduced. Another note: it's not a good idea to ask people to kiss a lot of strangers.

• Plan ahead for individuals who are not sufficiently mobile and/or energetic enough to stay on their feet for the entire ritual. Provide some seating and, in the case of dancing, standing space or seating that is protected from individuals too much into the spirit of the dance (and beside the drums isn't necessarily the best place for this). Plan wheeled transport for people with mobility challenges so they can get to and from the ritual.

• If you plan for wine, mead, or other alcoholic beverage in the cup, provide nonalcoholic alternatives for those who prefer that option.

- Don't be tempted to plan for synchronized pyrotechnics; chances are it will rain and you might end up blowing up Stewart Farrar. Consider (stabile) lighting if you are doing pageantry. Be willing to change nights if the concert is under cover and the ritual is not, and on the night of the ritual it's pouring. Talk to the musicians about this possibility beforehand so they won't throw a tantrum when you go to them with the situation.

- Don't depend on getting everyone together days or hours before the ritual to listen to explanations of what it's about, what they're supposed to do, etc. Limit the need for explanations to something that can be either handed out at registration or said briefly, immediately before participants process into Circle.

- Test all proposed special effects *personally* several days before the ritual. Plan to have the central fire lighted well before the beginning of the ritual unless the individual in charge of it has proved at prior rituals that they can build a fire that is guaranteed to light instantly.

There are a lot of practical matters you need to consider when you begin planning a public ritual. These are important for their contributions to the effectiveness of the ritual. Many of them also contribute to the safety of the ritual participants, a concern which I hope is important to you.

Energy is very easily raised at a large ritual but there's no guarantee that it's the kind of energy you are used to handling. It's usually fairly chaotic and unfocused, no matter how carefully you've tried to prepare people. More and more public rituals have *tylers*, or people selected ahead of time (and hopefully trained) who monitor the energy levels at the edge of the ritual space and are available and prepared to help the HP/S responsible for directing the energy. They can even provide a filter of sorts to feed more organized energy to the HP/S if necessary.

Tylers can also cut doors to let people in and out of sacred space as necessary and can even take care of any participant having either a physical, spiritual, or emotional problem. If someone takes ill or experiences any problem during the ritual, one of the tylers should take the individual out of the ritual and stay with them. Usually there are tylers or guardians both inside the ritual and outside it. Tylers situated outside of sacred space are responsible for managing latecomers and those who want to go in and out of the ritual, as well as meeting with police, firemen, park rangers, or upset neighbors. These people should be wearing conservative *civilian* clothes and should be prepared to address the concerns of unexpected visitors.

Find out how you are expected to pay for the items needed to put on the ritual. At a weekend gathering a percentage of the fees should be earmarked for ritual expenses. You'll need candles for sure, and something for cake and cup. A good ritual which will cost very little can be designed, but sometimes you'll want to carry through with an idea that will require a tub of Jell-O or fifty yards of black fabric. Unless you are willing to personally contribute whatever money it will cost to put on the ritual, be sure you know exactly how much money you've got to spend.

More considerations: will the ritual be indoors or outdoors? what's the floor or the ground going to be like? will it make a difference if it's rainy or windy? how is the area lighted? how large is it? If it's outdoors on rough ground, you won't want to ask the participants to do much moving around; you may even not want to have the leaders move around much. The nature of your ritual site can make a big difference in just what you can expect to do during the ritual. If it's outdoors in a windy area, you'll want to have something besides candles for light; if it's indoors, you'll want to manage some very, very low lighting so that people don't hurt themselves before the candles are lighted. Give some thought to how people with mobility concerns can be handled so that they can participate.

You may, of course, know what the main purpose of the ritual is: if it's at the Beltane gathering, it's going to be a Beltane ritual. However, most gatherings have a theme and you can design the ritual to further the focus on the theme. Moreover, with good design, a ritual's effectiveness can be increased *because* of the theme. You'll probably end up with a better ritual if you start by figuring out what you want it to be or do and then determining how to do it. This approach produces better results than starting with a special effect or bit of theater and writing a ritual around it.

Most important of all, you need a pretty good idea of how many people are likely to attend the ritual. To simplify writing about this, let's arbitrarily create four classes of public ritual based on size: Medium = 25 to 50 people; Large = 50 to 100 people; Huge = 100 to 200 people; and Gigantic = 200+. Any ritual under 25 people can be treated as a coven ritual with a lot of guests. However many people you're told to expect, be sure to make plans in case you have more.

Some of the challenges you'll meet when leading larger group ritual must be considered any time the numbers are much greater than 25. Getting people into the sacred space is a serious potential bottleneck if you don't make appropriate plans. For medium-sized groups, having two lines for smudging or anointing will move people in quickly enough that those waiting both inside the Circle and in line to get in won't get bored and lose their focus. When attendance rises over 50, you may want to consider having 4 or 8 people working this job.

When you have significantly more than 100 people it's probably a good idea to think of new ways to handle the process. I've seen a number of ideas, including placing plenty of the appropriate materials on a table near the entrance and encouraging folks to smudge or anoint each other. Another group set out scented bowls of water on the way to the ritual area where people could do a symbolic cleansing.

Processions around the area also work. In fact, one fine public ritual I attended recently (masterminded by members of Oak, Ash and Thorn tradition) used an in-and-out spiral laid out with fallen branches to divide off the paths. Quantities of tealight candles lighted these paths through which participants wound in and out on their way to the ritual area to form a Circle. It was very effective and people seemed to enter the ritual in a very good mind-place. At one of the first rituals I attended, bowls of red Georgia mud consecrated to all four elements were prepared and, in theory, the participants anointed each other's foreheads with it. Unfortunately, we were summoned to the ritual area a long, *long* time before the leaders were ready. (The mud fight was really fun though.)

With larger attendance, it can be difficult to get people to spread out evenly in the Circle and even, sometimes, to actually *make* a Circle with the altar, fire, maypole, etc., in the center. Good results are usually obtained by having helpers that pick folks up at the entry and guide them around. If the original size estimate is too large or too small, they can cue people to move inward or out. Be sure your helpers know they have the authority (if they do) to make decisions about Circle size.

At all large group rituals it's extremely important that everyone can hear every word spoken, from the Circle-casting rhyme (if there is one) to the dismissal. I've seen a lot of leaders overcome the problem of participants not hearing the quarter calls (the calls are usually muffled because the caller will turn their back on the people in order to face out to the direction) by having the speaker stand at the opposite side of the Circle to call the quarter. That is, have the person calling East stand at the Western edge of the Circle facing the East. A second person is stationed at the actual quarter altar and this person lights the candle, presents the element, and performs any other action required. Work with everyone with a speaking role before the ritual and encourage them to speak loudly and strongly.

Another good tactic in this regard is to reduce the spoken parts of ritual as much as possible. This requires most of us to think about ritual in a different way, as I've noticed that an awful lot of us are very word oriented. But if we can turn our imaginations loose on such substitutes as theater, mime, dance, music, or simple direct action, I know we can cut the word count way down.

This leads right into the substantial problem of just how big a Circle of people you can deal with. Two hundred people make a circle around fifty yards in diameter and if you don't have a parade marshal's voice, it's going to be difficult for people to hear you. Even with good voice control, there are always going to be people behind you. I personally think that using some sort of public-address system is a good idea for large rituals. Some modern boom boxes have this capacity and there are karaoke machines available at quite reasonable prices. It may be possible to design a ritual where all the spoken lines can be said from the edges of the Circle, eliminating the problem of turning your back on people, but I suspect it's going to seem unnatural to both celebrants and attendees unless it fits into the story the ritual is telling.

At some point the numbers can be so great that a Circle composed of people standing one-deep, even if they are standing really close together, is going to be so large that all the people won't see or hear everything that happens. Even if you aren't expecting that many folks, it's a good idea to have a plan just in case. Just about the only solution to this problem is doubling people up. If you know ahead of time that you'll need to do this, you can write a way of dividing people up into more than one ring into the ritual. For example, you can match them up using Maiden, Mother, Crone; the elements; or anything else that will harmonize with the ritual.[2] You can gather people somewhere before the ritual and let them divide themselves up. Have someone take charge of each group and lead the participants into the ritual area and into the appropriate ring.

Another possibility is to mark out as large a Circle as you feel you can work with and place torches, lumieres, or benches to limit it to that size. It's easy to determine the maximum size for your Circle. Have the primary HP/S read something as loudly as they can. A second person should walk straight away from this person in the opposite direction from the one they are facing. The walker should stop when it becomes difficult to understand what is being said. Measuring the distance from the HP/S to that point will give you the maximum diameter for your ritual area. Have helpers aid people in sorting themselves out reasonably, like with tall ones in back and short ones in front. Remember that even though traditional ways of having people move around in ritual are unsuitable for large groups, they can still sway, clap, and even dance in place. Giving people some movement to perform helps keep their attention on the ritual and keeps them from stiffening up in the night air. It also tends to raise good, easy-to-handle power.

Obviously, the cakes and cup is another moment when a large ritual can degenerate into a Greyhound Bus Waiting Room. One large ritual I attended used four chalices but the one which should have come to me completely disappeared about 20 people to my right. You probably need a chalice *and* an attendant for every 30 to 40 people or less — and the chalice bearer needs a bottle in their other hand for refills, as the average cup only holds enough for 10 to 12 people. Sharing food is still a good idea even in Gigantic rituals, but it's important to find a way to get a sip and a bite to everyone quickly and efficiently. I rather like the idea of baskets of cherries (lewd remarks and all), as fruit can be said to combine both cake and cup. And don't forget that not everyone cares to share an alcoholic cup, which makes the cherry option look better and better.

While there's rarely any difficulty getting people out of the ritual area and back to wherever they are supposed to go next, for many people the darkness seems to increase after ritual; make sure that there are good people at hand to help those who might need assistance over rough, dark ground. Please don't forget to have a few people tasked to clean up everything in the ritual area: torches need to be extinguished and lost capes, jewelry, and shoes need to be gathered up, as does the altar and all the tools used for the ritual.

A medium-sized ritual can be a lot of fun to do: it's small enough not to need too much special planning and large enough to let you do some of the things you've always wanted to do but for which you need more people than you usually have in Circle. You can probably design your ritual much as you would a coven ritual, taking into consideration my comments above about keeping things going. This is a great group size for organized dancing; that is, something with steps that everyone does.[3]

Finally, a note to the wise: don't depend on "picking up someone" to drum. That's how the Druids ended up with me as drummer at one ritual and you wouldn't want that to happen to you! If drumming is important to the ritual, make sure you bring both drummer and drum — or other music, of course.

Pagan rituals are made up of a number of specific parts or sections that fit into a specific order, although the point at which the bulk of individuals attending the ritual are brought into the sacred space can differ according to the background of the people who design the ritual. Defining sacred space, called *casting the Circle*, is almost always the first thing done in a ritual. However, most of the large rituals I've attended have brought all the people in before casting. While Witchcraft calls this casting the Circle, other Pagan paths may not visualize sacred space as a circle nor speak of its creation as casting. Regardless of terminology, a particular area of ground or portion of a room is marked off in some way to be the site of the religious ritual. I suspect that Witches will continue casting the Circle long after we own our own premises within which to conduct rituals.

Bringing the participants into the ritual space may be handled as a procession led by the ritual leaders that ends up at the ritual area, or may involve some special activity to prepare the participants for the ritual. Planning the ritual should include not only the process of preparing participants to enter but also a way to make this process move well.

Invoking the Quarters and Deities is the next step in most Craft ritual. While other Pagan groups may or may not include the four classic elements, many do have a set of powers which "anchor" their sacred space and I'd say that pretty much all of us invite two or more deities to attend the rituals we are dedicating to them. A "Drawing Down the Moon" frequently fits in with the invocations of the deities unless it's actually the focus of the ritual.

The next section of public ritual should be a *statement of purpose*. Even if it's just a full moon ritual, which means everyone knows why they are there, it's a really good idea not only to announce that "This is a full moon ritual" or "This is a Lammas ritual," but to expand that announcement a little and tell people briefly about what you are going to do. Most important of all, tell the participants whether or not power is to be raised and if so, where it is to be directed. In very large group ritual this can be done visually or orally; people can carry in fruit and vegetables for a harvest ritual or perform songs or chants which state the purpose.

Whatever the purpose of the ritual, there should be a section that serves as a *centerpiece*. It can be the raising of power, sacred theater, seasonal celebration, or anything else you can think of. Those in attendance will remember this part and their feeling about whether it was a good or a bad ritual depends on the success of this centerpiece.

Be very careful about what kind of power you raise, how much power you raise, and what you do with it. One of the drawbacks of public ritual is that you will almost certainly have quite a few newcomers participating in their very first magical ritual. Since most of us have already handled enough cases of "after-ritual air-walking," think very seriously about how you are going to handle this situation. Even if you don't deliberately raise power, it will be floating around the ritual like mist, so you need a plan. I suggest something between *healing the earth* (hard to visualize) and *healing Lady Goldenrod* (they may not care). I like public ritual to be focused on empowering the individuals participating or empowering a community concern, but there are plenty of other alternatives.

If you chose to deliberately raise and direct magical energy in a large ritual, be sure to select a *recipient* or *focus* that everyone can understand and hopefully visualize. Endeavor not to get participants overly excited about something too personal or emotional like "Never again the burning," as it may be very difficult to ground them. Directing power at large concepts has a tendency to just splash the energy over everything; this is not a disaster, certainly, but it probably dilutes the energy so much that nothing very significant will result and people are likely to leave the ritual feeling let down. Directing energy raised from over 100 people at just one individual can cause flash burns, which I seriously don't think would be very comfortable.

After the centerpiece should come either the *grounding* or the *cake and cup*. These two sections can come in either order. However, even though eating and drinking tend to be "grounding" in themselves, at a public ritual it's a very good idea to have a formal grounding just to make sure that those attending a ritual for the first time are well grounded.

Closing the ritual and releasing the sacred space is the last step of any ritual. It's important to remember to fully disperse all the energies if the ritual was held in a place that will be used by somebody else the next day. On occasion, this step can be completed after the participants leave the area. It's OK to not fully tear down a Circle at your own home, but in a public park, other public place, or on land belonging to someone else, you should take care to completely clean up on all levels. I suggest you let the HP and HPS stay around for a few minutes after the close of the ritual to make sure all the energies are grounded or otherwise dispersed.

In some form these eight steps are a part of every ritual, although in some rituals a step may whiz by almost invisibly. I list them here because they can help you look over your half-created ritual and be sure that nothing important has been left out. It can be useful to visualize ritual as a *bell curve*; one which starts at the baseline, raises up evenly, and then returns to the baseline with the same smooth curve it had when it rose.

Now for some facts of Neopagan life. I know you're going to want to denounce me as a sour old pessimist, but some things that you'd like to have happen just aren't likely: you probably won't be able to get folks together for enough rehearsals; if you give someone else responsibility for laying the fire, it won't start (even if you pour kerosene on it); somebody with a speaking part won't show up; it will rain. Well, things really aren't all that bad, but *do* plan for things to go wrong as well as right.

With regard to Huge and Gigantic rituals, put away the watercolor brushes and get out some ten-inch rollers. Everything you plan for rituals this big needs to be done in bright, bold strokes. People will *not* be able to see absolutely everything done by the celebrants; people will *not* be able to hear everything that is said; and some people will *not* understand what all of the symbols mean — or they will think they mean something entirely different from what you had in mind. At a ritual this size you can bet on having someone there who does not share your cultural background and who is on a Pagan path about as far from yours as they can get.

Some solutions for the problems inherent in rituals with this many people include costuming all the helpers involved in matching and easily recognizable dress. For a night ritual outdoors, that probably should include some white so they will be easier to see. The people doing each set of jobs — bringing folks into the ritual area, getting folks to stand in the right places, passing the cup and plate, providing music or chants — can wear costumes which further the story the ritual tells. I've heard of a large Samhain ritual in which the assistants all wore skull masks with solid black dance wear, which was very effective. Once you have established the story line of the ritual, suitable dress may be obvious. Yes, this is probably going to cost someone a bit of money and it does require a lot of pre-planning, but that's all part of putting on a really big ritual.

Music and dance, alone or together, can be one of the best ways to communicate in ritual (the dance will probably be "performance dance" rather than something that includes everyone). In fact, once there are more than 100 people attending a ritual, it's really chancy to let them move around, as I've described above. (I'm specifically excepting rituals like the totem dance at Pagan Spirit Gathering, which is a different sort of ritual.

Here, power-raising and -directing are essentially accomplished on a personal basis, as is the "story line.")

Please don't let yourself feel self-conscious about speaking loudly enough to be heard,4 making "grandiose" gestures, or generally hamming it up. Good ritual, particularly good public ritual, is always good theater. Practice your lines in front of a mirror and decide what stance, arm gestures, and vocal interpretation will best communicate their meaning. Think of the movements of the primary celebrants as a dance and coordinate your actions. When one of you has an important speech, the other(s) should show, in body language, that they are listening. If you are addressing a sky deity, make your body an arrow to carry the message up there; a message to Mother Earth should be accompanied with gestures and posture which focus downward (without putting your face down or no one but Mother will be able to hear); and messages to the spirits and ancestors around us require some sending-out and gathering-in gestures. (Think of Vanna White when the puzzle is solved or when she sends us off to watch a commercial.)

Wardrobe is particularly important in big rituals and careful selection can do a lot to make the ritual work better. Celebrants, of course, should look wise and dignified but they also need to be able to move freely. Take the anticipated light levels at the ritual site into consideration: black, hooded robes are great for projecting mystery but without a fire and a lot of candles, all you'll be is a nearly invisible shadow! White is great for the helpers who assist people entering the ritual and for those who take around the cakes and cup. Alternately, ask assistants to wear robes, body suits (or an approximation) in the quarter colors with white sashes or headbands. A choir (a great idea at a new event where people probably won't know the same chants) can wear rainbow robes, perhaps with matching stoles. A few yards of fabric can go a long way in bringing a visual unity to those involved in putting on the ritual. For the most part no sewing is necessary, as these items only need to survive the one evening.

Music can add a great deal to a public ritual — or make it a living hell! If you don't have any good musicians available, use recorded music collected onto one tape. If the music isn't to be constant throughout the ritual, put one person in charge of starting and stopping the recording. Make sure you've discussed what to do if the ritual moves more slowly than expected. If it moves faster, it's up to the HP/S to slow things down. Perhaps the best solution is to use recorded music to bring people into and out of the ritual and live music of some sort while it's in progress. Live music can be as simple as a single drummer, but be sure you find someone who understands the role of drumming in enhancing ritual. Each stage of ritual has its own rhythm and speed; a drummer insensitive to this is much worse than no drummer at all. A choir or song leader(s), as mentioned above, can make chants work a lot better.

Always remember that large public ritual always gets complicated; don't add any elements to the ritual which don't contribute to the result you've defined. If you've decided to have each participant take a particular action, be sure you make it clear what the desired action is and that it needs to be kept short and sweet. For one thing, other participants are quite likely to lose focus or get bored if another participant hogs center stage. Plan such individual participation very carefully, as its success is always threatened by exhibitionists, shy people, folks with a disability, inevitable delays in the flow of the ritual, and the actions of any one of the various trickster entities who might have dropped in on the occasion (which is another reason for not attempting any really complicated special or untested effects!).

Ritual is theater but it is also mystery. Suspense is an implied part of most good ritual and is especially important in giving the ritual impact when you haven't planned to work high-power magic. Many ritualists plan for a special effect to mark the high point of a ritual. Let me again caution you to be careful when using special effects. Try them out carefully in advance under many different conditions (i.e., high wind, misty rain, indoors, outdoors). It's good to know in advance that brandy won't generally burn unless it's preheated and that you can smell kerosene on the firewood (tip: hide several tealight candles under the kindling — there'll be no "poof" of flame but you're guaranteed to have fire). If you want the fire to poof, splash some warmed spirits (80-proof or more) onto it after it's begun to burn. Don't use large fire effects in a field during a drought — grass fires move unbelievably fast! In fact, even if candles are the most flammable item in the ritual, have water, sand, or fire extinguishers handy.

While it is unlikely that you will be able to hold a full rehearsal of the ritual, be sure that everyone with key parts gets together to do a walk-through. This will give you a slightly more realistic idea of how long the ritual is going to take and you will have advance warning that the next sentence you are supposed to speak is certain to cause a bad case of the "adabadabas"! Some sentences look great in print but aren't so great when spoken aloud.

When packing up to take all the equipment you'll need to the ritual site, make a list and physically check off every needed item as it's packed. Consult the list again about ten minutes before the ritual's scheduled start time to ensure that everything you need has actually made it to the site. While you can probably find a knife with a corkscrew blade in any group of fifty Pagans, you're going to feel silly having to ask for one. Call everyone who has agreed to take a role in the ritual the day before and make sure they still plan to be there, that they have their wardrobe packed, and that they are still willing to do their job. Double-check with the appropriate person at the festival to make sure that there have been no schedule changes and review your plans for inclement weather. Don't leave anything to chance. Take extra candles, wine, nonalcoholic cup, chalices, cake, plates — everything you might need more of than anticipated.

After the ritual, your job probably isn't over. An effective large group ritual will probably produce a few people with questions, a few with unpleasant comments, and frequently one or more persons who experienced a spiritual event during the ritual which they need to discuss with someone appropriate. Occasionally it can be even worse, as when some idiot high on drugs or alcohol manages to sneak into a ritual, or when someone who's supposed to be taking psychoactive meds goes off them for the weekend, or even when somebody losing their emotional balance wants you to figure out what to do about it.

Pre-plan to make a couple of experienced people who worked in the ritual easily available to talk to participants afterward. Give someone else the job of providing these folks with a beverage and snack and taking their ritual garb back to their tent or cabin. Questions can range from "Why did you do this?" and "Who was the Goddess you called?" to "The Goddess touched me. What do I do now?" It is very important that someone be available to people with these sorts of questions.

Plan an evaluation of the ritual with as many of the people involved as possible. Some leaders like to do this almost immediately after the ritual is over and others like to postpone it until at least the next morning. At this review try to cover most of the following concerns:

- How smoothly did we get people into the Circle and spread out?
- Could most everyone see and hear what was going on?
- Did the cakes and cups get around smoothly and quickly enough?
- Did people ground? Did they have any idea of what grounding is?
- Did most people seem to get the message we intended?
- What didn't some people understand?
- What energies did we feel from participants when it was over? Are these the energies we intended them to take away from the ritual?
- Did many people have experiences that they brought to one of us? What sorts of experiences were they? Was anyone seriously upset by them? What did we do about it?
- What comments did we hear about the ritual?

Each of these questions should generate a second question: What could we have done that would have been better?

I suggest that this discussion be kept to the ritual itself and not find a focus on any single person who might have done something wrong. If indeed someone messed up and needs to be spoken to about it, do it privately. I suspect that, in general, messing up publicly carries its own chewing out. On the other hand, this is the time and place for public praise, by name, of anyone and everyone who did a particularly good job.

Even if you personally have firmly resolved that it will be a long cold day before you ever volunteer for something like this again, hold the review session. Every little bit we can add to the lore of conducting effective large group ritual is needed. It is almost certain that some members of your ritual staff will help put on public rituals in the future.

Really try to stay relaxed about putting on a public ritual and give yourself permission to enjoy doing it. There's lots to worry about and it's a lot of work, but the rewards ain't bad. Amber K* once gave me permission to be Witch Queen of the Universe for a whole afternoon after I pulled off a good group ritual and I'm giving you permission to do the same after you perform your first one.

POINTS TO PONDER

- Read poetry in ritual as if it were prose; that is, do not put your pauses at the end of the poetic line. Instead, pause at those places appropriate to the meaning of the words. The ritual will be more meaningful when it's read that way.

- Make a list of everything that needs to be inside the Circle at any time during the ritual. Before ritual begins, check to make sure that every item is there.

- Outlining the ritual area with small candles set on the ground or floor can present a fire hazard when people in long skirts walk too close to them.

- Make sure everyone who will need to move around during the ritual has practiced walking in whatever garb they are to wear.

NOTES

[1] Roger Finke and Rodney Stark, *The Churching of America, 1776–1990: Winners and Losers in Our Religious Economy* (New Brunswick: Rutgers University Press, 1992).

[2] I once divided a large ritual into five groups, loosely based on age, and each group made its own Circle inside the sacred space and danced to its own nursery rhyme.

[3] I have a personal prejudice against calling it dancing if people are just turned loose to galumph around the circle without pattern or step.

[4] There's a special way of producing voice which lets it be heard over a wide area without having to yell. When you yell, you make the air go through your vocal cords faster; alternately, using actor's voice, you push the air from your diaphragm and make it stronger. This is called using a *stage voice*. Stop by a community theater; you should be able to uncover someone who can help you develop this skill.

CHAPTER TEN

I think it was the silence which woke me up: no traffic sounds, no sirens, no bumps and thumps from upstairs or next door. I stick my nose out of my sleeping bag and pry my eyes open to the faint lessening of darkness inside my tent. Suddenly, clear tones break the silence as a wood thrush greets the rising sun.

Even though I'd been up rather late sitting near the campfire listening to the drums and talking with people, somehow I have no desire to go back to sleep. It's chilly in the tent so I throw my cloak over my sweats and unzip the door. To the east, a pink flush foretells the sun and the silver predawn light makes the early groundmist look like the illustration in a book.

I see movement and there, half in and half out of the mist, is someone in a white ghi doing a kata in slow motion and a group of four or five sky-clad people are on the hilltop to the east, quietly singing a hymn to the rising sun.

I climb the hill to add my own greetings to the sun and then look down across the acres of rolling meadow sprinkled with the colorful mushrooms of tents. Here is the Pagan nation, a world in which for once we all can just be ourselves; where our religions won't make us the butt of dumb jokes and where the dangers of persecution are distant and all of us can experience the feeling of safety. A Pagan village: self-run, self-governed and the reality of the many dreams we share of a world to come.

GREY CAT

BLOW THE HORNS AND CALL THE PEOPLE HERE

Organizing Events

Whether it's a community ritual that brings together 35 or 50 people from local groups, or a week-long festival that draws 500 or 1,000 people from all over the US, sponsoring an event tempts many of us sooner or later. Putting on an event isn't easy, but it's also not as difficult as it may look before you begin. The secret is being organized.

In the following discussion, I will focus on the idea of a two- to five-day festival. If you're working on a one-night open ritual there are many things in this chapter that you can ignore. The general principles, however, are the same: the date and site need to be as convenient as possible; you must let people know it's happening well ahead of time; participants must get to the site and get their vehicles parked; you must take the local laws and the neighbors into account; you must make sure that you've done all you can to keep everyone safe while they are your guests; you have to cover the cost of holding the event and have a plan for any leftover money; and you have to prepare for the event and clean everything up when it's over.

There's just a little bit more to planning an event than everyone agreeing that it's time to have a party. I know there are those who believe that all you really need to do is find a place and a date and let everything else just happen.

Unfortunately, this isn't a very responsible way to do it. With attendees who have never been to a similar event before, folks who don't know much about camping or spending an entire weekend with a bunch of weird people they don't know, and with the possibility of bad weather, exposure, accidents, injuries, and interpersonal strife, we're just lucky that nothing too dreadful has happened . . . yet. If you are determined to host a "freestyle" event you might as well skip this chapter. It will still be here next year.

Alternatively, begin by discussing just why you want to have the event and what purpose you want to accomplish through it. If this is just your idea, sit down with a pen and paper; if there are several people sharing the idea, get together with a good bit of time (and a pen and paper). Why do you want to host an event? Does it fill a need in the community (define what community you're talking about)? If it's impossible to choose a date because there's already something going on every weekend, the community probably doesn't need another event. (Perhaps you can think of something great to do indoors during the winter instead.)

Currently, there are many regional and national festivals so it can be important to have a theme (either a permanent one or a different one each time) in order to identify the particular portion of the Pagan community you wish to attract or to define a greater objective to which the festival is designed to contribute. If you don't have a good reason to sponsor the event, perhaps there's a better way to invest the time and energy of your group. Also keep in mind that while you may be pretty sure you'll be sponsoring only one gathering *ever*, you might want to leave room in case of success beyond your wildest dreams.

Next up is determining what kind of an event you want to host. This question can be more complicated than just deciding whether you're going to put on a local sabbat ritual or a big festival. At most rituals, of course, everyone knows what the purpose is — at least partly. It's a good idea to know exactly why you feel it's a good idea to gather a number of separate groups together, whether it's simply to get to know each other better or to begin the formation of a closer cooperation for some later purpose.

Once you've established the why and what, you get to the hard part: what will you call the event? While clever acronyms are fun and evocative references to misty mornings and dragons are great, they can be slightly overdone. Straightforward geographical or seasonal names have the advantage of actually conveying hard information.

If you're hoping to sponsor a major festival (one with 300 paying participants or more), you absolutely *must* research your date. Conflicts with long-running local events will cut into your base for recruiting major workers; conflicting regional festivals will compete for participants; and coincidence with another national event (if it's geographically convenient and neither your event nor the other focus on special and different groups) can cut your attendance below survival levels. This generally isn't just a matter of competition but rather that many people will already have plans in place for the festival which has been happening for some years.

Of course, the desire to bring together people connected with a particular teacher, coven, or tradition is a perfectly good reason for sponsoring an event, and these small gatherings are probably the easiest type of event to manage. Weekends involving local members of two or more groups whose leadership have discovered a good deal of agreement and liking are also easy and worth doing.

Regardless of the size and scope of an event, almost all the same jobs have to be done. The main difference is that at smaller events, each job takes less time and it's possible for one person to combine several jobs. All events require that you have a core group of people who will accept real responsibility and can be depended on to follow through without being nagged. Do not try to do everything all by yourself. Another difference between big and small events is that for small events, most of the work can be accomplished the day of the event or, at worst, the day before. To host a really big gathering, quite a few people are going to be working for months in advance as well as through the entire event itself.

Here are some basic questions about staffing that you need to ask: are there enough people with enough energy to put on the event? just how many people is it going to take? where are you going to find them? are you sure that enough of them will have time to take a major role? is everyone already stressed out with too much work? Please do not depend on volunteers from among those attending the event to fill your personnel needs. Chances are that just won't happen and if it does, you'll be worn-out from trying to make it happen!

It's very, *very* important to be absolutely sure that you're going to be able to fill your minimum people-power requirements at the outset of planning. If you've only got four or five people you can depend on to take genuine responsibility for jobs connected with an event, plan a small one. With any luck, by the next year you'll have the staff to do something more ambitious. A good small gathering is better for you, better for your hard-working staff, and much, much better for those attending the event. And a good gathering — one which balances substance and fun, relaxation and growth — will grow by its own impetus and will bring in helpers who believe in the event and don't begrudge the time and effort involved.

Call a meeting of all the people interested in putting on an event and all the folks you hope will be willing to help staff it. When your group initially met, you decided to definitely sponsor an event and you talked about just what sort of event it's to be. Your second meeting (which can theoretically be held the same day) needs to be devoted to making some crucial decisions. Complicating these decisions is the fact that each is partially dependent on the others. For example, the type of site chosen will have a direct effect on the entrance fee; the season of the year will have a lot to do with the type of site desired. These decisions include:

Sponsorship. Exactly who is going to sponsor this event? While it's tempting to keep everything in your own hands (or inside your own group), for most events, bringing in others to help is generally a very positive action. For one thing, it takes quite a few ready workers long before the date of the event to get everything together and make sure it runs smoothly. Recruiting as co-sponsors a few other groups or individuals with whom you've already worked and with whom you have enough in common will make for a much better event and everyone will be less exhausted when it's over.

At this point it's a good idea to appoint one or more overall leaders — probably one from each participating group — who have enough authority to make decisions that follow the guidelines developed during the first couple of meetings. I call these folks *buck stoppers* because they are where passing the buck stops. While these leaders probably will want to discuss any decisions with each other and with people whose jobs will be directly affected, it's needful that there be someone who can make fairly quick decisions about problems as they come up. (Finding the time and energy to hold a meeting on the spot to discuss these problems probably will be too heavy a burden on everyone considering how much work there is to do.)

Experienced event sponsors assure me that after a nucleus of people who know their jobs and enjoy doing them is assembled and trained, the buck stoppers essentially can resign from most decision-making and become support persons for the coordinators. After continuous fire-fighting at the first event, they will then have time to ask around among the coordinators and inquire how they doing, if they need help, etc.

Money. How much money will it take to set up the event and where will it come from? It costs a good bit of money to put on an event — *any* event. Even though you and your core group are going to pay your own gas costs, phone bills, postage, and connect time personally, there are other costs that will have to be paid in advance, as preregistration money comes in slowly, if at all. These expenses include printing and postage for the gathering announcements; reserving the site (deposit); possibly obtaining insurance (most places require that you get private insurance if the event is anticipated to run more than a minimum number of attendees — this insurance was less expensive than I expected); reserving porta potties; etc. Of course, the amount of seed money required will be different for every event, but all events need some.

The other very important thing to decide about the money *at the outset* is what you are going to do with any that's left over at the end. And, yes, if you plan well there should be some. Good preplanning, reasonably accurate attendance estimates, and proper costing (*costing* means figuring out in advance how much you'll have to spend to put on the event) should ensure that there will be at least enough left over to provide the seed money for a repeat event the next year. Good planning can also provide moderate sums of money for other projects, which is perfectly ethical so long as you are honest about it up front *and* actually spend it the way you said you were going to.

Attendance. Will the event be by invitation only? open notice to the Neopagan community only (or to some subdivision of that community such as "all Asatru" or "all British Traditional Wiccans")? wide-open welcome to anyone who has seen the poster in an occult bookstore or other location? Be prepared to draw people from a much wider area than you may have expected.

Location. Will the event be held in a hotel or a conference center? at a park or campground with cabins, mess halls, and gyms? on someone's back forty with porta potties, bad roads, and no water on-site? The season of the year will have an effect on what sort of site you'll look for, as will your goals for cost, comfort, and accessibility.

Food. Will you need to provide meals? If meals are provided, more time is required in the event scheduling and more volunteers will be needed. Additionally, you will need adequate cooking facilities and refrigeration. Remember that with food included, the fee to attend will look quite a bit higher. Thought will have to go into how to please everyone — omnivores, vegetarians, vegans. Finally, is there a place to dispose of garbage?

There are folks in the pagan community who specialize in food preparation for gatherings and will work with you to provide and charge separately for the meals. Generally the provider donates a percentage of the profits to the organization as well, but that's an individual decision. Just know that you will not please everyone and if you will be offering carnivore and vegetarian but not vegan, or if you cannot cater to individual special diets, make that known because you *will* be asked. It's important to make the food options clear in your announcement materials.

If you decide not to provide meals, you must check to see if the proposed site has any permanent outdoor cooking aids such as stone barbecue pits, picnic tables, etc. It helps a lot if there is a convenience store close by. Should no drinking water be available on the site, you may want to arrange for one of the venders expected to bring bottled water to sell.

Accessibility. Think about making the event accessible to people with mobility challenges. Tent camping at heavily wooded sites (or in once-plowed fields) is not accessible to a lot of people. You may have to discourage any special needs people from attending or think about a slightly less heroic site.

Entrance Fee. There are a number of decisions which will have a direct effect on the entrance fee of an event; making these decisions is a process called *costing*. One thing you have to figure out is how many people you can expect to attend. If you have to reserve a site and either pay a portion in advance or commit to a certain rental regardless of attendance after a particular date, you need to know how many advance registrations you'll need in order to cover this cost. If you don't have enough reservations, cancel the event, pay the cancellation fee, and be glad you aren't stuck owing more.

Frequently the amount of the attendance fee is decided first and all other plans are made to fit the event into that fee. It's still necessary to determine how much will be set aside for people who can't afford to pay a full fee but are willing to do extra work to earn their attendance; for discounts extended to workshop presenters; for special enrichments and materials for ritual; and for the cost of basic first aid supplies, child care materials, firewood, etc.

It's important to restrict the number of free and reduced-fee participants, otherwise you may find yourself hosting an event for which no one is paying full price. However, many event sites charge per person attending and that includes you, the coordinators, the scholarship people — everyone. As these fees can add up pretty quickly, decide *early* how many of these you can afford.

You arrive at your entry fee by adding together the cost of the site, publicity, needed materials, food, out-of-pocket cost for scholarships, and anything else you can think of and then dividing this amount by the minimum number of paying people you feel you can count on attending. If this figure comes out too high, find a way to cut your costs — don't just cut your entry fee and hope you get additional people to meet your obligations.

There's absolutely nothing wrong with coming out a little ahead at the end of the event. For one thing, you'll have seed money for the next event without digging into your own pocket! As I mentioned previously, as long as you're honest and up front about exactly what will be done with any excess, there is no ethical issue. It's not even unethical for the people who put in all the advance preparation time to pay themselves a small salary so long as it's based on hours worked and no one is cheated or deceived. If the excess is going to a "good cause," be specific. Say that it's going to a fund to keep low-income Pagans on-line when their computers misbehave or to a scholarship fund for kids of Pagans, and then be sure it actually does go to that purpose. Plan to donate some of your profit to the site; this helps to ensure that you can get it again, and if your liaison has been good, they've probably done more for you than they promised.

Decide exactly what you're going to do about people who make reservations, pay, and then cannot attend. Are you going to refund all or part of their money? Don't leave this question for a panicked, off-the-cuff grab at a decision after the event has begun.

At the second meeting, when you definitely select the date and really commit yourself to sponsoring the event, you also need to work out a timetable of the various jobs which must be completed before the moment the event begins. Then you must find people to take responsibility for each of these jobs. (The various jobs, the extent of the commitment each entails, and the exact responsibilities are discussed later in this section.)

At least six months in advance (for a national event, double all these times):

1. Select the site. This job done by the site coordinator (big surprise). You can't really get going on event plans until the site has been selected *and* reserved. Make sure you've got a copy of the site rules, as you're responsible for seeing to it that everyone at the event obeys them. It's a good idea to include these rules — plus your own rules — in an informational message to those who register for the event. As soon as the site is selected, reserve porta potties and any other rental needs — these are in demand and you'll be up a creek if you leave it too late and can't get any!

2. Make a final decision on the date. Obviously, this and committing to your site selection go hand in hand.

At least four months in advance:

3. Finalize the name and focus of event and solidify general thoughts on publicity. Decide when the announcement should be made. (Two to three months in advance is the usual interval for the announcement of a regional event. Local events need less lead-time and national events need six months to a year and more than one announcement.)

4. Fill all the important jobs. Arrange for insurance; guest speakers; and liaisons with park rangers, police, neighbors, media, local medical facilities, etc. All those with responsibilities should visit the site, if at all possible, to help with the planning.

5. Finalize menus if meals are to be provided.

At least three months in advance:

6. Settle all issues to do with the ritual. Check on how each coordinator is doing and where problems are cropping up.

One month in advance:

7. Confirm all things which must be reserved ahead of time (guest speakers [nationally known people need a year or more to add an event to their calendars], porta potties, ice delivery, food venders, etc.). Add additional people, if needed, to supervise the volunteers.

One week in advance:

8. See to final details. In the time immediately before the event, things speed up and there will be all sorts of things to attend to, like compiling the final count of preregistrations, buying food and other

necessary supplies, accepting deliveries at the site, finding someone with a truck to take all the stuff out there and so on.

The day before:

9. Transport the core group to the site, do all the necessary basic set-up, pick the best cabin for yourself (oops, did I say that?).

The bigger the event, the more people you need working on it. Below I've divided up the work for a more or less average weekend event planned for fewer than 200 people. If you think there will be more attendees, put two people on as many of the jobs as you can. Divide up some of the jobs if that appeals more to your working style. For events under 50 people, you can combine many of these jobs, but it still isn't a good idea to try to do everything alone.

Buck Stopper(s). There needs to be one to three persons who will be able to make independent decisions should a time crunch require such action. Buck stoppers need to be able to take over any of the other jobs if something happens, act as traffic cops to keep things moving reasonably smoothly, and generally take all the heat from every malcontent who comes to the event.

If there are two or three buck stoppers it makes sense to divide their responsibilities: one can be responsible for all the paperwork issues and the another for all the physical facility issues. When you have three, make the third responsible for the schedule and volunteers. This divided load helps prevent any problems due to confused lines of authority.

Publicity Coordinator. This person does all their work before the date of the event. They design and write the invitation or announcement, have it printed, mailed and so on. They are also responsible for getting posters put up in local bookstores or other spots and handling the media if it comes into play (although possibly one or both of the buck stoppers will be part of any interviews). The publicity coordinator is also usually responsible for preparing the pre-event material, telling people what to bring and what not to bring, and arranging for any printed materials to be given out when people arrive at the event. Make any restrictions — no sky-clad, no pets, no children, etc. — clear in the announcement. There will still be people who just don't get it, but you'll be in better shape if you fully inform them up front. (See also Internet Coordinator, below.)

Registration Coordinator. As soon as the first note or phone call comes in from someone who says, "I'll be there," the registration coordinator's job begins. They need to have an up-to-date count of how many people are expected — both paid and total. They also need to know how many preregistrations have actually been paid, how many scholarship people there will be and how many free and reduced-cost entries have been granted. This person should receive all mailed and on-line registrations and forward merchanting, workshop, special health and child care information included on the registrations to the appropriate coordinators, as well as keep an independent list of these details.

As the event gets underway, this person will be very busy getting a registration area set up, making sure that those who have paid in advance aren't made to pay again, and that those who haven't paid do so. Their list will be the only record of who and how many people attend the event and will make the difference between getting enough money to pay for it and coming up short. Of course, working the registration desk is one of the work-jobs attendees will be asked to sign up for and the coordinator will need to have figured out beforehand how to make these jobs clear and easy.

Set up a fail-safe system to make sure that everyone does pay their entrance fee before they are allowed to truly enter the site. If registration cannot be accomplished at the actual entrance to the site (due to the need to plug in a computer, for example), figure out how to control where those who haven't paid in advance will be until they have paid. Don't count on "Pagan ethics" to bring these folks up to registration a couple days later with the money. You'll be disillusioned and why tempt people?

Meals Coordinator. If you will be providing any food for those attending the event, someone has to be in overall charge of this. The meals coordinator will submit menus which fall within the amount of money set aside for meals in the event's costing, research the proper places to purchase the food, and make arrangements for it to be at the site. They will also work out how many helpers will be needed for each meal and what the specific jobs will be so that enough volunteers can be found. Double the meal coordinator's estimates for numbers of volunteers to cover preparation and cleanup.

Site Coordinator. As well as looking at possible sites and choosing between them, the site coordinator also needs to map out the site (and provide a map to the publicity coordinator so it may be included in the handouts if it's needed) and indicate the tenting spaces, workshop sites, ritual area, drumming space and so on. This person will also be responsible for getting the site set up for the event and for getting everything picked up when it's over.

The site coordinator is also generally in charge of talking with the site owners, the park rangers, the local police and firehouses and so on. I know it's a scary thought but it's really better to talk with them before the local Klan turns up or something upsetting like that happens. Most people who have done this have found that these various authorities are glad you thought to talk with them and, while they may think it sounds pretty weird, take the whole idea of the event reasonably well because you weren't afraid to get in touch with them in advance. You may even decide to invite them out to visit while the event is going on. In any case, give them a phone number in case of need and they'll probably decide your group is in the "harmless nut" category — a really good police category to be in. When you go to talk to these people, please dress like a real grown-up: it makes a much better impression and these are folks who have to make snap evaluations about the people they run into and clothes *do* count in such cases.

Health Care Coordinator. At every event there should be a person who watches out for all the guests' well-being. At a simple event like a local sabbat, a pocket full of Band-Aids and maybe an Ace Bandage will be all the equipment you need. The longer the event and the further it is from "civilization," the more seriously health care should be taken. Make every effort to find someone with some sort of medical training for this job. They'll be able to decide when it's time to call an ambulance instead of you having to decide. We've been used to being a young community but that's not true any more and having someone around who can tell a heart attack from heartburn will become increasingly important. The health coordinator should schedule some time to check out the nearest hospital, the kind of emergency facilities and staffing it has, and if there's a nearby rescue squad, paramedics, helicopter and the like. It's always better to know about such services and not need them than need them and not know about them.

Child Care Coordinator. You usually need someone to do this job. Even for an evening ritual it can be difficult and expensive for parents of young children to find a sitter — particularly in those cases where the grandparents don't approve of Neopaganism. We're a little undecided about the "place" of children in a way; we don't want to indoctrinate them in our religion but surely we don't want to hide it from them either. Plenty of rituals are "suitable" for children to attend but the kids may not want to or the ritual may be complicated enough that the kids will need some help figuring out what's going on. Having someone in charge of making sure the children are both safe and are enjoying the experience is worth some time and trouble.

The child care coordinator will probably eat up most of the work-jobs set up for volunteers, and these are often the hardest positions to fill. The coordinator might want to make some good plans for activities so volunteers who aren't parents will have help in providing the children with a fun experience and will have an enjoyable time themselves. For larger events, there will be a need for more than one option to take care of the age range expected. The coordinator will need to provide everything from baby sitting for very young children to activities for preteens. I tend to offer a special, reduced entry fee for families but also charge a small materials fee for each child under twelve or so in order to buy crayons, construction paper, magic wands, and fairy dust.

Security Coordinator. Whether you call them "safety," "security," "guardians," or something else, large events and public events need a few really good people to take care of some pretty important jobs. To begin, the security coordinator and volunteers look over the site with an eye to danger and then try to find a way to eliminate it or keep people away from it. At a public ritual, they will not only monitor the energy levels in the circle and cut someone out if it becomes necessary, but at least one of them will be outside the ritual to be available in case the police or fire department turns up. They will also be alert to any individual(s) causing problems inside or outside the ritual itself.

At a larger or longer event, the security coordinator's job begins with checking out all the points of access to the site and determining if any of these accesses need watching. They place quiet, passive wards on the area and maintain a watch for anything or anyone which triggers them and decide what areas need to be patrolled during the event. They figure out where to park the cars, where to put child care, and how to get someone with a broken leg to a hospital quickly and efficiently. They monitor the weather service radio and warn the buck stoppers or someone else, as appropriate, if bad weather seems to be coming.

The security coordinator is there if the mythical pick-up truck full of rednecks with guns in the rear window drives up or if someone is allowing the energy levels to overwhelm them (a much more frequent occurrence) or if a fight seems to be building up. Obviously, these folks have to be very carefully chosen but they need not be limited to the physically blessed; a little old lady in sweat pants is likely to have success defusing the redneck situation and she's in a pretty good position to not get hurt if a husband and wife find themselves in real trouble.

Finance or Accounts Coordinator. Unfortunately, there have often been accusations made against gathering organizers about the handling of funds. Sadly, some of these accusations have been true, although most have not. It's a really good idea to have someone other than the leaders of the sponsoring group in charge of taking care of the money. Posting accounts to date at the event can also help dispel any gossip. The accounts coordinator should, if possible, be someone who has a talent for figures. Strict attention to every expenditure and asset goes a long way toward preventing unpleasant gossip.

The following coordinators may not be needed. It depends on the size of the gathering, the number of people in your core group, and perhaps a need for jobs with less responsibility for good people that you want to keep involved.

Workshops and Scheduling Coordinator. Before the event this person will go through the various activities planned, choose from among the workshop proposals received, and work out a schedule for the event. If workshops will be a part of the event, this person will advise those individuals chosen to make presentations that they have been scheduled and when. This coordinator will produce a schedule at a time agreed upon with the publicity coordinator so that copies of the schedule can be handed out to those attending the event.

Herald Coordinator. This job can easily be merged with that of scheduling coordinator unless the event is very large and long lasting. This person's job is simply to keep up with schedule changes during the event and to send a volunteer "town crier" around to remind people that it's time for the next set of workshops, ritual, dinner, etc. The herald coordinator is the person who has a chance at keeping the event from degenerating too far into "Pagan time."

Sweat Lodge Coordinator. If you can't find a person who is trained in this area, has the confidence to decide if a stranger really does know what they are doing, and can be trusted to lead a safe and worthwhile sweat, don't allow sweat lodges. I live in fear of someone dying in a sweat at one of our gatherings — I've heard of some Neopagan sweats which were dangerously hot and/or long. Like leading a major ritual, leading a sweat lodge isn't a job for a beginner. Additionally, there are special rules about how to build, cleanse, and take down a lodge which an untrained person may not know. I don't feel that there is any excuse for not treating sweats with the same degree of respect we'd wish for formal high church Gardnerian ritual. There have been outcries from assorted Native American individuals or groups about the nonindigenous taking over items from their spirituality, although sweats with a religious or spiritual aspect are a custom not limited to Native Americans and are definitely not limited to the tribes from whom the noise has come.

Merchanting Coordinator. It may seem silly to suggest you need someone to manage this part of an event, but a lot of problems can arise if no one is paying attention. Above all, having a good selection of Pagan merchandise can be a draw for an event that happens more than once. It's still difficult for many people to find the various small luxuries and necessities of our paths. Of course, most everything is available on-line but you don't get to touch before you buy.

I strongly suggest that you treat merchants fairly; asking them to pay full entry fee and a 10 percent contribution (why call it a contribution when they aren't given any choice?) only means that they have to put prices high enough to cover these expenses. Events aren't *fun* for them — they're doing their job through the whole thing. Requesting an item for auction is much easier on them and can easily raise more money than the tithe would. Good merchants can be as important to a successful event as good workshops and food.

Balancing Area Coordinator. Particularly at gatherings where a large number of beginners are expected, it's a great idea to set aside a quiet spot on the site and have it staffed at announced times with people who can help anyone being overwhelmed by the energy levels, upset by the language or lifestyle, or otherwise feeling inadequately centered. Those staffing this area do need to be experienced.

Ritual Coordinator. The event will have all or some of the following: an opening ritual, a *big* ritual, a closing ritual, a drum circle, and miscellaneous handfastings and dedications. Not every event needs a special person to keep these rituals straight, see to it that the ritual area is prepared and cleaned up, and schedule the rituals those attending the event want to put on — but it sure can help. Sometimes the ritual coordinator is the person responsible for the big ritual or even all the rituals. At other times, this person is in charge of organizing volunteers in advance to put on the big ritual.

Transportation Coordinator. If you're holding a national or even a regional event, some of your participants may be flying in (or even coming by train or bus), in which case you'll need to organize getting them picked up at the airport and taken to the event site.

Internet Coordinator. This person creates a Web page about the event, makes a form for preregistration and attempts to arrange a way to accept credit cards or arrange with an Internet payment service for prepaid registrations. They also answer e-mail queries about event, get it mentioned on appropriate mail lists, etc.

Volunteers Coordinator. This person consults with each of the other coordinators to determine how many volunteers will be needed and prepares appropriate sign-up sheets. During the event, they attempt to make sure that enough volunteers show up when expected to get the jobs done. This job requires a very diplomatic person with a will of pure iron, for not only do a lot of gathering attendees manage to neglect to sign up for anything, a lot of those who *do* sign up don't bother to turn up at the time promised.

Our community has been troubled with an awful lot of "free riders" in recent years and I personally think that we should attempt to make it difficult for people to shirk doing their share. Make sure everyone signs up for a work shift before they are allowed on the site. If someone doesn't show up for their work shift, send a herald around to call their names, dig them out of whatever they're doing, and get them to where they are supposed to be. Yes, it might embarrass them a little. So what? Free riders do us no good whatsoever. If they want to get mad and leave I really doubt we're going to miss them. I suspect that most of our problems at events come from the ranks of these free riders, petty thieves, folks who start silly arguments, those who leave litter on the ground and don't put their pop cans in the right recycling bin, and people who keep talking right through workshops or try and walk in and out the ritual circle — basically, the same people who, after the event is over, tell everyone in town that "it really wasn't all that good."

It's extremely important to select the best possible site for your event. I developed a checklist from a similar document used by someone in the Society for Creative Anachronism and my revised site report form is as follows:

Site Report*

Gathering date_____

Name of site_____
Address_____
Contact person's name_____ Title_____
Telephone number_____ Site phone_____
Reservation due date_____ Cancellation cut-off date_____
Is insurance provided?_____ How much?_____

LOCATION

_____ miles from _____
Directions_____
_____

COSTS

Deposit $_____ Due by_____
Per person charge for bed & meals: Adults $_____ Children $_____
           Meals only: Adults $_____ Children $_____
           Bed only: Adults $_____ Children $_____
           Camping fee: Adults $_____ Children $_____
           Electrical, water connection: Adults $____ Children $____

---

*Site Report, pages 240–243, may be reproduced for personal, noncommercial use only.

GENERAL

Size of site_____acres   Size of exclusive area_____acres

Parking facilities_____

Types of structures available_____

_____

_____

Privacy_____

Special access or privacy issues_____

_____

How pretty is it? Is there shade, swimming, boats, etc.?_____

_____

Comments_____

CABINS

How many cabins? _____ Beds_____ Bunk rooms_____

Beds per room_____ Bathroom facilities per cabin_____

Shower rooms_____ Toilets_____ Fresh water source_____

Amount of hot water_____

Comments_____

CAMPING

Approximate number of tents accommodated on flat ground_____

Availability of toilet and shower facilities_____

ACCESS

Paths: Gravel___ Paved____ Concrete_____ Ramps_____

Stairs_____ Hilliness___

Distances between activity areas_____

_____

Comments_____

ACTIVITY AREAS

Place for ritual_____ Place for drumming_____ Meeting area_____

Merchanting area_____ Child care area_____ Health care area_____

Comments_____

DETAILS

Staff arrival and departure times: Arrive from _____ on _____

Depart by   _____ on _____

Participant arrival and departure times:

Arrive from _____ on _____

Depart by   _____ on _____

Trash and garbage arrangements_____

Ice availability_____ Vending machines_____

Toilet paper_____ Telephone_____

MEALS

Number facility can feed: Adult_____ Children_____

What meals? Breakfast_____ Lunch_____ Dinner_____

First meal at_____ Last meal at_____

Choices available: Vegetarian_____ Vegan_____ Omnivore_____

Other information: Tables, paper or regular plates, etc._____

_____

KITCHEN FACILITIES

(In many state parks meals are not provided by the site, but kitchen space is available.)

Dining space: Number of tables, chairs, benches_____

Refrigeration facilities_____

Stoves and appliances_____

Cutlery, dishes, pots_____

GENERAL CONCERNS

Limitations and/or special rules_____

_____

Site ambience_____

Magical impression_____

Attitude of owner/manager_____

What is the best feature?_____

What is the worst feature?_____

What about clothing optional?_____

Comments_____

There is probably no such thing as a perfect gathering site. There are, however, some things which particularly help or harm a gathering, which I've listed below:

- A lack of level tent sites can make the morning hours a bit less happy.
- A shortage of showers or showers at extreme distance can be a real problem. The same is true of toilet facilities.
- Extreme hilliness and/or long distances between activity areas can be very hard on people with mobility challenges and on older folks in general.
- A lack of any area with visual privacy from the outside world is a real disadvantage.
- Non-Pagan owners living on-site can cause difficulties.
- More than enough toilets, porta potties, etc., is better than not enough. This is a really bad place to skimp.
- The workshop areas, ritual site, and drumming area all need to have enough distance between them to prevent the sounds each produce from spilling over. It's usually better to have the drumming

take place in a low spot; if it's on the ridgeline it may be heard from miles away.

- Too large a site prevents people from mixing and getting to know new people, while too small a site may cause all the problems associated with overcrowding.

If you do no planning at all for your event, there'll be at least one bonfire where people will drum and dance all night, a few serious types will announce they're holding workshops, a half-assed attempt to hold a ritual will be made, a couple of people who think that they have overdosed will worry about health care, and you'll be busy answering questions and breaking up nasty arguments — all this for however many days the event goes on. If you announce no workshops or other continuing education events in advance, the majority of your guests will be there only to party and it will be a toss-up whether the merchants are cheating their customers or vice versa.

On the other hand, if you try to plan every minute of a gathering it not only doesn't work well at all, but it really cuts into the enjoyment. A careful balance between planned time and free time, relatively serious activities and activities more focused on fun, generally makes for an all-around more enjoyable experience. If you've got a theme for the event, you might build the rituals, the workshops, and even part of the fun around that theme.

Except for get-togethers which are just for the purpose of holding joint ritual, events usually include at least three rituals: Opening Ritual, Big Ritual, and Closing Ritual. I personally tend to downplay opening and closing rituals, letting them be primarily the business of the security staff in warding the site and then making it clean. Although I seem to have some strange personal reluctance to attend opening rituals, they can go a long way toward really setting up the theme of the event. If you plan to use the opening ritual in this way, I suggest that it's best to schedule it as late on the first arrival day as is practical to allow as many people as possible to attend.

Give it just as much attention as you do the main ritual; get a really good ritualist to lead it and help them write in some really good stuff that will help the participants get into the appropriate mind-set to contribute to the theme. This is also a good time to go over the rules and announce any last minute changes.

I go into some techniques for effective large group ritual in Chapter 9. In case you don't have time to review that right now, I do suggest that you keep it simple and keep it clear. Remember that it's most likely that some of the participants will be at their very first magical ritual! Short rituals tend to be more kindly remembered than long ones; rituals which encourage everyone to participate in some way may well be perceived as "stronger; and rituals in which participants can hear every word seem more "professional." The form of the opening ritual may be simply put as (1) we're delighted to be here, (2) this is what we hope to do while we are here, and (3) may the god/desses bless what we plan to do.

The big ritual — generally held on the Saturday night of a weekend event — is more difficult to plan and put on. You need to start by finding ritual leaders who are really good at it. Unfortunately, this particular job often becomes a political matter. Some folks see the job as some sort of status symbol rather than a pretty difficult undertaking; strangely enough, these folks are generally the least qualified. Experience has led me to believe that it's worth facing up to a possible political thunderstorm in order to get the best ritualists to do the job.

In a themed event, this ritual should be planned in such a way that it really attempts to do *something* about reaching the goal(s) implied by the theme. By this I mean that it should be designed to promote the ideal, create the organization, or accomplish the spiritual change that the theme indicates.

The closing ritual gives everyone a chance to say goodbye and, hopefully, to thank you for going to the trouble to put the event on. It is also a good time to help attendees begin the transition back to the "normal" world. Leaving a gathering can be rather emotionally stressful, and reminding people that it's going to be different "out there" will help them begin the process of changing worlds.

Some gathering organizers welcome all workshop proposals and suggestions for other sorts of activities. While this usually works out alright, there have been cases where the individual leading the activity has overestimated their knowledge and/or abilities. People attending a Pagan event open themselves to experiences and frequently make a real attempt to cooperate with all the activities. Unfortunately, a badly led and/or badly conceived guided meditation or similar activity, under these circumstances, can leave some participants dangerously ungrounded or insufficiently guided back to reality.

I suggest that you exercise some discretion about who leads activities and what activities are done. Ask people for biographical information or information about their background regarding the activity in question. Check around to see if they've got a good reputation in their community. Sweat lodges, vision quests, some types of guided meditation, and shamanic journeys all can be dangerous when the leader just isn't good enough to support people who aren't properly prepared and properly brought back.

Workshops which include people touching each other, such as massage training, can be the occasion for unfortunate occurrences. Responsible massage training spends a lot of time teaching a massage therapist how to touch other people without that touch exceeding reasonable limits or being misinterpreted — something that can't be taught in a one-hour workshop. Workshops of this type have given rise to allegations of improper sexual behavior in the past and many gatherings have chosen not to approve them.

Some workshops can greatly benefit the event overall, so much so that you may want to go out and find people to offer them. Circle 101 is a quick introduction to Pagan ritual and explains to all the newcomers what will happen and what they will be expected to do. Pagan Manners is another subject which seems to need a certain amount of explanation to event participants, and not necessarily just to the newcomers. (Toward the end of the chapter there is a brief discussion of this topic).

Usually you'll want to have a schedule of workshops and rituals prepared and duplicated to pass out at registration as people arrive for the event. It's a really good idea to go on and make it a *booklet* and include the rules for both the festival and the site and some advice about good manners. Including short biographies of the workshop presenters and ritual leaders makes the booklet more interesting and may inspire people to actually *read* the rules. This also gives you a chance to remind everyone that they are expected to sign up for work-jobs. It's also a good place to list the names of your loyal and hard-working volunteers and give them a hearty "thank you" (do this again at the opening and closing rituals).

Events can be particularly difficult times for those recovering from addictions and I, certainly, feel it's important to help provide the kind of support that they may need. I generally appoint a suitable site for twelve-step or other types of support groups and include in the schedule a time for them to meet in that spot. This can be a lunch and/or dinner meeting or a meeting that takes place immediately before or after the evening meal. I suggest late in the day, as temptations tend to increase in the evening. I've rarely had any problems finding someone willing and qualified to lead these sessions, particularly since "giving back" is part of most recovery programs. At larger events, I suggest you find a qualified moderator before-hand to help with the planning of this element.

Announcing your event is obviously crucial to making it a success. It's important, first of all, to get as many people as possible to register for the gathering in advance. It's even better if they'll pay in advance so that everything doesn't have to come out of the hosts' pockets! When people have registered, you probably need to send them a map telling them how to get to the gathering. Remember that most of the people coming to the gathering are city people and they need the best possible directions to get them to the site.

At a gathering or festival, there's more to protecting the health and safety of your guests than protecting them from outside visitors, fights, and minor accidents. Protection starts with the material you send to folks when they register, which should tell them what to bring. These days, festivals attract many people who are not only new to Paganism, but are new to spending nights outside of a real bedroom. Unless you want to run out and buy two dozen blankets the second day of the gathering, it's a really good idea to tell everyone what they'll probably need. I've made this simple for you by listing everything that an attendee should bring (just leave off the tent if roofs and beds are provided and the cooking gear if meals are provided):[1]

- Tent or other shelter (you must have advance reservations for an RV if you plan to camp in one)
- Bedroll or sleeping bag and blanket
- Mattress or sleeping pad
- Camp stove and fuel (building cook fires at the gathering site isn't permitted)
- Nonperishable food
- Cooler and ice
- Drinking water
- Rain gear
- Jacket
- Sport clothes (enough to allow for changes in case you get wet)
- Long-sleeved and short-sleeved shirts; long and short pants
- Swim suit
- Underwear, night clothes
- Lots of socks
- Personal medication
- Sunscreen

- Pen and paper
- Ritual gear

Some of these items may seem obvious to you, but people don't know how badly they can sunburn when they take all their clothes off. They also think that heat exhaustion only happens to hard hats and desert nomads and they've apparently never heard of hypothermia.

Most of us know that it's a good idea to ask all our guests, as part of their registration, if they have any health problems. Knowing if I have diabetes or a heart condition helps the health care people if I'm found unconscious on the ground. Actually, I make sure they know I'm more prone to heat exhaustion. It doesn't make the condition less dangerous, but at least they know what to do first! When you know beforehand that you have participants with disabilities, you can plan appropriately.

Advise people to leave valuables, laptops, expensive cameras, jewelry and so on at home or to lock it in their car. Remind them never to leave such things lying on the ground outside their tent — that's practically entrapment, except there won't be a video camera on the would-be thieves and the participants won't get their stuff back.

Provide all the rules for the gathering and for the site in the package with the map and what-to-bring list. Print facts such as no alcohol, no pets, no children, etc., boldly in every advertisement. It will save everyone involved headaches if you plan things so that you are not making rules that will be impossible to enforce. If you don't want people smoking cigarettes in the ritual area, then don't site the drumming circle in the same place. If there are clothing-optional areas as well as clothing-required areas, make signs and post them visibly and liberally at the boundaries of both areas. Don't be afraid to have your staff say, "I'm sorry, you must have missed that 12 x 12 ft. neon sign that says you are entering a clothing-required area" while smiling.

In the course of the gathering, some people may not realize that dancing naked too close to the fire can result in second-degree burns they won't notice at the time, or that being undressed isn't necessarily sending a sexual message. Saddest of all, numbered among us are a few sexual predators whose Pagan beliefs fail to prevent them from attempting to indulge their appetites. It's important for someone to keep an eye out with the hope of preventing anyone from being threatened seriously by one of these people. Perhaps the best defense against the predators is to make sure that any victim (near victim, hopefully) feels comfortable coming to someone on the staff. It's the victim's decision, of course, whether to involve the police or not in these cases.

Those of us with considerable experience at gatherings have some idea of just how many hazards lie in wait for the inexperienced; with thought we can help guard against at least some of them.

We've been lucky so far and few Pagan gatherings have had serious run-ins with the law. With as many gatherings as there are now, I worry a lot about whether this may change for the worse. It's not all that difficult to make sure you're in the right and it's definitely worth taking the trouble to do so. If the neighbors panic and call the police and fire department, you've got a really good chance that they'll apologize and leave if you've contacted the proper people in advance. Here are some tips for avoiding messy legal situations.

Parade Permits/Assembly Permits/Park Use Permits. Check with someone at city hall, the county courthouse, or the state park office before you plan to hold a ritual on public land. Check with the zoning commission before you hold anything very big on private land. Some residentially zoned areas have all kinds of use restrictions. If you *have* to fight the zoning board, you're in a better position to win if you haven't already broken their ordinances.

If you're holding a large ritual in any type of public park it's a really good idea to have someone check in with the police a day or two in advance. If you don't feel that you can talk about your event with someone at the police station, it's better to postpone it because you're taking a chance of having to talk to the same person in far less favorable circumstances (e.g., standing in a park surrounded by a crowd of neighbors yelling "Satanist," a bunch of people wearing really weird clothes whose rights you're attempting to argue, and a bunch of cops who have *no idea* of what's going on or how much danger they're in).

Alcohol. Generally speaking, it's illegal to consume alcohol on public land. Generally speaking, the police can arrest people who are obviously drunk and may be perceived as likely to drive in that state. Generally speaking, having alcohol in your possession is going to greatly decrease the effect of your arguments about first amendment rights.

Recreational Drugs (a.k.a. Illegal Drugs). Your opinion on the use of drugs, the history of the illegalization of recreational drugs, and the proper medical use of pot do not matter. If the police find drugs they can, if they wish, seize your car and/or your property and put you in jail. Keep your drugs at home where you're the only one taking the chance and insist that others do the same, particularly at an event on Pagan-owned land. It's truly wrong to be in possession of drugs in that situation, as the owner can lose their land, their investment, and the product of their hard work.

Pets and Children. Not all pets are trained to the same standards and not all people can face a friendly Rottweiler without panic (and homeowners' insurance *does not* cover Rotties!). Chained-up dogs often bark or howl — something the people in nearby tents are unlikely to enjoy. If you decide to allow pets — something I recommend against for a lot of reasons — make sure you've thought it through and make absolute rules covering all possible types of pet.

No one can accept responsibility for someone else's child. If a child is hurt, a hospital will not treat them in the absence of a parent or legal guardian unless the injury is life-threatening. People who bring their children to an event must not be allowed to abandon their children to the child care staff or to anyone else involved in the event.

Most state law can be interpreted to consider it child abuse if an adult who is not a parent of the child in question appears unclothed where the child can see them. If your event allows people to be sky-clad, it's wise to define an area for this and bar children from entering that area.

Knives and Other Weapons. In many states our athames are illegal. Wearing swords, gitanas, and other miscellaneous weaponry may or may not be illegal depending on state law. If you know someone in the Society for Creative Anachronism, they'll probably know all about these laws. Otherwise, check with the city and/or county attorney; it's their job to answer questions of this nature. Having a handgun outside your home requires a permit (unless you're a policeman and then you know what the rules are) if it's even legal at all. Long guns are more likely to be legal, but you won't need them at a Pagan gathering.

When you finish sponsoring your first event, you'll be able to join Rhiannon Bennett, myself, and a lot of other fine people in telling "bad Pagan manners" jokes. Until you've hosted you just can't believe the displays of bad manners that can happen. Everything you can say about what makes up good Pagan manners boils down to *respect*: respect for the hosts; respect for people of other paths; respect for others' fears and preferences; respect for yourself by not doing dishonorable things.

Rhiannon, from her many years experience, has written the following suggestions for proper conduct, which you might want to share with the coordinators of your event. You can also use the ideas for compiling a short discussion to include in your event mailer or gathering booklet:

Neopagan gatherings are not commercial endeavors, or at least few of them are. Most are more like a normal "guest" and "host" situation. The entry fee is there to cover the expense of hosting the festival (which is considerable) and does not give those in attendance carte blanche to "do as [they] will" according to their personal philosophy. Different sites have rules and regulations that the festival organizers must agree to at the onset of the contract. My mother Priestess once said, "Being late sends the message that you think you are more important than everyone else." In the case of insisting on a behavior that threatens the entire use of the property, it is more than rude — it's unconscionable.

That notwithstanding, different festivals have different focuses and each will have different rules. Do whatever you can to encourage the attendees to *read* the rules, preferably *before* they get to the site so they won't be surprised to find that clothing *is* or *is not* optional. Some people come to a festival and then *bitch* about everything in the world that doesn't meet their expectations. Even at a small gathering, it is not the responsibility of the festival hosts to make the event "live up to" everyone's personal hopes and dreams. Giving them fair warning about what to expect will, at the very least, reduce your own feelings of inadequacy if someone complains.

Attendees often expect the main ritual to be a profound, enlightening, awe-inspiring, personal spiritual experience and then criticize it if they don't *tingle*. The focus of a large rite is to bring people together. If it moves some of the participants, great; but if everyone doesn't get tingly over the sheer energy generated when a large number of folks come together, help them realize that it's not the fault of the ritual coordinator and their committee.

Scheduling a festival is very difficult. If a major festival offers six-plus workshops per block with four or more time blocks a day, as well as national speakers, musicians, festival rituals, bardic circles, drumming circles, and merchants, how in the world can people in all good conscience call it a "party" festival?

Volunteers give up mass amounts of their lives on a regular basis year-round. They are willing to work the entire festival so that hundreds of people they don't know can have a good time. They then take the blame and criticism for anything that goes wrong. So why do they do it? I've heard the notion that they're on a "power trip." Well, while I can't guarantee that some folks aren't drawn to the possibility of recognition, unless they are masochistic they will soon realize that volunteering entails more work than it does recognition. Of the many wonderful people I know that have worked and continue to work on festival planning, the ones that stay with it do it to see the genuine smiles on the faces of the people that come. That's the reward.

Communicate to those attending that they must clean up after themselves. The staff will be exhausted from planning, preparing, and running the festival and chances are that they'll have had about five hours of sleep per person for the entire festival. They don't need to spend two more days picking up after everyone.

Ultimately, people must be responsible for their own personal safety. Not everyone that comes to a gathering is honorable, and these days, anyone can buy what we once considered identifying jewelry. Try to impress upon people that if they find themself in a situation that makes them uncomfortable, they should leave and alert security if they feel it's an overt incident. Anyone are faced with a situation that feels that it may be beyond their control, should say "*No*," repeatedly, firmly, and *very loudly*. People will be there in a second. On the other hand, those who engage in loud personal squabbles will discover that security is going to feel obligated to come and check it out. Staff will be too busy to referee a family squabble.

Those who are so certain that they can do everything so much better should be encouraged to go out and host their own event.

To wrap up this section, here's a list of items that you may want to share with those in attendance in an attempt to make their experience of the festival more enjoyable:

- Don't walk barefooted in the woods after dark without a flashlight.
- Don't underestimate the wildlife in the area.
- Don't jump over a fire in long, flowing robes unless they are asbestos.
- Don't jump over a fire whose pit is over three feet wide or ignore PADFJ (Priestesses against Drunk Fire-Jumping).
- Don't urinate on the fire, especially if you're a woman (don't ask).
- Don't abandon your children at child care. Many of us love children and they may be adopted and gone by the time you remember them.
- Don't drop trash or butts on the ground.

The bottom line is that you will get out of a festival exactly what you are willing to put into it. The staff can procure the site, coordinate the workshops, speakers, musicians and group rituals, but the magic is *you*.

I bet you thought I'd forgotten the most important part of a Pagan event: the fun! It's important that your guests have a good time and some of that fun is the better for advance planning. But it's important to make sure that your event isn't scheduled too tightly. People need enough time to wander around, look at the merchants' displays, and just meet new folks and talk with old friends.

Plan a party, a drum and bonfire circle night, a bardic circle, or an emceed talent show. Lots of people in the majority culture don't know how to just have fun — everything's always been done for them. So you'll not only need to schedule these recreations, you'll need to find someone to facilitate each one. Hanging around is fun to some extent but it's generally worthwhile to plan some specific "fun times" as well.

Maybe even more important is to plan some fun for all the people working to make the event happen. First of all, advance planning and organization should reduce the chaos during the gathering and allow all the staff more leisure time to actually enjoy the event. Insist that absolutely everyone have formal, designated time off — yes, even the buck stoppers and security coordinator! Obviously these folks are going to be "A" types and getting them to go off duty isn't going to be easy; make every attempt to arrange for their jobs to be covered and encourage them forcefully to follow orders!

Even if yours is a one-time-only event, it's a really good idea to have a meeting of the organizers and all the coordinators a couple weeks or months after the fact. You can go over what things went right and what things didn't — and you can compliment each other on a good job well done. Of course, if it is to be an annual event, this meeting will also cover the preliminary planning for the next year. Putting on an event tends to be habit-forming and there's every chance you'll want to do it again.

My special thanks to Rhiannon Bennett for her contributions to this chapter. She worked with the Heartland Pagan Festival organization team for ten years and continues to this day as an outreach coordinator. The Heartland Pagan Festival is held every Memorial Day weekend at the Gaea Retreat Center, outside Tonganoxie, KS. Rhiannon is also the founding mother of Earth Rising, Inc., the nonprofit organization that raised the money to purchase the Gaea Retreat Center, which is completely volunteer-managed and -operated. Its payments and ongoing maintenance costs are supported by regular group rentals and donations.

POINTS TO PONDER

- You won't actually be able to stick totally to the schedule, but if you've built in some gaps, you can catch up in those intervals and get back into real time. Starting the big ritual at 2 A.M. isn't recommended, as it pushes the concept of "Pagan Time" a bit too far.
- Handicapped access requires more than a couple of ramps. Wheel chairs require paved roads and concrete sidewalks. We aren't, however, in a position to make most of our events easily accessible to people of every conceivable disability. Seek a reasonable compromise.
- Not everybody will be pleased. Accept this fact before you get started.

NOTES

[1] You might want to recommend a book about camping and outdoor cooking such as Dian Thomas, *Roughing it Easy: A Unique Ideabook for Camping and Cooking* (Cincinnati: Betterway Books, 1994). If you are going to recommend this title, you may want to also include the following information: ISBN 0962125733; $14.99 (list price).

CHAPTER ELEVEN

You have hit on one of the key points, of course, when you discuss the power and magic of the Word, and the necessity that all parties agree on its meaning, and that this can only be insured through dialogue, including not only the definition, but an agreement on the meaning of the words used in the definition.

B. STEVENS

PATHWAYS TO THE FUTURE

Teaching Our Religion

Most modern Witchcraft groups place a very strong emphasis on training students in the knowledge, rituals, customs, and skills of a Witch. It comes as an unpleasant surprise to many newly come to Paganism that an ambitious course of study should be expected, although other religions have similar requirements. And while there are many books covering each author's idea of the basic knowledge of Witchcraft, it's generally agreed among experienced Witches that, even ignoring the mysteries, few people can really learn everything from books alone.

I don't mean to imply that there aren't some very good books available and that anyone willing to read several of them, preferably by an assortment of authors, won't learn a great deal about Witchcraft beliefs and practice. But it's difficult for any author to teach as well through the written word as they can when given interaction with the student. Certainly I do not intend that anyone use this book as their sole educational resource for elevation! In reality, most Craft teachers assign their students a number of books to read in addition to other methods of teaching.

Traditionally, once a student was accepted, they spent a "year and a day" learning about the group's ritual and much other knowledge about Witchcraft. At one time, most students also copied the leader's Book of Shadows by hand in order to have a copy of their own. The current scarcity of personal time and ease of photocopying seem to have put an end to this custom for many groups.

"The Inter-Tradition Guidelines,"[1] developed some years ago, list the following general requirements for first degree training (pre-initiatory training for the groups who developed it):

1. One must be adept at meditation.

2. One must thoroughly understand the basic symbolism of the Circle, including

    a. the Quarters and their calls of the tradition in which the student is being trained (here, some teach the standard Neopagan ones first and following initiation they teach the ones particular to their tradition);

    b. altar layout and position;

    c. robe and badge of position (where used); and

    d. protocol and etiquette.

3. One must know the sacred elements.

4. One must know the coven and tradition totems, deity figures, etc.

5. One must know the history and philosophy of the Craft.

6. One must know the pantheon of the tradition in which they are being trained. Knowledge of other pantheons can be follow-up teaching.

7. One must know the sabbats.

8. One must know the esbats.

9. One must have an introduction to healing arts.

10. One must have general knowledge of the power of symbols (may include runes).

11. One must know how to cast sacred space and perform basic ritual.

12. One must be moderately knowledgeable about one form of divination.

13. One must have a thorough knowledge of both Universal Law and Coven Law, and live these to the best of their ability.

14. One must know and adhere to the Code of Honor.

15. One should have served as a dedicant for a year and a day.

16. One must be adept at conducting ritual.

17. One must be free of substance abuse.

18. One must be capable of self-sufficiency in life or be actively pursuing such goals (i.e., enrolled in FC 101).[2]

Of course, you'll be passing on the teachings you received. But before we start talking about what you're teaching and how best to teach it, let's talk for a few minutes about accepting students. I can assure you that out of ten people who turn up for their first class in Witchcraft, you'll probably initiate one. This doesn't seem to change no matter how high the group's requirements or how long students are expected to study. Obviously, few students wishing to work as little as possible are going to ask to study with a group with particularly tough requirements, thereby sorting themselves out somewhat.

I do recommend that you put your prospective students through a good screening process, which is the only way I know of to really affect the dropout statistic. Losing a student halfway through training is always a painful thing. No, I'm not recommending that you keep people on a string for years and years, graciously accepting the occasional candlelight dinner from them as they try to achieve your acceptance. However, the tradition that one shouldn't accept a student until they've asked three times isn't all that bad an idea. Holding an "Introduction to Witchcraft" or "Introduction to Paganism" set of classes is one way of identifying students likely to succeed with the more difficult coven training. After observing the individual over a number of classes you can better estimate their abilities and commitment. These short courses of general information are often offered in connection with adult or free university programs or a Pagan business. There doesn't seem to be any problem within the Craft community in charging a small fee for these classes.

It's important to be aware that professional troublemakers actually exist. In *Antagonists in the Church*, Kenneth Haugk discusses this not uncommon phenomenon that occurs in many sorts of groups — and not merely religious ones.[3] Sometimes these troublemakers are simply difficult personalities or highly neurotic people. Others deliberately cause discord in group after group, presumably to achieve some goal of their own. Either way, group leaders can find themselves losing self-confidence and not infrequently, a group so attacked can fall apart. This book is pretty condensed and I'm not going to try to précis it here. Written by a Christian minister, only a small amount of change is needed to totally adapt it for Pagan use. Even the chapter devoted to finding support in the Bible actually speaks clearly to the need for a religious organization of any sort to find a method of dealing with discord within its belief system.

If someone comes to you for teaching and tells you they have been in several other groups, ask if you may talk to the leaders of those groups. I usually do this in order to be sure that the group knows the individual is seeking elsewhere. At that time you can give the leader an opportunity to mention if they've had any particular sort of problem with the person in question. In common with most Witches, I believe that people can change their behavior, but it does little harm to have as much information as possible when making such an important decision.

Chronic antagonists are neither amusing nor something a group can survive unscathed. At worst they destroy the group and cause the permanent retirement of the leaders. At best they will put all involved through a very stressful and miserable experience. I do strongly recommend you get a copy of Haugk's book.

You'll want to have a good idea of what your student already knows — about Witchcraft in specific, but also their general knowledge of history and other academic disciplines, as well as their mundane skills and experience. You may be more comfortable developing a questionnaire for prospective students to complete and return, or you may prefer to sit down with them for a long talk. Either method is effective and the only advantage of the questionnaire is that you have a record to refer to later.

Of course, we all know that serious legal problems can occur if we accept a student under the age of eighteen. Yes, I agree that the majority religions don't necessarily observe this limitation but I think that a parent *does* have a right to oversee their child's religious education until some age, and here right now that's eighteen. Although I have initiated one person who was under eighteen, the young lady in question was born to a practicing Craft family and not only knew her stuff, but was a good deal more mature than many students regardless of age. I'll accept a student under eighteen only if I meet with at least one custodial parent and have their knowing permission (which expressly includes the "W" word, Witchcraft).

I've begun to make sure that new students have at least a bare minimum of control over their own lives, at least so far as to know where breakfast is coming from and having a clean plate in the kitchen off of which to eat it. If a prospective student's family is in a state of real change, I recommend that they put off their studies until things settle down. I also ask outright if they have any illnesses or other problems which may interfere with study or practice. Not that I would turn down someone with diabetes or depression, but it's a lot better to know about these things ahead of time.

Unfortunately, there are many things a prospective student probably isn't going to tell you about, including alcohol or substance abuse problems, chronic bad boyfriend or girlfriend records, marital discord, and/or psychological problems greater than you, as a teacher, are willing to cope with unless a professional counselor is added to the mix. Introductory classes are ideal for sorting out many people with hidden problems. Those with problems are going to miss sessions — oh, with a perfectly good excuse usually — but it's very hard to teach Witchcraft to someone who isn't there. (Don't ever, *ever* let yourself continually rearrange the class schedule for one individual. It simply isn't fair to the others.) My advice, which I don't necessarily always take myself, is to ask troubled students to fix what's wrong in their lives first and then come back to you for study. Even if you accept someone with personal problems for study, at least you'll be forewarned.

I don't think that we should be called upon to provide a course in Basic Civilized Life. Students should come to us with some basic manners and the ability to balance their checkbook, budget their money, boil water, and get to work on time every day. I've looked up books on-line in a category called "life skills" and have seen several which looked like they would help someone having a hard time getting a handle on these basics.

Sometimes it really is necessary to ask a student to leave the class or group and there probably isn't any way to make this easier for the teacher. The teacher feels badly because they know that they probably shouldn't have accepted the student in the first place. Many teachers assume that it is the fault of their teaching and assign no blame to the student. Sadly, there are only two common outcomes to this situation: (1) the student goes away angry and bad-mouths you all over town or (2) they go out of town and tell everyone that they are an X-degree initiate of your group. If you can recommend them to another local group with whom they may be expected to do better, you might avoid these results. This isn't often possible unless the primary problem is that the student really does seem to belong on a different path.

My first group of students and I tried to be a support group but I'm not at all sure that was — or is — a good idea. We found that one person was sopping up most of the support and it wasn't really helping her get better. Too much support can be very seductive and to the individual receiving it, it can seem worthwhile to continue needing and deserving such support. Not that a group, coven, or class of students doesn't make a good support group, but they shouldn't allow that to become the focus of their meetings. We meet to study Witchcraft and need to keep that in mind as much as is practical.

One question which often comes up about teaching Witchcraft is whether it's best to have a class of several students or to work one-on-one. It seems to me that there are good and bad points either way. With a group you can have discussion and the students themselves will bring up a lot of the points you want noted and they'll find some issues you've never thought of. The primary drawback to holding classes is scheduling. Between changing meeting days and times every week until everyone forgets to even come to the meeting and becoming so strict and hard-nosed about schedules that everyone is required to attend each meeting, you begin to annoy even yourself.

Teaching one-on-one at least reduces the problems of scheduling and it doesn't matter if you meet at a different time and day each week. You get to know the student better and you can be absolutely sure that they understand everything. Drawbacks include the fact that if you end up with more than one student it will really begin to eat up your time. With a group you can rehearse the ritual forms, but that's a lot more difficult to do with a single student. In actuality, you usually don't have free choice: either six people will show up at once and the only way you have time to take them is as a class, or only one student shows up at the first class but they really seem to be a good one — and there you are. When you have a choice it's probably best to go whichever way you are most comfortable.

Where do you start now that you've got your student or class sitting in front of you waiting for jewels of wisdom to drip from your lips? Actually, you're not quite ready to begin teaching even yet. People learn in different ways. There are people like me who tend to learn best from print material. There are people who learn best through listening and those who really learn best with a maximum amount of hands-on time. If you have a class, varying your teaching method and approach can help, although there are some people you may end up working with individually for some parts of study. A multimedia approach undoubtedly goes a long way toward meeting a variety of needs and keeping the material interesting, thereby keeping the students' attention.

You will even, at least to some extent, be teaching them how to learn and how to figure out which style of learning suits them best. For the more important elements of what you have to teach, there's a progression: listen to the message, question the message, understand the message, and then restate the message; this process helps you teach and helps the student learn. For such things as doing ritual, the progression is as follows: I (the teacher) do, you (the student) watch; I do, you help; you do, I help; you do. We have an advantage in that we teach a specialized set of materials and our students come to us with a real desire to learn them. What we need to do is constantly revise our own approach to the materials. In fact, it's by constantly reexamining what we are teaching that the greatest benefits come to the teacher. Each time you teach Witchcraft 101, you'll understand more about it.

If you've gotten your student(s) fresh from a short introductory series of classes, you can jump right into tradition materials. But if they are starting at the beginning, I like to commence with a lot of information about what Witchcraft is and isn't, then take a brief look at the different Wiccan traditions and usually a look at Neopaganism in general. After that it's pretty difficult to decide on how to sort out all the different things you want to teach. I get into ritual pretty quickly so students can participate more fully and practice to take parts themselves. While all the teachers in my group use the same set of classes, I think everyone has taught them in a different order with each student or group.

My friend with a Master's degree in education has looked at how we've been teaching in our group and he says that first we teach our students about the philosophical tenets of Witchcraft. This is done through ordinary teaching methods: lecture, discussion, reading, etc. Then we go into the ritual aspects, both as a matter of understanding the rituals and learning to participate in and lead them. This requires a combination of continuing the philosophical material and rote learning both the words and the physical components of ritual. When that part of the process is well begun, we help them start the inward-looking process, which is a training issue rather than a teaching one. Of course, we can't teach students to actually do this work; we just help them with the tools it uses, such as meditation and vision quest. This is an area which we can lead them *to* but cannot lead them *through*. The fourth step in our teaching process is applying what was learned in the first three steps to divination, ritual, magic, and leadership.[4] At this point, we really begin to step out of teaching and into something more like mentoring. Even in a class situation, one-on-one interactions will increase at this time since each student will probably be focusing on an individual interest.

I like to have each student do an individual dedication ritual when they've gotten through about six classes or have been working for a couple months, whichever comes first. This is simply a promise to study seriously and protect the confidentiality of the materials and information being shared with them. It's also a chance for the teacher to remind the student, in a way they will really hear, that it's possible they'll realize by the end of the training that Wicca just isn't their path. It happens. Nobody's wasted any time, though. The student has lots of useful knowledge and a solid base from which to seek the spiritual path which will be right for them. And strangely enough, the person who doesn't continue on may well have been one of your best students, meaning you, as a teacher, have gained a lot from the relationship as well.

We make a pretty big deal out of the dedication ritual; even if we decide to dedicate more than one student on a particular night, we run them through the process separately. First degree studies are difficult and the student is experiencing a lot of new things to think about and, if we're doing our job well, the way they experience the world is changing. The dedication ritual provides a reward for those first few difficult classes when they are realizing that we really mean they must develop self-discipline, learn to meditate, and memorize ritual all at once. The ritual itself is usually a very positive experience for the student and it seems to be a source of strength for them over the bumpy road to first degree.

One of the costs of being part of a religion without rules written in stone is that we have to help our students develop a sense of personal responsibility, self-discipline, honor, and community service. Unfortunately, there's just no easy way to teach these things. No writing from some great mind can be depended upon to totally communicate the spark that energizes people to pursue such difficult goals. As human teachers, the only technique available to us is to do our best ourselves to live in harmony with these ideals and to join our actions to our words in the hope that our students will adopt them for their own. We can also reward them when we observe them acting in harmony with these principles by letting them know that we've noticed.

I cannot tell you in words what the true mysteries of Wicca are and I certainly can't tell you how to bring your students to them. I believe it to be as much an intuitive process for the teacher as it is for the student. What we can do is help them develop a sense of wonder and a greater acceptance of the evidence supplied by their own senses. In a society which professes only to accept *scientific* evidence, we must help them open up to what science cannot yet measure.

Our role as teacher is to help them accept their experiences that can only be seen with the inner eye or heard with the inner ear. But we must also help them maintain a sense of proportion. I guess I can best explain what I mean here with a comparison: it's one thing to believe in the possibility of visitors from somewhere in outer space (i.e., UFO sightings) but it's a different thing to accept all the alien abduction stories going around.

We believe that there is an unseen component to our world; that there are deities, totem spirits, thoughtful entities which don't live in the world exactly the way we do. Sadly, any religious belief can be taken too far. Witches believe in the balance of all things and this principle of balance should also be applied to our religion and its beliefs. We seek illuminations from the other worlds but we should live within this one. The ideal of Witchcraft is to be well balanced between all worlds. However, this ideal is not a static and unmoving balance, but a dance spinning among the spheres, never still and never falling. The only way to arrive at this dynamic balance is to dare the dance and we, the teachers, must do this and find our balance before we can hope to pass it on.

It may sound like I'm asking you to achieve some point of perfection, but remember balance. If perfection were achievable, it wouldn't be perfect for a Witch. It is, however, important that you have done a reasonable amount of inner work before taking on a student. Not that this is an easy resolve to stick to: the moment you know things to pass on you may well be deluged by folks who want you to teach them. Remember that learning and then passing on Witchcraft is a trust we have accepted, one which we in our turn will pass on. Teaching the Craft, whether or not it is a part of leading our own group, entails so much more than merely conveying information. As a result, we owe it to our students to give ourselves some time to make sure we've internalized the mysteries and the real import of the knowledge we've received.

Witches frequently speak of *The Mysteries* but other Pagan groups may not. However, there is a mystery element to many religions and teachers of other Pagan paths may find this discussion helpful. This is not meant to imply that the mysteries of the Craft are the same as those of other paths, nor that they should be compared in any way. I believe that, like the Gods, there are many Mysteries — they are different, but important, to an individual's understanding of their own path.

How *do* you know that you yourself have reached the true mysteries? It's really not a thing that someone else can tell you. I believe the best evidence is your own inner surety. For me, an important part of it is an understanding of what I am and what I'm called to do. I feel that I can know when I've been honored with a communication from some mysterious entity and when my imagination is trying to get me out of something — or into something. However, self-image sags and the wise always question their sureties and there can be days of doubt. Obviously, personal surety isn't enough — your connection with the invisible needs to fit somewhere in the general range you can observe among leaders you respect. As well, it's important to remember that not every entity necessarily has your good in mind!

Unfortunately, no matter how well you've done your inner work, you still may make a mistake when it comes to judging correctly about granting initiation. All you can really do is *never* initiate anyone you don't feel completely comfortable about and then just accept it if you make a mistake. The fact must remain that you know for sure that you have trained the student to the best of your ability. While individuals are our students, we give them the best we have and once they are initiated, they are free to do as they will — good or bad. Strangely, even for a teacher who has come from a long line of Witches who left the tradition of their initiation to found new traditions, it's not easy when an initiate leaves to practice a different Witchcraft.

It seems to be almost a tradition of its own in the Craft that when an individual leaves one group for whatever reason, they feel the need to loudly criticize the group they've left. Perhaps it is partly unfulfilled expectations which pushes an individual who had left a group openly and without rancor to suddenly bristle with criticisms. On the other hand, it does seem that there are some people who hope to gain status in our community by criticizing everyone else. I believe that we are gaining some maturity and paying less and less attention to these folks. More and more we are withholding recognition from people whose only claim is the distribution of gossip.

One of the most unpleasant things that can happen to a teacher is when we must refuse initiation or elevation to a student, particularly if the student comes to us requesting it. As a rule of thumb in this situation, you *can* question an individual's readiness. Especially in the case of second or third degrees, I feel that anyone who really wants the elevation just doesn't understand what they will be getting themselves into. It's my conviction that the Goddess drags in her priests and priestesses kicking and screaming and that's the way it should be. It's a sort of a theory of mine that anyone who wants it isn't qualified for it. That's not quite true, of course. Obviously an individual must want it in some ways, but it's important for them to realize that the demands are going to be overwhelming at times and they will be giving up their private life in some ways. As much as any Christian minister, we must focus ourselves on our job as clergy over and above our personal ambitions.

Is there any good way to break the news to a student that you don't feel they are yet ready? In my experience, no. I can recommend that you handle the situation in a way which will allow you to feel that you did the very best you could. I'd begin by following absolutely the "letter of the law" of your tradition on how initiations are to be approved. Bringing in the other upper degrees in the group can not only take some of the heat off you, it can also let you double-check your own reasons for refusing the initiation. After all, we are just people and have likes and dislikes which don't necessarily match others' impressions. If it turns out badly, you'll probably feel better that you checked up on your own perceptions.

I personally feel it's important to very honestly review with the student exactly how they have failed to fulfill your requirements for initiation. If possible, I'm sure it's best to do this in as positive a vein as possible. Stress how much good work they have done and be straightforward about what hasn't been done. It helps if you were careful to go over the rules very carefully when the individual started studying with you, although even that can't be depended on to lessen their anger and resentment over the refusal. The chance of any refused student leaving your group is very high. They feel disappointed, disrespected and devalued, and their emotions are very likely to overwhelm their intellect no matter how well you've explained why they aren't ready.

I have come more and more to believe that it's a good idea, when someone leaves your group, to put out a very quiet announcement that "So-and-so, an X-degree initiate of this group, has resigned." There's no need to state the reason; just let the community know that the association is at an end. This is a courtesy to other leaders in your area as it lets them know not only that the individual is no longer a member of your group, but exactly what degree (if any) they hold. It also gives you credibility if you must defend yourself later against inaccurate claims made by the person who left. It sure would be nice if we could get along a bit better and if people weren't somehow convinced that their lies will never be found out. In my experience, lies have a very bad habit of finding their way home.

Why am I including these unpleasant possibilities in my chapter on teaching the Craft? Because I've come to believe that dealing with disgruntled ex-students is just another part of the job. Witchcraft is a path which attracts rebels and those who somehow don't fit in elsewhere. A few of them don't manage to fit in with Witches either, and it's a lot easier for them to get mad at a specific high priest/ess who "mistreated" them than it is to put down the entire public school system. All we can really do is to treat every student as fairly as we possibly can. When it's obvious that a student isn't working out, we owe it to them — as well as to ourselves and to the group — to help them find another path. When this doesn't work, we still need to ask them to leave before they bring unnecessary turmoil to the group and perhaps damage it.

The new millennium, as might be expected, has brought us new challenges. Among them is the possibility of teaching our students on-line. There's a lot to be said in favor of this method. For one thing, once you get everything set up, that part of the work is done for good. Despite the 2001

"death of the dot coms," there is an amazing selection of free services on the World Wide Web, and convenient and private facilities for on-line teaching are among them. My group is developing some specialists in on-line teaching, particularly Ceffyl Starr, who is shepherding her third set of students through our first degree course.

So far, she has added personal contact to web-based learning for any student who reaches the point of requesting first degree initiation, and the plan for the future is to have in-person contact with any student who reaches this point. I plan to use the web-based learning facilities for any in-person student who has an Internet connection since it's a lot easier for me to put materials on-line than having to go out and get photocopies made. Ceffyl uses on-line chat and telephone calls to augment the written work, schedules group chats on a regular basis, and has a class bulletin board for discussions. We find our ratio of students who seriously begin the course work to students who complete it is just about the same as that reported by other teachers in the Craft regardless of teaching method.

We are both very pleased with the results of teaching on-line, particularly since we started using a specially designed Internet facility.[5] Ceffyl has a new class and while the early dropout point seems to have been reached, it's going pretty well. We've had to keep after the students a bit in order to get them to post on the bulletin board and to make it to the chats, but it's working out better with each group, Ceffyl says.

I'm told a great deal has been written and is taught in teacher education classes about techniques of teaching. There are two aspects to teaching techniques: first is to keep the student(s) interested and second is to match the method to the subject. Keeping the student(s) interested has two aspects: (1) getting them to pay attention during lectures and (2) getting them to stay interested enough to keep coming to classes and doing the work in a timely fashion.

Television has adapted the American human to paying attention in eighteen-minute (approximately) blocks before tuning out the commercial.

You can attempt to cure students of this habit and I wish you all the luck in the world. Alternately, you can keep in mind that it's a really good idea to schedule a break or change of pace at fifteen- to twenty-minute intervals. I have to admit that my personal technique is to throw in a joke, wisecrack, or four-letter word when I feel students drifting away. This, however, works better if you're a sweet little old lady; the technique probably doesn't work as well for normally loud-mouthed biker types.[6] Even as simple a thing as having a five-minute break for people to fill their glass (of soda) or just stretch and find their pen will let them come back ready to pay attention again.

It's easy to figure out the best method of teaching for some material; as mentioned above, you teach ritual by having people do it in your presence and then you discuss what they did right or wrong. But you can also think about videotaping a demonstration ritual if a video camera is available. In teaching Tarot, you're going to be displaying the individual cards and you will probably be doing sample readings. You may even be collecting a lot of different decks to demonstrate how much the symbolism of a particular card can differ. But there are a lot of things which are difficult to teach by any means other than the lecture class. These topics can be made more interesting by adding photos, drawings, music or whatever you can think of to illustrate a point. Making sure the teaching method suits the material being taught can make some things easier to learn and any introduction of variety can help maintain students' interest.

While groups less often require copying a BOS by hand,[7] assigning a certain amount of homework still strikes me as a pretty good idea if for no other reason than it winnows out the lazy individuals quickly. We require students to handwrite a pledge at dedication which sets out clearly what the group is, what they may expect to learn, and what they are allowed to do with that learning. We also require essays on the First Law and on ethics. Individual teachers in my group often add questions or other essays at the end of each class.

I've concentrated here on entry-level teaching; I suppose this book, as a whole, is about teaching those working toward elevation, higher degrees, or circles. My own elementary classes attempt to train students to become excellent ritualists and to gain a really good general knowledge of Paganism and Witchcraft. I also have included some material on the theology and philosophy of the Pagan path and some exercises I hope will help students with their spiritual work. My advanced curriculum has a tendency to grow and change as I add material pertaining to situations I myself have experienced (particularly the ones the have come crashing down on me).

I haven't said much about exactly what you should teach to those working toward their initiation in Witchcraft or their basic education as a Pagan. You'll know a lot of the things you want to pass along. I can share with you what I teach with the understanding that I don't think these are the *only* things we should teach, nor do I believe them to cover *everything* we should teach. These topics represent what I considered important while I was actively teaching and include the additions made by others in my group since. I'm sure some things can be left out without damaging students in the least. So, merely to give you an idea, here is a list of the classes NorthWind teaches:

1. *Witches, Pagans, Druids, and Other Peculiar People.* A brief survey of the contemporary scene with an even briefer foray into the history and mystique of the origins of Witchcraft.
2. *What is Witchcraft?* A short historical survey of the emergence of the modern Witchcraft and its relationship to ancient pagan religions.
3. *Generalized Pagan Ritual.* An explanation of tools and terms and the basics of ritual.
4. *Doing Ritual.* The basics of ritual and altar set-up; the first ritual in which students participate; the Frame of the Ritual and the three Moon rituals.

5. *Laws of Witchcraft.* Exploration of ethics. Enclosures include "The Covenant of the Goddess" statement of ethics; Judy Harrow's "That Old Black Magic"; Tony Kelly's "Pagan Musings"; Council of American Witches' "Principles of Wiccan Belief"; Grey Cat's "Discussion of the Laws of Wicca."

6. *Pagan Manners.* The basics of good manners in and out of circles.

7. *God, Goddess, and Community.* A look at the life of a coven and approaches to deities.

8. *What is Magick?* Affirmations of Power and Pendulum.

9. *Symbolism.* Explanation of numerology, Planetary hours, tables of symbols.

10. *Magickal Personality.* Learning the Four Element personality profile and balancing act.

11. *Ritual Cleansing, Aspecting.* How to clear one's self and habitat of unwelcome influences; learning to let the Powers into one's self.

12. *Vision Quest.* How to go into the silence; reasons for doing a quest or vigil and how it is done.

13. *Working with the Power.* Learning aura work and healing and protective techniques.

14. *On Turtle Island.* A survey of American Indian practices and beliefs: prayer sticks, tobacco ties, pipe; working with totems, drums, shields, masks, spirit bag, etc.

15. *Clearing the Channels of Power.* A look at the integration of the three parts of Self.

16. *The Wheel of the Year.* Discussion of elemental and mystical associations with the Sabbat and structure of the annual celebratory cycle.

17. *Divination.* A brief look at several systems of divination.

18. *Tools of Magick.* Making, attuning, and dedicating magickal tools.

19. *Elementary Herbalism (magick only).* Using herbs appropriately for ritual and spell-working; correspondences.

20. *Time*. Discussion of the movement of the Moon and Sun; calendars.

21. *Sex and Sacrifice*. A look at the Great Rite, the symbolic Great Rite, and animal and blood sacrifice. Additional materials presented on appropriate sexual mores and behavior in Pagan groups.

22. *Getting ready for Initiation*. A look at what initiation is and what a student should expect to get out of it.

We also try to do some workshops which last several hours and get deeper into the skills and knowledge we hope our students will have. Workshop for first degree students include:

1. *What is NorthWind?* A trip inside the heads of the Founder and some of the earliest students; a short history of NorthWind and a review of its goals and purposes.

2. *Ritual Theater*. How to use voice, visualization, gestures, and pacing to increase the magickal effect of ritual; discussion of the need for initiative and responsibility in ritual.

3. *Ritual and Magick*. The Why, How, Who, What, When, and Where of working Magick through the technique of ritual.

4. *American Indian Skills and Philosophy*. Learning sweat lodge, fire-tending, making and using tobacco ties, smudging; the Medicine Wheel and the Sacred Circle.

5. *Dance and Music in Ritual*. Using music, drumming, dancing, and other movement to increase the power and effectiveness of ritual.

6. *Creating Ritual*. Learning to determine if it is time to do a ritual; how to write ritual and which sort to do.

7. *The Stone Peoples*. NorthWind's concept of the words Community and Brother/Sisterhood; the Who, Why, and When of Rites of Passage. Additional material presented on the God, Goddess, and Community concept of deity.

An abbreviated set of six classes is taught to those who want to come to rituals but don't want to study toward initiation.

I absolutely am not implying that you must teach the same things I do. Groups have different bodies of lore and different emphases as to the importance of that lore. I thought hard before I included our class list in this chapter but decided that you might find it useful as a starting place for organizing the material you are planning to teach. Each of our classes has written material and several have handouts of material written by others. Several books are assigned, although at present we're looking at our list and are considering making some changes. Altering course material is important, as knowledge isn't static. My upper degree candidates are going to wish I'd never written this volume because I've found so many really useful books I'll want them to read!

POINTS TO PONDER

- Choose your students carefully and help any who don't work out (given a fair chance) to find a different teacher and path.
- Give the best you've got to your teaching and be a good example to your students.
- Don't initiate anyone you aren't really sure of and once they are out of your hands, don't let them worry you too much.
- It's extremely easy to be a very popular High Priest/ess: just tell people what they want to hear. It won't help them (or you) grow, but they'll think you're wonderful.

NOTES

[1] Guidelines by Lady Rhiannon of Serpentstone, Lady Cassandra of the Temple of Hecate Triskele, Grey Cat of NorthWind, Lady Silver Ravenwolf of Black Forest, and Grandfather Michael Ragan of the Temple of Danann. 15 Oct. 1997; 1997 — www.northwind.faithweb.com/guides.htm.

[2] FC 101: Feces Coagulation or getting one's shit together.

[3] Kenneth C. Haugk, *Antagonists in the Church: How to Identify and Deal with Destructive Conflict* (Minneapolis: Augsberg Fortress Publishing, 1988).

[4] Many thanks to B. Stevens for this analysis.

[5] See www.blackboard.com.

[6] *This is a joke*! I'm not exactly a sweet little old lady myself.

[7] BOS: Book of Shadows. A name for a book of lore and rituals belonging to a Witch, handed down by the tradition in which they trained. Gerald Gardner evidently heard this name and applied it to *Ye Boke of the Arts Magickal*, which he kept in connection with his coven. Ceremonial magicians keep a *grimoire*, which contains records of what work is done, when it is done, and how it is done. Many Witchcraft groups past and present also keep grimoires rather than a BOS.

CHAPTER TWELVE

Community is not the same thing as mass or mob. It is anything but a featureless aggregate of interchangeable individuals. True community, like all other living things, has a complex and well-articulated internal structure. It consists not of individuals but of families, congregations, ball teams, neighborhoods, unions, garden clubs, choruses — all those many groups into which people coalesce around different kinds of affinities and common interests. We can only know each other, share our lives, a few at a time. It's so easy, otherwise, to get lost in the sauce.

JUDY HARROW[1]

A COMMUNITY OF LIKE-MINDED PEOPLE

Building Community

I remember it taking me the better part of a year to come face to face with my first *real* Witch. At that time we were a small number outside of a few large cities. It's really not like that any more. I suspect that there are very few Pagans who don't live reasonably close to others of like mind. Of course, in some areas we're still pretty hard to find — partly because of safety issues and partly just to guard ourselves or family members from unpleasantness. Particularly since the explosion of the Internet, it's generally very much easier to find other members of our community.

The difficulties that Pagan, Wiccan, and other related religions and spiritual paths have in getting along began with the first group to come out of the closet. This group, led by Gerald Gardner, split up in 1956 over a debate on whether or not publicity was desirable. The question continues to be debated endlessly, most recently because of the way public television handled an interview with Wiccans on a program about religion and ethics.

I do know some of reasons why we don't get along. One of the major ones is that a large number of us were the folks who weren't popular in high school, neither with other kids nor with teachers, so we didn't get elected president of any club or picked to go to the special events put on for potential leaders. In fact, a lot of us didn't even join clubs, meaning that we have rather limited experience working with voluntary groups. Additionally,

many of us tend to have a lot of problems with questions of leadership
and power.

> Issues of interpersonal power are difficult for Witches to think or talk
> about, since we cherish an image of ourselves as free spirits, guided
> only by our own individual True Will and perhaps the leadings of the
> Goddess. Or we may feel that questions of power and authority are
> essentially political questions — as they are — and that spiritual
> people should somehow be above all that.
>   In reality, where there are people, there are politics.[2]

When ignored, however, power issues, like politics, just go underground where they can fester, swell, and eventually create a necessity for
amputation. I'm afraid a part of the unrest and actual warring in our
community cannot end until more of us recognize that politics is what
happens when two or more persons attempt to accomplish something and
that leadership is an important ingredient, much like flour is in a cake. If
we leave it out, the recipe doesn't work.

That is *not* to say that all or any of our groups need to follow any specific
organizational pattern — the pattern your group chooses is completely up
to you. It's denying that you need an organizational pattern that causes the
problems. No matter how equal we see or wish to see the members of any
group, it's rare that all members can be considered the same. In most Pagan
groups there is, first of all, a difference in knowledge and experience among
the participants and more frequently than not, the group actually coalesces
around a very knowledgeable and experienced individual — a teacher. No
matter what the agreed degree of authority the teacher is given, they just
plain have authority and (if the group is to have any chance at longevity)
the respect of the people who have come to learn. How much authority the
teacher is given, overtly or in practice, is something the group should
discuss and settle right at the beginning.

In the community at large, issues of authority and power — and the wish of many to pretend that in a perfect world there would be no politics — are the root of much of the unpleasant behavior exhibited by so many people. Politics[3] is actually only a word that describes individual interactions relating to a group process, such as electing a leader or adopting a particular course of action. The problem arises in part because we don't differentiate between politics and *toxic* politics. Toxic politics includes all the underhanded methodologies: using false arguments designed to appeal to emotions; lying; power-brokering; forming lobby groups; putting people under perceived obligations and then calling in the favors; and making personal attacks against the opposition.

So long as so many of us insist on pretending that we don't have politics, there will be no way to discourage those who employ unethical means to get what they want. So long as we refuse to accept that leadership is required if anything is to get done and therefore refuse to define what appropriate leadership looks like, we are at the mercy of anyone who tries to obtain leadership status through the techniques of toxic politics — which are all the more effective when we deny that they might be employed.

In order to have a discussion about our community, I believe we first should define it. Judy Harrow has said that Paganism is the religion and that Witchcraft is a particular subgroup (as Sisters of Charity is a subgroup of Catholicism). While I can agree with this statement, across the breadth of Neopaganism some groups differ sufficiently that few of us would be entirely comfortable considering them a part of the same religion. On the other hand, the vast majority of unaffiliated Pagans are comfortable in public ritual led by a variety of different paths. While Witches and Druids will certainly disagree about a whole lot of things, for the most part they can agree that they resemble each other as much as Catholics resemble Baptists.

However, if you attend any fair-sized Festival or Gathering, discrete questioning will reveal that there really is a very wide variety of people present, including an occasional Buddhist, a more-or-less Christian Ceremonial Magician, a Hindu, or any number of other idiosyncratic ("peculiar to the individual," not idiotic!) religious focuses. In my discussion on the Pagan worldview (Chapter 5), I briefly outline many of the beliefs on which Pagans can almost all agree. One thing we continue to be unable to agree upon is the question of where groups that consider themselves *left-hand path*, *black magicians*, etc., fit. I do note that while they may be polytheist, they differ from most Pagans in several important ways. So far as I know, none of these groups would consider themselves earth-centered and while they do have ethics, those ethics differ greatly from the ones accepted by other Pagans. I tend to feel that they do not share sufficiently in the Pagan worldview to be accurately called Pagan, but I'm willing to listen to other points of view. It has occurred to me to wonder why some of them wish to be part of the Pagan community considering how little we share in beliefs and goals. I believe that the word *pagan* applied to the modern religious movement means a lot more than simply being polytheistic.

Many of the disagreements in our community are based on personality conflicts and are waged because a few idiots think they'll look like Big-Nosed Pagans if they criticize and tell wild stories about everyone else. Obviously I'd be delighted if everyone in the community could be sufficiently mature to be able to handle a personality conflict without attempting to bring everyone they know *and* Aunt Sadie in on it, but while we're waiting for that day of glory there is a lot that individuals can do to improve things.

First of all, keep your personality problems with another just that — personal. You can disagree with another individual without calling them unethical, dishonorable, or wrong. Either your personalities don't mesh comfortably or you have beliefs and customs which don't easily go together, even though yours is right for you and theirs for them. In neither of these cases does the community need nor, I assure you, want to know all about it.

Problems that should probably concern the community as a whole include sexual mistreatment or harassment, mistreatment of students, and actions involving the majority society or others in the Pagan community which are clearly outside of community standards. Such things as claiming untrue initiatory status, charging unreasonable amounts of money for teaching or rituals, putting money contributed for a community purpose to personal use, and making questionable behavioral choices clearly can give the entire community a bad name. These kinds of problems should not only be brought to the attention of the community, but the community should listen, take the charges seriously, look into whether they are correct and if so, take appropriate action. Too often the guilty party claims that the problem is not really a question of behavior, but a mere personality conflict over some trivial matter — and our community lets them get away with it.

As a group, we don't seem to be able to discriminate between *discussion*, *argument*, and all-out war.[4] Too many people react to every slightest differ-ence as *confrontation*[5] and seem to feel that such confrontation is to be avoided at all costs. This is to ignore the meaning of the words and is an overreaction, to say the least. Discussions and arguments can become heated and rather loud without in the least signifying that there is any sort of trouble between the participants. While I don't personally engage in argu-ment as a sport, I know a lot of fine folks who do and their discussions may be louder and longer than ones that revolve around a fairly important point, such as "Who's going to wash the dishes?" or "Shall we get a divorce?"

The human intellect is organized in such a manner that open discus-sion one of the most important ways in which people learn and, even more important, evolve their own ideas and views on a subject. Cutting off this process demands either that this work be done out of sight or that an idea or opinion be accepted on authority without the individual being allowed to make it a part of their inner landscape through exploration and vocalization. Argument gets into trouble when overaggressiveness carries the interaction toward verbal, personal, or even physical violence.

I find it amusing that the person who attempts to carry a discussion into violence of one sort or another (attacking the personality and character of the opponent, attempting to drown the other out, attempting to draw in on-lookers, etc.) invariably perceives themself as losing the argument. The effect of such violence or implication of violence is highly detrimental to the individuals concerned, not to mention the community.

If we can just learn that violence, coercion, and other unacceptable behaviors are like sand (they get into everything), we might be able to approach community relations a little more practically. As you may well have discovered when talking with one half of a relationship, you can't make other do squat — the only person you can change is yourself. Luckily, change is contagious. As long as there are those of us who can keep our heads during community crises, more and more people will realize that that approach makes one look good and contributes toward solving the problem.

It's not appropriate to overlook the actions of people or groups who have seriously trespassed the standards of the community. I've mentioned such trespasses above. Yes, there are problems involved with implementing this policy; you'll have to take the trouble to find out if the story is true or not. Our only way of showing our disapproval of truly bad behavior is to exclude the offending individual from our community. This is unlikely to change that individual's behavior, but at the least more vulnerable members of our community will be less available to them. Further, those who might consider doing the same will know that it may well mean losing access.

Obviously, learning the facts in such a situation may not be easy, particularly when children of Pagan parents are involved. Making a criminal case out of it may be seen as more dangerous to the victims than to the perpetrator, meaning we may have to research the incident(s) personally. I believe that conscientious and responsible leaders will do this. If a leader is convinced that a wrong has been committed and knows by whom it was done, they should confidentially report to other leaders and as a group, those leaders can decide what steps to take. This isn't a pleasant task and hardly anyone is going to be thanked for doing it, but I believe that we owe it to the vulnerable people in our community to take thought of their needs.

Another prominent problem is groups who lie about their background, educational level, and/or in some way abuse or cheat their students. When this happens and someone speaks up, they run the risk of being accused of jealousy or of trying to get even with a leader or some such thing. My group has worried about this issue for some years and the only thing we've come up with is to simply say (about a group we question) that we're not comfortable with some of a group's teachings.

I do know of an incident involving a group that claimed training they very clearly hadn't received. When contacted very diplomatically by an experienced Craft leader, this group was very open to working with him to bring their practices and teachings into line with general community standards. There were some favorable circumstances surrounding this case, however, including the ability of certain leaders to determine that a charge of sexual harassment made against the group was completely untrue. This kind of positive outcome resulting from contact with an unqualified teacher or unethical group isn't going to be frequent.

I have always truly believed that almost anyone should be allowed a second chance. I take it as an article of faith that people do sometimes change. My group accepts students who have failed with other groups and, in general, we have found this to carry an acceptable level of risk. There are, however, a few people who seem to be driven to disrupt any group which allows them access. When a student leaves or is asked to leave my group because they have caused great disruption, I quietly (and without going into unnecessary detail) advise other teachers in the appropriate area that the person in question had presented our group with a problem. I do *not* imply that the student will cause such a problem in another group and should another group accept them, I make myself available to help in whatever way I can to ensure that it works for the new group.

As I mention in Chapter 11, I've found a most helpful book, *Antagonists in the Church*,[6] which examines a common problem that causes the pastor or other leader and their respective groups enormous emotional pain and stress. The problem centers on a single person who is actually present solely to cause as much trouble as possible. It's important for our own peace and sanity that we learn to recognize these individuals. Groups can literally be torn apart while attempting to appease such a person, which is a completely wasted effort since they do not *want* to be satisfied. Their aim is disruption and whatever idea they appear to be supporting is simply a tool they use to this end. Kenneth Haugk's book is inexpensive, short, and very well written. Its Christian approach is easily adapted to a *spiritual* approach suitable for any religious-based group.

I should mention here that too much group solidarity can sometimes be a problem when it comes to making important decisions. If the solidarity and harmony of the group should become of very high value to each of the members, it may be very difficult for the group to seriously examine all possibilities, alternatives, or any sort of argument which appears to threaten the atmosphere of consensus. A group isn't best served either by uniting in opposition to other groups through unfair criticism or by a false consensus which ignores all disagreements in favor of harmony.[7]

With any luck, we'll all be facing fewer and fewer situations of this sort as more and more leaders live up to the responsibilities they have claimed or accepted and as we refuse to allow our community to be abused by the remarkably few really nasty people who have tried to harm and exploit us.

It seems to me almost half the witch wars that occur these days are caused by plain, old-fashioned, ill-natured gossip. Person A tells High Priestess B that High Priestess C said that Lady B has done thus and so. HPS B immediately calls HPS C a bitch-and-a-half and off they go. I keep a simple pledge designed by Dr. Medicine Hawk Wilburn which essentially says, "I promise that should I hear that you have said something bad about me, I'll check with you personally before I get mad." That doesn't seem to me to be asking too much.

Think about the last piece of colorful gossip you've heard and how plausible it seems. If you know the individual mentioned in that gossip, think about whether or not it even sounds like something that person would do. Some of the gossip that's gone around about me has simply flabbergasted me. I can get mad and I can do a lot of things, but some of the items that appear in this gossip would never have occurred to me. Moreover, if I *had* thought of them, I wouldn't have had the brass to do them!

I find that all in all, 90 percent of the interesting gossip you hear is either entirely wrong or so exaggerated that it bears little resemblance to the actual event. Why do we listen? In part for perfectly good reasons, like being able to offer support to someone who is ill or in emotional pain. Unfortunately, the purveyors of the really good gossip are far more interested in "getting an in" with you than they are with conveying a true account of a situation or event. I don't at all understand what motivates people who don't have a personal animus against the subject of their tales. I suspect there are some things we just aren't just meant to know. But for all of its potential to cause problems, gossip may just have a time and place:

> I don't think gossip is bad. I think it's the glue that cements us together as community. I think malicious gossip is toxic and definitely agree that one should go to the subject of the gossip. But when someone tells you another friend had a baby, lost their mother, had a car accident, signed a book contract, whatever — that's gossip, and it's what makes us a human community, in my opinion. We share these things because we care about the people involved. So I'm a gossip. A righteous gossip in most instances.[8]

Untrue gossip can actually be stopped if those who hear it are willing to make the effort. Research has found that if the true story is sent back up the grapevine, it can significantly suppress the untrue story's spread. Merely refusing to *lower oneself* in order to pass on the untruth is not sufficient; it's necessary to seek someone who really does know the truth, find out what that truth is, and then specifically send it back along the route by which the untrue story came. If we participate in this process as much as possible, we might just take enough of the fun out of gossip to cut down on the worst of it.

Right now our worst — or at least most apparent — problem as a community is excruciatingly ordinary prejudice or bigotry. Damn near everyone hates Wiccans even though each individual's definition of *wiccan* may be different. Hard-working people who have spent years studying, learning to do good ritual, leading ritual, teaching, and doing their inner work define Wiccans either as teenyboppers, leftover new age wispies doing their religion-of-the-week, or folks who've become Witch Queen of the Universe after having read one book and watched *Sabrina* on television. Talk to a Druid or a Gaelic Traditionalist and they'll tell you that Wiccans don't do their research and are too lazy to pay any attention to even not-so-ancient traditions. Others will tell you that Wiccans are vicious, untruthful, abusive, stupidly secretive about things that have been in print for years, and altogether beneath contempt. What none of these people realize is that there are a lot of Wiccans and wiccans, Witches/Witchen and witches, and they are rarely very much alike.

I remember an older lady who lived across the creek from me and belonged to the Presbyterian Church (one of only two churches in my community). She yelled at a noisy bunch of us kids saying, "Stop that! You're acting just like Baptists." Was that any way to represent a religion that stresses love? I don't think the church would have thought so and neither did we.

I just finished rereading my favorite Louis L'Amour book, *Last Stand at Papago Wells*, which tells a story about thirteen random people trapped at a water hole in the desert, threatened by renegade Apaches.9 You'd think they'd have realized that their best chance to survive would have been to work together, but of course that's not what happens. I still think that Pagans should attempt to keep some harmony in our community even though we're not at the moment seriously threatened by any organized outside enemies. Why must we fall into the ugly pettiness of bigotry? And that's what it is: we pick out groups of people, judge them by the behavior of a few individuals, and yap all over the Internet or at any gathering of people about how awful *they* are and how superior *we* are. It's grade school playground behavior.

Wicca, or more accurately, *Wica*, was a word Gardner used occasionally, but it was not used by very many people as an identifying term until the early 1980s. At that time, most of us called ourselves *Witches* and our religion *Witchcraft.* I made the change to *Wiccan* and *Wicca* only because it seemed to me that the first half hour of a conversation was wasted trying to re-educate people about the word *witch*. It was obvious to many of us back then that Paganism and Witchcraft were destined to grow very fast during the next couple of decades and we felt there was just too much for us to accomplish beyond wasting time debating two words which were essentially synonyms.

Problems arise when an individual or group thinks it's got the "One True Right and Only Path"10 and that path is right for other people whether they know it or not. The Christian book doesn't just tell Christians that only those who follow its path will escape hell; it directly orders them to convert everyone else to it. Pagans don't have a book and we probably wouldn't do what it told us if we did. Pagans *never* proselytize, but they sure do bad-mouth other people's choices.

Now that it's come up, I figure I'd better put in a few words on proselytizing right here. The circumstances surrounding the whole question of proselytization need to be looked at very carefully. Let's begin with a definition. *Proselytize*: To induce someone to convert to one's own religious faith.[11] A look through the *Oxford Dictionary of the English Language* didn't give me anything worth adding to this definition but I do note that all the examples given clearly disapprove of the activity. At the time the rule about Witches (and later Pagans in general) never proselytizing was accepted, it would have been very easy to tell when the rule was broken. Since everyone was hidden and told almost no one about their religion, speaking about Paganism just didn't occur often. Some groups even went so far as to forbid members from mentioning their real religion.

We are now living in a rather different world and most of us practice our religion a lot more openly than we did then. Going back to our definition, note that it uses the word *induce*. Other definitions use the words *make, cause to come over, bring* — all far stronger words even than *persuade*. On my first try writing these paragraphs, I interpreted proselytize extremely strictly, suggesting that one should be careful when talking about one's religion. But as the evening wore on and I kept thinking about it, I decided that wasn't really appropriate. I still don't think we should bring up the subject of our religion — even with friends — except when asked, and I certainly don't think we should discuss it with strangers. If we're talking to anyone but close friends or family, I think we should keep our talk focused on answers to questions and never keep on after it's apparent that the listener is beginning to lose interest.

However, I don't think it's fair to think that by merely answering questions or talking with close friends, we are proselytizing. There is always an element of pushiness implied by the word and I don't think very many — even those in the midst of their first enthusiasm — really go that far over the line. To proselytize really means to try to convert another to your religion, a crime of which I suspect we'll rarely be guilty. We do need to avoid being a bore about it and we certainly don't want to copy techniques from those religions deeply involved in numbers.

Wiccans generally do not look to history to validate the path as a whole, although there exists a feeling that there is a connection between many ancient religions and the new religion of Witchcraft. The traditionalists, who also may call themselves *reconstructionists*, are highly dedicated to the concept of historical accuracy, and research is a primary focus of most active members. Witchcraft is much more focused on what works best today, and only a few consider research the highest priority. Things get difficult when one group uses its own standards to judge the worth of the other. Witches will probably find a traditionalist group's rituals shallow and powerless while the traditionalists, of course, will feel that Witches are uneducated and grossly ignorant of historical fact. That the traditionalists don't use ritual in the same way or for the same purposes, and that ritual is a major focus of all Witchcraft, doesn't seem to occur to either group.

And yet, at the exact same time we're proud of our diversity and the fact that people of so many different paths can cooperate, celebrate religion, and just have fun together. So which is it? As things are now, we're letting careless, stupid language tear us apart mentally by trying to love and hate the same people at the same time. As far as "good research" goes, I suspect Mother Teresa didn't put a whole lot of time into studying the faint, far, and fantastic backlands of Christian theology. Her work was to get a certain job done, which both fulfilled the meaning of her God's incarnation and contributed immeasurably to the glory of her religion and her particular church.

Sure, there's a need for our scholars (and I'm not really one of them) to learn from the past and for our theoretical philosophers (that's me) to see below the surface of our rituals and Books of Shadows to the real meaning of our faith, but we also need a lot of other people to make our symbols and tools, to cook dinner for 300 people at a festival, to walk the festival grounds in the middle of the night to ensure our safety, and to just be hardworking, honest, voting, good citizens of our nations — which makes Paganism look good.

Actually, it occurs to me to wonder why Gaelic traditionalists (for instance) worry so much about the research capabilities of Wiccans (for instance) — they are not Wiccans so why should they care? I'm afraid that one of the main things we're seeing here is the old game of attempting to gain status by putting somebody else down. This is combined with the more easily forgiven human fault of judging a vast group of people based on a single experience with one person who says they are a member of that group. Based on that single experience, this instant "expert" is ready to declare that "all Xs are Ys." Actually, I can't think of even one true example to finish the statement, "All Wiccans are . . ." I can't even finish it with the word *human*, because I once had this cat that . . .

It's difficult not to suspect that some critics from various Pagan paths might be using their criticism of a different path — which has so far attracted the largest numbers — as a way of seeking more members for their own groups. All of us have our bad moments when the values of the majority society seem to take us over and cause behavior we thought we'd left behind us. Placing our self-value in terms of numbers is certainly a bad habit carried over from the majority society.

I have no quarrel with resenting the idiots who read two books and immediately start calling themselves Lord Thundermug or Lady Golden Fairie Unicorn. We're far from the only religion to have to deal with this sort of thing. I suspect half the *fakirs* in India are just beggars with a good line of patter. I believe that our coven-trained leaders are a valuable part of our religion and while I want to see some minimum standards be accepted, I have no wish to see us start requiring university training for our Priest/esshood. So while these sorts of personalities will continue to surface, they never last very long. Even newcomers soon realize that a particular Witch Queen just doesn't have it and leave to find a teacher who really does know what they are talking about. We just need to stop overreacting.

On the positive side of the account book, indiscriminate Christian bashing seems to have become much less prevalent. We obviously have issues with certain Christian groups or categories and even some historical bones we pick over now and then, but I'm hoping we've gotten bored with going over and over the same issues. With any luck, we'll get bored trashing each other too. Most Pagans agree that there is more than one way to connect with the God/desses, that each one of us has to walk our own path, and that only we ourselves can judge whether that path is the right one for us. One of the rules I received from my initiating High Priest was "Judge not the path of brother or sister for all paths are sacred."[12] Many other groups have similar guidelines. I believe that this endless harping on how terrible those [fill in the blank with group of your choice here] are violates both the meaning and the implication of this rule. We'd do a whole lot better to spend our time and energy following our own path and letting others take care of their own business.

There is a large "floating population" in our community; that is, individuals who join us for a time to try the religion out. They aren't sure they really want to be Pagans, they don't really know what's involved in being a Pagan and, in fact, they probably think it's just like being in the SCA:[13] you go to a great party and then go home and return to being like anyone else. Some find something which speaks strongly to them and they become true Pagans and are active in the work of the community. Others keep coming and enjoying the fun and the ambience and the energy, and are as much Pagans as many people are Christians. Others still think we're just too weird and never come back — and that's OK!

All of these things are part of the process. Undoubtedly, the undisciplined, insufficiently serious people can be irritating and can get in the way, but that's what some people are — at the particular moment. If we had a Pope, we could have all sorts of standards; we wouldn't have to be bothered by anyone who doesn't fulfill requirements — the Pope's requirements. No thanks; I'll take the confusion, irritation, and lack of solidarity any time over electing one from among us to set up the rules of just who is and who isn't toeing the party line.

The time spent bitching about fluffy bunny Wiccans and newbies who don't know what they are talking about could be put into doing something about it — ignorance has a cure. Wren, my right-hand High Priestess, is planning a set of Vacation Pagan School Classes, each standing alone, which could do a good deal to help provide solid educational resources for many people. We can do a lot of things, which include holding a series of classes on Wicca 101, Ritual 101 (to be held before public rituals), healing techniques, meditation and grounding techniques, divination techniques, history, Pagan theology, and different traditions (which could be structured as "meet the tradition" afternoons). I believe that you and I can put an end to the complaints about newcomers pretty quickly. All we need to do is notice such complaints and interrupt them with a simple statement about how pointless they are and how childish they sound, adding that such opinions are rooted in simple bigotry, which is something we should be able to put behind us. While we continue to obsess over airheads and pretenders and ignore individuals who seriously violate ethics, we dwell in the worst of all possible worlds.

Who speaks for the Pagans: self-appointed Queens? miscellaneous authors of books with one of the magic words in the title?[14] the person standing outside the Circle when a newspaper reporter crashes it? Well, let's face facts: yes, these people speak for us. We have no Pope, no elected Pagan Leader of the Year, no process whatsoever designed to aid the press, government, or general populace to understand us. The spokesperson role goes, by default, to whoever is handy. Next week, it's just as likely not to be you.

While there are individual people in the media who have demonstrated that they can be trusted to keep their word about how an interview is going to be treated, the fact is that the reporter speaking to a Witch isn't actually in control of what will appear in print or on the television. Unfortunately, the media haven't a very good record for handling news about Pagans in a responsible way. Most of them go for the maximum shock or maximum nutcase angle and whatever facts you'd hoped to get across go down the drain because they aren't shocking or funny.

Nevertheless, it's sometimes necessary to speak with the media and when you're the one picked, there are a few things you can do to minimize their opportunities for negative handling. First of all, do not let them interview you in ritual robes with all of your magical jewelry. Jewelry comes over rather strangely on television and even a medium-sized pentacle is likely to look huge and cheap. We always look best when we appear in nice, ordinary business clothes. Looking weird or different really doesn't do us any good when our message is that we aren't evil or dangerous and we aren't going to hurt anyone's children. Think about it.

If a particular program doesn't usually present a religious guest without inviting others who hold opposing beliefs, don't agree to appear with such opposition. Of course, many shows say they won't bring in people with opposing views but do so anyway — usually extremely bigoted fundamentalist Christians who are allowed to take over the show and shout down everything the Pagan attempts to say. Consider walking out on camera if such a thing happens to you. I don't believe a Catholic priest would just sit there if the host brought in a Satanist to debate belief systems.

Before doing the interview, think about what questions you are likely to be asked and write down possible answers. Check to see if the end of your answer could be chopped off, thereby changing enormously what you intended to say. In other words, if they *are* out to get you, make it as hard for them as you can. Do your best to speak in sound bites which will be difficult to cut apart and twist to mean something different than you intend.

I think I do more good speaking to the World Religion class every year at my local community college than I could do in any number of street demonstrations in front of this or that building. Each year I speak to approximately fifty young men and women who then know what a real Witch looks like. They also know that what she told them about Witchcraft just isn't all that scary, even if it is different. One of my initiates frequently speaks to Christian church groups about Paganism. He appears before them as a Witch, a policeman, and a Sunday-dressed person talking about a religion which is different, but not evil. And there are 100 more people who have seen a Witch and lived to tell about it.

Perhaps you've noticed that the moment any individual Pagan makes a name for themselves, however temporarily, there will be little knots of other Pagans whispering and sneering and putting them down just as fast as they can. Mention a Pagan author on a mail list (i.e., any Pagan author writing for a publisher) and some folks will pop up with harsh criticisms — it's like they feel such Pagan authors unfairly get rich off their books. Believe me, no Pagan author has ever gotten rich off books. Considering the time spent writing and editing and, for most, the cost of the research materials, making something a bit above minimum wage takes pretty darn good sales.

There will never be a "perfect" spokesperson for Paganism, partly because people just aren't perfect and partly because Paganism includes many different paths and no individual can really be knowledgeable about more than a few. In actuality, most of the individuals who have, usually by no real choice of their own, been in the position of speaking for all of us have done a fine job of it. We really need to support our spokespersons and leadership; it's a pretty thankless job all in all, and even those who asked for it didn't realize what a hornet's nest they were getting into.

Really, look at the people who run the festivals and speak with reporters, government officials, and leaders of other religious groups — they aren't doing a bad job and I doubt that many of us could do better. And while some Pagan authors and publishers are just riding the easy bucks the popularity of our paths has brought, most of them had every intention of doing the best job they could. Show some respect and your example will help others learn it. I think that envy and jealousy has poisoned the attitudes of many Pagans toward leaders, authors, and others. I really don't understand why this attitude persists — it surely doesn't make any sense at all.

Many of us who follow our path quietly away from the great cities are going find ourselves called upon to interact as Pagan clergy with non-Pagans. I'm not actually in favor of scheduling *any* prayers before secular meetings, but if there are going to be such prayers, Pagans should be leading some of them. Or we may simply need to visit a friend, covener, or student at the hospital to bring religious comfort, and since we are not immediate family, we become clergy in those people's eyes. It's just plain *wrong* to let one from our community die without a Priest/ess bringing the reassurance of their religion to the hospital bed and it's you people, the ones drawn to read this advanced book, who will have to be there for them. Because there is getting to be a great many of us, it follows that we (those of us for whom our religion is the central focus of our lives) are the people who must find the courage to step forward and do the necessary jobs.

I'm not saying that this will be either safe or easy. Years and years ago someone asked me if I thought the next twenty or thirty years (from then) would bring a resurgence of the Burning Times or acceptance by the mainstream population. My answer was simply, "Yes." A few of us are going to get hurt and a great many of us are going to find an acceptance which surprises us. Because there is a danger, I absolutely do not recommend that those with small children or other personal obligations become known in their immediate community. In fact, if you have children or grandchildren in school locally to you, that in itself is sufficient reason to remain hidden for a time. The children of weird rebels like us have enough problems in school without our adding any other stresses.

Each individual must make their own decision whether or not they should come out. But let us keep in mind that increasingly, the police department, the medical services and hospitals, the local government, and many local churches actually need to be able to contact a Pagan *clergy-person*. How can a Methodist minister properly counsel a Christian-Pagan mixed marriage if they have no one to help them understand the beliefs and customs of Pagans? How can the police learn to tell the difference between a satanic ritual site and a mess made by silly children? (*We* know it's not a Wiccan ritual site because *we* wouldn't leave anything there for them to find, right?)

How can a conscientious newspaper treat stories with occult connections well if there is no reputable source of information on Pagan beliefs and practices for them to contact? Some variety of Neopaganism is mentioned in a news story in North America several times every week. We can't expect these stories to be treated properly (in our eyes) if there's no one for the reporter to check them out with.

The reason that Pagans aren't invited to do the opening prayer at the school board meeting is partly because no one in charge of setting up the list of clergy to be invited knows our names or even knows that we are around. And only we ourselves can correct this situation by coming out into the open *and* showing ourselves to be relatively normal people, dressed decently and neatly like any other minister. We must be knowledgeable, without prejudice, about our own religion and its similarities and differences from other religions. We need to write prayers which conform to Pagan beliefs without unnecessarily insulting the beliefs of others. Saying, for instance, "May the powers of goodness and good judgement bless this meeting and aid you all in wise and ethical decision-making," is going to be a lot easier for administrators to take than something partisan like, "Gracious Goddess, ruler of all, bring enlightenment to these people that they may honor your wisdom." Better yet, why not say, "As an opening prayer, I'd like to ask each of you to privately seek guidance and assistance for the work of this meeting from the universal power. Let us spend a moment in silent prayer." After all, we really do not want to ask these people to pray to a god other than their own; what we want is recognition as a legitimate representative of a religious body, qualified as much as any other to request that the current activity be blessed by deity.

Any sort of disruption caused by our participation as clergy in any public way works against our goals. Sometimes disruption is unavoidable, but we would be well advised to let some other religion be the one to cause it. In early 2001, an Eastern Catholic priest objected to a Pagan clergyperson meeting with an association of religious professionals (ministerial association, council of churches). The result was a strong showing of religious tolerance by all the other members of the group — a much more positive outcome than some off-the-hip reaction by the Pagan cleric would have been.

If one of us decides to join a clergy group such as this one, the way to begin the process is to first meet privately with the elected leader or the administrative person associated with the group. Find out what the process is and do what's necessary to present your application in the usual way. Only if you are refused a hearing or membership due to your practice of a Pagan religion would it be the time to maybe go more public. Even then, I think that continuing to keep things as private as possible is the best strategy. Making a stink in the newspaper should be the absolute last resort. The same is true of getting on the clergy list at the hospital, with the police or sheriff's department, the rescue squad, etc. Go through the regular process first; come back, if necessary, with an attorney or gather up support from other accepted clergy and don't move on to other tactics until these have been exhausted. Otherwise, even if you win, you must face a lot of resentment from other clergy to the detriment of your ability to do your job.

Pagans are becoming more involved in the local communities, frequently meeting acceptance and cooperation, but also fear and hatred. More often we're meeting ignorance and doubt and those we can pretty easily do something about. Situations arise, such as when the police or fire department is called to an outdoor ritual. Before you know it, somebody has to act as spokesperson for the group and attempt to keep the situation peaceful while resolving the issues.

It's absolutely imperative that the Pagans involved in such a confrontation have met all reasonable requirements so that the only issue remaining is religious. That means they should have permits for use of public lands and/or for a group to gather, have festivals only on land zoned for such activities, etc. Every jurisdiction[15] has laws against public nudity, so sky-clad rituals should only be held inside *or* in places where privacy is truly assured. Backyards in the suburbs, even with fences, just don't protect you from prosecution.

Not many people understand that if a law or court ruling violates the promise of freedom of religion set out in the Constitution, refusing to obey that court order isn't the way to get the case to a higher court and ruled unconstitutional. If you break a court order, you'll be tried for contempt of court and the issue of whether or not the court order was correctly issued won't even come up. If you want to test a local law, get a lawyer's advice first — there are ways to *not* do it if you really want to make your point. If the case isn't really clearly based only on religious discrimination, you can be sure that the peripheral issues will get all the attention.

Like any other citizens, we should make every effort to obey all the laws of the land. Just because you may think that kids under eighteen years of age *ought* to have the right to make religious choices for themselves, this won't save you from persecution for corrupting the morals of a minor or from civil suits from the parents. A wise male keeps the words *jail bait* clearly in front of him when faced with a bevy of lovely, but very young, ladies and *any* religious teacher should always keep in mind that parents have all the rights when it comes to exposing kids to religion. You may think there is some basic right to run around sky-clad because it's part of your religion, but if you do it in front of other people's children, you are vulnerable to charges of child abuse. After ten years in prison, you're not going to be quite so delighted if the law is changed because of religious discrimination.

Actually, current interpretation of the US Constitution holds that religious activities, to be constitutional, must offer no harm to the community and I suspect that those who seriously offend community perceptions of decency may not get by citing religious activity. I suspect such things as public, nonsymbolic Great Rite need wait until community perceptions change. In a more personal area of the law, Pagan parents would do well not to present themselves to the community as too strange because the rights of Pagan parents have often been abridged by courts in the past and so far as I know, no one has had the support and money to carry one of these cases into an effective appeal. Until higher courts have ruled, there's nothing to prevent a family court judge from making whatever disposition of the children they choose.

I believe that the only cure for Pagans living in fear — of attacks by neighbors, authorities, or ex-spouses — will be the majority community getting over the notion that we are strange and deviant people. And that can't happen until a lot of them get to know one of us personally. We're not the only religious group undergoing difficulties from city government, zoning boards and the like. The freer US immigration policies have meant that many more Buddhists, Hindus, Muslims, and those following other non-European religious paths now live here. People are afraid of what is strange and we, along with Buddhists and Muslims, are strange to a lot of people in North America.

So, all in all, what am I asking of you in this chapter? I'm asking that you consciously present yourself to both the Pagan and non-Pagan community as a particularly wonderful person. I want you to be concerned for the health and well-being of others in the Pagan community without participating in ugly gossip. I'm asking you to refrain from putting down other Pagan paths even if you *do* think they are a bunch of day-dreaming idiots. In fact, I want you to discourage those in our community who diss others in your presence. I want you to have the courage to present yourself as clergy to both the Pagan and non-Pagan community and to do so with great dignity, humor, good information, and the common touch. And I want you to obey the small laws and rulings of the town or county you live in, unless you have worked with a lawyer to plan a challenge of a (probably) unconstitutional law. I want you to do public weddings and funerals which satisfy the needs of Pagans without totally affronting the sensibilities of persons not of our path. I don't know — is it really just me asking this?

POINTS TO PONDER

- On the whole, Pagans have many issues with power, authority and leadership, making it more difficult for our groups to run smoothly.
- The mistaken idea that one can gain status by putting down others has poisoned many Pagan organizations.
- One individual can crash an organization if they are allowed.
- Confrontations include the threat, or at least the possibility of actual physical violence; everything else can be classified as an exchange of ideas and opinion.
- We value the diversity of Pagan paths — let's act like it.
- Each individual's right to freely choose their religious/spiritual path shall not be abridged through gossip, put-downs, or infantile criticisms — or anything else.
- We want others to respect our own individual religious/spiritual choices and practices; we damn sure better respect those rights when they are practiced by others.

NOTES

[1] Judy Harrow, *Wicca Covens: How to Start and Organize Your Own* (Secaucus: Citadel, 1999), 7.

[2] Ibid., 21

[3] Word Web (www.wordweb.co.uk/) defines *politics* as social relations involving authority or power.

[4] *Discussion*: An exchange of view on some topic. *Argument*: A discussion in which reasons are advanced for and against some proposition or proposal. (Source: Word Web. See note 3)

[5] *Confrontation*: 1. A bold challenge 2. A hostile disagreement face-to-face 3. The act of opposing groups confronting each other. (Source: Word Web. See note 3.)

[6] Kenneth C. Haugk, *Antagonists in the Church: How to Identify and Deal with Destructive Conflict* (Minneapolis: Augsburg Fortress Publishing, 1988).

[7] Irving L. Janis, *Groupthink: Psychological Studies of Policy Decision*, 2nd ed. (Boston: Houghton Mifflin Company, 1982). My thanks to Judy Harrow for firmly

recommending I read this book. For me it was fascinating to read, and provided useful insight into group dynamics.

[8] M. Macha Nightmare, personal correspondence with author, 15 Apr. 2001.

[9] Louis L'Amour, *Last Stand at Papago Wells* (Greenwich: Fawcett Publications Inc., 1957). I've actually got a first edition!

[10] Isaac Bonewits's phrase.

[11] *The American Heritage® Dictionary of the English Language*, 4th ed. (Boston: Houghton Mifflin Company, 2000).

[12] Michael Ragan, classes of the Temple of Danann, Irish Witta, Hanover, IN, circa 1983.

[13] SCA: Society for Creative Anachronism. This group gets together to create temporary, historically correct reconstructions of medieval European life. In other words, they engage in elaborate make-believe.

[14] Magic words in this context: Wiccan, Pagan, Witch.

[15] A jurisdiction, in the sense I'm using it here, means the geographic area covered by a court and set of laws. In a city park, you are in that city's jurisdiction and out in the country, you're in the county sheriff's jurisdiction; either way, you're in the state's jurisdiction.

CHAPTER THIRTEEN

When I was in college, it was the fashion to debate such important questions as "Why are we here?" "What is the purpose of life?" and "Who am I?" As time passed, we stopped asking those questions and realized it was because there are no answers. Eventually, a few of us recognized that these weren't even the questions to ask. We ourselves, by the way we live, give meaning to our lives.

GREY CAT

WHO AM I WHEN I'M
BY MYSELF?

Personal Growth

Personal growth — that is, spiritual growth or *exploring the mystery within* — is the goal of both the Witch and the Mage, so it's doubly your concern as a teacher and student. Becoming more yourself and more the best self you can be is the real goal of all our work and in most Pagans' personal belief, the best expression of our respect for the Gods. I recently read a comment on a mail list that was a reaction to some conversation about the work involved in achieving personal growth and skills. In effect, the writer was really glad she wasn't Wiccan because she thought it sounded like a lot of awfully hard work.

Of course, she was right: personal growth and the development of appropriate high priest/ess skills is very hard work which must be addressed on a daily basis. Sometimes I wonder why I ever let myself get pushed into this job. Sure I wanted to learn as much as I could about Witchcraft and magic, but I didn't realize quite what I was getting into. By the time I accepted third degree I had a pretty good idea that it wasn't exactly an empty honor, but I doubt that any of us realize just how much effort, care, and interior work we're letting ourselves in for.

And why do Wiccans and many other Neopagans consider this work important?

> The purpose of spiritual practice is to restore, maintain, deepen, and clarify that conscious connection to Deity in each one of us, and to let it guide and empower all aspects of our lives.[1]

It's very easy to loose sight of the importance of one's own relationships with the God/desses when kept busy with all the day-to-day tasks of Neopagan clergy.

Once an individual is fully launched into teaching Witchcraft and/or filling other necessary roles within the Pagan community, they usually realize that however much training and life experience has been required of them, it hasn't been enough. In fact, from time to time everyone in this position gets so involved in doing the job and learning fast enough to stay a step ahead of their students that their own life may take a back seat. This is not a good thing!

I'm the worst person to be telling you that you need to set aside some time every day for personal work of various kinds. Devotions to personal deities, meditation, and time to just chill out obviously should be a priority when we're scheduling our days. Don't yell at me — I *do* know how nearly impossible it is. And I've also noticed that when I *don't* schedule in some time like this, I'm doing myself a grave wrong.

You can understand the necessity of scheduling time for personal work when you consider that burnout is one of the main reasons we lose experienced leaders. Maintaining a personal life, holding down a job (for most), taking care of a family, *and* devoting much time and energy to unpaid work as a Pagan leader creates very high levels of stress. Frankly, we can't do our best work when we're stressed out. And while it's certainly true that I'm emphatically in favor of our feeling a dedication to our community, doing our inner work is a part of FC101[2] and it cannot stop just because we may have "topped out" on initiation. You know all of this already, so use me as the excuse to really do it!

I rather like the fact that our religions aren't all choked up with things we've *got* to do. We don't have to appear in a particular building every Sunday morning, we don't have to go to confession, we don't have to say our prayers at night, we don't even have to attend lunar or sabbat rituals every single time (or at least not after initiation). If you're one of the people leading the rituals, these ceremonies are less personal religious activity than they are a part of the job. As a result, we can become a bit like a front yard in a dry spell: we're still grass, shrubs, and flowers, but we aren't quite as green as we ought to be.

Sooner or later, most of us come to a moment when we look confusedly around us and wonder why in the holy heck we are working ourselves into the ground to serve deities we're not even totally sure we believe in. It happened to me in the middle of my first set of students at a time when I was writing a book, writing a Witchcraft class every week, and writing rituals for every single Circle — and I was barely a second degree! In fact, a thought occurred to me yesterday as I was looking at the very few days I have left to make this a book I can be proud of: are the Gods really there? does all this work really serve them?

It is totally normal for any religious professional to have moments, days, months of doubt. If we didn't manage to get them all by ourselves, I'm sure the Goddess would send them to us. Coming through a loss of faith is an important part of our training and the result is always a stronger confidence in our choices. It also gives us the perspective we need for pastoral counseling. No one told me that third degree initiation wasn't the last initiation I was going to get. It's the last formal initiation for most groups, I'll agree, but everyone I've discussed this subject with concurs that other initiations lacking numbers, forewarning, and confirmation by our community can happen. This leaves you with your head spinning, chaos piled up somewhere in your life, and a whole lot of new knowledge or understanding to cope with.

How do you start back at exploring the inner mystery? First, simply ground and center. Sit there a moment and let the energy flows stabilize.

Get up and go light yourself a candle. (Personally, I've come to prefer tealight candles and fancy candleholders, single ones that I just really like. Using these saves you from finding that you have only three candles in the right colors when you need four.) Journals are also good (as you've told your students!). I'm not saying that you need to either write in one every day or record every important event; only that if you are taking care of personal needs, writing down your thoughts will probably help.

Sometimes it's really hard to get well-grounded, clear, and peaceful in mind and emotion. I've always preferred working with the elements and I've evolved a cleansing and clearing exercise which utilizes them. It is useful for personal work and it's also a good exercise for a student, class, or a whole group before ritual.

Elemental Cleansing Ritual[3]

Prepare each of the four quarters as follows (if it is possible to walk around the outside of quarter markers, I think that works very well):

- At North, place a small container of salt. If your tradition has any way of consecrating the salt, do it.
- At East, place a candle or incense. The candle or holder should be yellow or white; the incense light and "intellectual" or airy.
- At South, place a cauldron with a tiny fire or a red candle in it.
- At West, place a container of water. You can add a sprig of herb to sprinkle drops of the water.

Begin at North. Stand or kneel at the quarter point and consciously drain all the heaviness, discouragement, stasis, and physical discomforts out of yourself. When you feel that you have accomplished this, pick up a few grains of salt with your fingers and let them melt on your tongue. (It's important not to rush yourself too much at any of the quarters. On the other hand, when a group is doing this exercise it may be necessary to encourage someone to get on with it.)

At East, drop all your worries, complicated intellectualized chains of thought, confusion, and cages — let your brain relax. When you feel you have accomplished this, wave some incense in your face or concentrate for a moment on the light of the candle

At South you'll let go of chaotic energies, anger, fear, and that aggravating super-consciousness that's always yelling at you about what you "should" do. When you have completed this, pass your hand over the fire or flame, and rub the heat onto your face.

At West, let go of all your emotional discomforts. Look inward long enough to find all the day's or week's little niggling emotional stuff and let it all go. Let even love cool down for the moment until you're in a simple, receptive state. When you are finished, sprinkle a little water over your face.

In a group, each person can go from West into the Circle for ritual. When working on this alone, you may want to go to the inside of the Circle and spend some time meditating or merely thinking.

After a little practice you'll find it possible to do this process entirely "in your head" and it's an excellent preparation for class or when someone is expected for a counseling session.

So now that we've got ourselves sitting still for once and quieted down, just what *is* exploring the mystery within? It seems to me it's got to be different for every individual. What I may see as enormous growth, you may see as kindergarten stuff and that's OK — growth is what *you* need, not what somebody else thinks you ought to need or where you ought to be. Exploring the mystery within means getting yourself sorted out well enough that you have a chance to try and be the best *you* possible, not the best somebody else. You're the only one who can find that person deep within yourself who can become a reality — perhaps the idea you had of yourself before you were born.

I think the only way to make that idea of yourself real is essentially to become a sculptor in both stone and clay. Half the time you'll be chipping off stuff you don't need, which covers up the final figure, and the other half of the time you'll be trying to add stuff into the holes here and there, again to find the figure. Frequently, what you do, don't do, or get rid of isn't so important as keeping the picture of what you want to end up with in mind. It's so easy to lose track of who you *really* are in all the day-to-day wash of emotion and busyness.

These first years of the twenty-first century are terrifying because we're all so damn busy! We run from sunup till midnight but we aren't getting all that much done. And as if we weren't already busy enough, we get yelled at all the time about being better time managers! We work absolutely all the time and we've changed most recreation (exercise) into work or competitive sport rather than allow ourselves to just go fishing. I suppose I'm terribly old-fashioned, but it doesn't seem to me to be any way to run a life.

I'm going to suggest that the first exercise you practice with your new determination to put more into your inner work is to learn to say "No." If you've already got more to do than you have time for, don't take on even one more job. It's not going to be easy; the community will really need to have a festival, a student will really need to be taught, and you will really need to write up your ideas about something. Say "No." Then, after you've said no, take a look at the things you are already committed to and see if you can't give a few of them away.

Delegate is a magic word! Perhaps another person can't do a particular thing quite as well as you can — and they never will unless somebody gives them a chance to try. We often treasure the hope that some of our students will eventually assume leadership roles in the community; entrusting even beginning students with real responsibilities must surely help us in achieving this goal. Obviously, we must use a good deal of judgment when we do this and not overburden anyone or make demands they likely can't handle. Success builds strength and we can depend on life itself to provide sufficient rebuffs that anything we do covertly to confine a student's ego is probably redundant.

I tend to give an individual a job, making sure that they really know what is required and when it has to be done, and then I just leave them with it. If they screw up, well, they screw up. It was their job and their mistake and they probably won't make the same mistake again. If I hang over their shoulders, not only do they learn a whole lot less (I might just as well have done it myself) but there's almost as much chance they'll mess up than if I'd left them alone. Some people will mess up a job with the hope that it will keep them from being asked to do another. If one discussion about this tendency doesn't cure them, you might as well just write them off. They are unlikely to change any time soon and it's not your job to be their mother!

Many tasks can be divided into smaller areas of responsibility (pretty much in the same way I describe in Chapter 10), meaning that you can remain in overall control but delegate the less demanding jobs to whoever's handy. Some people will probably never be able to do this: they either crave the power and control that comes with keeping everything in their own hands or they genuinely fear that if they don't take care of everything, it won't be done perfectly. Well, it very well may not be done perfectly or exactly the way they would have it done, but so what? That it's *done* is the point.

Perhaps this is the right place to discuss the disease *high-priest/essitis*. This ailment touches every single leader at some time. It's perfectly natural and human to occasionally pull off a difficult task and have a rush of feeling that you really are pretty darn good! On the other hand, there are people who take themselves and their status too seriously and get to the point of throwing a hissy fit if anyone doesn't agree with their slightest statement. We can all catch ourselves doing this from time to time. And that's the trick: to *catch* yourself when you do it.

The Goddess and I have a pretty good relationship all in all, and She's got this really nice habit of giving me a hint when I'm in over my head. While this by no means makes me infallible, I've noticed that any time I get to feeling I'm pretty hot stuff She manages to quietly take me down a peg or two. She's usually kind enough to do this in private but I suspect that if I ignore the gentle hint, the Great Cosmic Two-by-Four will make an appearance (don't worry about not noticing the Goddess trying to get your attention this way — it's hard to miss).

Let's face it, you can't possibly do a good job as a Pagan leader if your ego isn't reasonably healthy. One of the main reasons I got into Witchcraft in the first place was because I wasn't required to pretend to be humble and modest — attitudes with which, I'll admit, I've always had a good deal of trouble. It's a daily balancing act to keep yourself equipped with enough positive self-image to do the job but without so much that you come across as arrogant and snotty.

My best suggestion is to choose a leader who you think is good at this balancing act and keep their picture in your mind as much as you can. They've probably had their lapses, but if you haven't seen them, it won't affect the usefulness of the image. The biggest problem arises when you are in public *and* doing your juggling act to pull something off. You just aren't going to have room in your mind to keep the visualization up front and keep track of everything else. Relax a bit, though; in general, people will forgive the lapses so long as you pull it off most of the time.

In fact, part of a leader's inner work is developing what has been called a *magical persona*. I'm *not* advocating that you develop two entirely separate personalities, just that you have a pretty clear vision of who you want to be when leading ritual and conducting workshops. Some of the rules covering this visualization include the idea that the image really has to be you, not some Big-Nosed Pagan⁴ you've seen. It needs to be an ideal, but not one that's out of reach (if your visualization seems impossible for you to attain, like any sensible human, you won't really try). Essentially what you are doing is attempting to *externalize* that vision of yourself being the best you can be.

This can be a very controversial idea. Many people will decide that I'm talking about *play-acting*, suggesting that you cultivate a false role which makes you appear a lot more able and wise than you really are. This isn't what I mean although I'll admit it's very difficult to write or speak clearly about it. To some extent the idea is based in the behavioral school of psychology, which says that if you behave as if you were kind and gentle, you'll at the very least develop a kinder and gentler personality. What I'm proposing is more like selecting a memory of yourself when you were achieving your goal(s) and holding that vision in mind where it can help you tap the sort of behavior you need to accomplish what needs to be done. When you are in a group that tends to require that you do all the organizing and talking, it's useful to have a *sentry* to help you keep your cool and prevent you from slipping away from your goals. It's also helpful if you have a handy procedure or process that allows you to slip into being a high priest/ess. That way, when you look at all the people you're going to be leading in ritual and find your courage at low ebb, it can help you get started.

Despite all I've mentioned, I can't figure out a really good definition for exploring the mystery within (i.e., working on inner growth). It's partially teaching yourself behaviors you consider desirable; it's partly learning to think more clearly and more in line with your cosmology; it's partly getting rid of all the inappropriate blocks that early life and society erect to constrain our inner sight, intuition, and apperception[5] of the nonmaterial. But in addition to the part of inner work which applies to the individual's mind and behavior, it's also necessary to pay attention to the portions of self which urge us toward religion and which encourage us to seek a personal relationship with deity and all the universe.

Obviously, one's personal relationship to deity will evolve over time, depending on individual experience and knowledge. If you work with a historical deity, it's usually important to find out as much as possible about that deity. As with all other historical research, consulting a number of sources is strongly suggested. Any single source can pass on the bias of the author, while your own relationship with the deity in question should, if possible, only include *your* biases.

As well as studying everything you can get your hands on about the deity, spend some time learning about the culture of the deity's adherents. If you've chosen a Sumerian Goddess, you really need to know if the culture was agricultural or pastoral,[6] and aggressive, defense-oriented, or peaceful. You also need to know what position women held (yes, even if you're male you need to know what the culture thought it knew about the differences between the sexes) and what was expected of the deities. Please keep in mind that in the ancient world, major deities were generally thought to be concerned with the survival and prosperity of the leadership rather than the needs of individual people. In other words, Athena probably didn't spend much time acting as muse for poets, particularly since there were Muses to do that job.

I suspect that Athena has a somewhat different take on her job these days but I also hope that she remains interested in the "big picture." I'm afraid the mind-set carried in the idea that "all Goddesses are one Goddess," repeated by several feminist/religious writers, has led many Pagans and/or Witches to get a little sloppy about selecting deities for specific ritual or other purposes. Certainly I do not believe that "all Goddesses are one Goddess" in any immediate sense. I don't think that it's wise to invoke Hecate when you're doing love magic; that's just not her job. On the other hand, I do think it's possible to communicate with unnamed deities and/or with deities you have not found in history or mythology.

I've never really gotten into keeping a permanent altar, or more accurately, *shrine*,[7] set up in my house, but this is an excellent way to work on developing your relationship to the specific deities you feel closest to. In Chapter 6 I mention that there is an agreement between an individual and those deities chosen for particular allegiance. In other words, there are certain things you hope the deity will do for you and there are certain things you do for the deity. Whether or not *worship*, *prayer*, or *sacrifice* are words you feel comfortable using, I believe we can agree that most of us expect to honor these deities and, insofar as it is safe, do so publicly. A personal shrine is also a good place to burn candles for specific intentions and to place spell workings, and it can function as an altar for personal rituals in general.

However, should you have or should you decide to create such a shrine, you must budget sufficient time to keep it properly. Gods may feel differently, but I suspect most Goddesses will be offended if it's dusty or has been left unchanged and unattended for any significant length of time. A shrine is similar to an open phone line — personally, I'd hate to have the Goddess think I'd put Her on hold!

To nurture our communication with deity and whatever other immaterial entities we choose, we must encourage our psychic senses. On the other hand, just because I'm a Witch doesn't mean I believe in everything I hear! There are people who see and hear things due to psychological problems and we wish neither to become one of them nor to encourage anyone to live in this world of psychological confusion. Here again we come to a balancing act as difficult as the one concerning ego mentioned above.

Unfortunately, there are even fewer hints I can give you about this balance. It's my experience that such communications tend to be almost imperceptible and don't remind one much of any sort of sight or hearing. I just get a *feeling*, either that there is something present with a certain appearance or that the gem of knowledge or the idea I've just discovered was *put there*, rather than having grown naturally. It happens to me most often when having a conversation with someone who has a problem. I'll have a question or comment sort of float to the surface and I'll feel sure that I should share it with the other person. I consider these questions or comments *communications* because they tend to be accurate regarding incidents or feelings about which I had absolutely no normal way of guessing.

> Such information should be respectfully considered but not absolutely followed. None of us is a perfect channel. Instead we are collectively responsible for interpreting, weighing, and integrating inspirational information — just as we do information from any other source.[8]

So far as I know, the only way to encourage communication with deities or other immaterial entities is to be open to them, to pay attention to what may appear as mere stray thoughts or occurrences (they might be *signs*), and to express gratitude for any communications which prove somehow useful. Don't confuse this type of communication with the manner in which some people can literally draw down the Goddess or God or otherwise *channel* information. Whether or not such communications for you require a trance state or simple receptivity, it's very important to keep clear on exactly what is or isn't *you*, as confusion in this regard can be quite dangerous to your sanity.

I feel — although I could always be wrong — that for the most part, entities don't communicate with us a great deal. Believing as I do that our deities value our willingness to rely on our own strength and intelligence, it seems to me that there are three circumstances under which they are most likely to feel moved to lend a hand. In the first, they can help us find and stay on the right track in our personal work. These communications are likely to be indirect "signs" rather than experiences such as the one I just described where words surface in my mind. For instance, if you've decided to take some particular action and something keeps happening to interfere with that effort, pay attention. Of course, sometimes accidents just happen; other times, you may want to reconsider the action you've decided to take.

Next, I think that when you do a vision quest, a meditation seeking an answer from the God/desses, or a shamanic journey, the totems or other entities may communicate with you. And finally, I think the deities sometimes decide that a particular person is a good candidate to undertake some particular job they have in mind. I do not think that these communications generally come with great clarity. Mostly I believe we just get a strong feeling about something in particular.

It's a good idea to remember that incorporeal entities (assuming they do indeed exist and can communicate with you) come in more than one kind. Many may be your friends, but others don't really care one way or the other and some are, at the very least, mischievous. Some actually teach through mischief and indirection, but if you can catch on to what they are teaching quickly it can save a lot of pain and aggravation. If you're hearing something telling you to do things counter to the First Law, it's *not* the kind of entity you should be listening to. Obviously there are psychologists who will call us borderline insane, but if you're hearing from entities who want you to do hurtful things, you need to figure out why they have chosen you. I'd even be a little worried if I thought I actually heard voices. Heck, I worry because I think I know a dragon!

I really think that it's our job to find our own way through life. When I get one of these hints I go with it, although for all I know the hint is actually coming from deep inside my own mind. I do know that in the past it's been, at a minimum, safe to consider acting on these communications. However, I don't think we can expect aid from our deities every time we have to make a decision or perform a difficult job. They value strength and we can't develop that unless we learn to depend primarily on ourselves.

My suggestion to you, therefore, is to be open to communication but not to seek it. Learn to think analytically and to make good decisions. Ask for clear thought rather than answers, which should go a long way toward preventing mistakes. I read somewhere that the majority of all prayer is asking deity to make two and two equal something besides four. Since most of us believe that our deities are constrained from performing miracles lightly, avoiding such requests ought to make them like us a bit better.

Do I believe that the Goddess must have sent a situation so I would "learn" something? No, not really. I don't believe that clouds come with silver linings, but if you're willing to work at it, you can give them the silver linings. If I wanted to believe in a deity who would send a catastrophe such as a flood or earthquake, or even an argument, just to *teach* me something, I could have stayed a Christian. I'm a great believer in the phrase "Shit Happens." I think I need to learn from what I have to deal with, but I don't think that some intelligence is deliberately messing around with my life in order to teach me lessons. There is room in a Pagan's cosmos for a certain amount of tinkering by the god/desses, but I truly resist the idea that this tinkering is going to include them deliberately doing harm to an individual or to those close to the individual.

It is the nature of deity that we cannot really know or comprehend them. We cannot do more than deduce their motivations and we cannot always accurately identify exactly what events might be of their doing. For me, it seems the only time I'm at all sure that something is the work of a deity is when the event is purely internal, which, of course, doesn't in itself make the event any less *real*. Each individual must design their own pathway to deity, which is one reason why I'm not including meditations or rituals in this chapter. I believe that most of my readers will be able to design those for themselves.

On the other hand, I suspect it would be useful to discuss such exercises generally, as you'll design them for your own use and you'll probably need to design them for others. The basic principles primarily rest on using words and other cues to evoke a suitable environment for the connection. For the Goddess Diana you might want to describe a woodland glade, the sounds of deer and other animals, and add in a lunar incense. If you are attempting to contact the Little Eagle (the Cherokee, along with some of the other Eastern Woodland tribes referred to the totem of a species by using "Little" in front of the species name) you will probably begin with a setting more reminiscent of Native American life.

You've probably noticed by now that in many ways I tend to be extremely direct. I'll admit, though, when it comes to writing ritual I have a tendency to go for a harmonious arrangement of words rather than direct- ness when I must make a choice. It's my feeling that the nonrational aspects of ourselves respond to "fancy" language and since it's those aspects we want awake and participating, it's worth it to forego directness. The primary purpose of the words and everything else you use in the exercise is to evoke the God/dess or totem. In the discussion of magic (see Chapter 8) I recommend that you coordinate all aspects of a working to intensify the purpose; in this particular sort of working you want to be just as focused as you would be for magical work.

However, the absolute truth is that you can probably best get in touch with your deities in the simplest way: sit quietly and let them in. If it's convenient, take a day and go sit in the mountains, at the edge of the sea, in a July field with the cornstalks rustling over your head. Go sit on a patch of green surrounded by concrete cliffs, on the floor, on the front steps, on the fire escape. Open your mind and heart to all of creation and listen for the voice of the Goddess, the hoofbeats of the God, the whisper of the stars.

There are any number of methodologies which can aid us in our search for spiritual realization. I have space here to mention only a few that have worked well for me.

Spinning with the Wheel of the Elements, Living within the Moon, and Walking the Medicine Wheel are three rather similar methodologies for personal metamorphosis. I'll talk about the Wheel of the Elements in some detail and then I'll touch on the others sufficiently that you'll be able to take it from there. I feel particularly drawn to work with the elements and have collected and devised a number of methodologies using them.

As you are aware, each of the four classical elements (earth, air, fire, and water) are associated with one of the cardinal directions (North, East, South, and West) and are further associated with specific personality traits. There are some variations on which element goes with what direction and the specific tool that corresponds, but for the most part, the associations with human emotions are pretty similar among all of us who use the elements. It really doesn't matter for this project if your associations aren't quite the same as mine; just make what adaptations are needed. I believe this process will be more useful to you if you use those associations which are most meaningful to you.

The general process requires you to focus on the elements individually for a reasonable period of time. The shortest period I can recommend is three months, which would allow you to complete the cycle in one year. However, devoting six months or a full year to each element really isn't at all excessive. The idea is to become deeply immersed into the element of the moment, which includes selecting clothes in its colors and choosing food, scents, activities — everything with the element in mind. And that's just the beginning. You're also to meditate on the qualities associated with the element and to examine your own relationship with them, including which of the good and/or undesirable qualities you tend to evidence most often.

In order to do this, you'll need to put together a list of attributes which go with each of the elements. The following table will help you get started.

Element	Positive Attributes	Negative Attributes
EARTH	Body	Boredom
	Death	Breaking oaths
	Diligence	Confusion
	Employment	Death

Endurance

Dormant fertility

Growth

Dullness

Healing

Irresponsibility

Law

Lack of conscience

Material things

Laziness

Mystery

Material things

Nature

Melancholy

Practicality

Mystification

Prosperity

Shallowness

Punctuality

Spinelessness

Purification

Stagnation

Respect

Stolidity

Responsibility

Solidity

Thoroughness

AIR

Creativity

Boastfulness

Dexterity

Depression

Discrimination

Frivolity

Intellectual gifts

Gossip

Joy

Gullibility

Kindness

Illogic

Logic

Indecisiveness

Mind, mental work

Lies

Optimism

Presumption

Psychic Powers

Setting limits

Teaching

Truth

Visions

Wisdom

FIRE	Action	Anger
	Courage	Cowardice
	Determination	Destruction
	Energy	Hatred
	Enthusiasm	Jealousy
	Exorcism	Lust
	Protection	Temper
	Prosperity	Vindictiveness
	Sexual love	Violence
	Strength	

WATER	Compassion	Fluctuation
	Dreams	Fluidity
	Emotions	Indifference
	Fertility	Instability
	Fidelity	Irresponsibility
	Fluidity	Laziness
	Forgiveness	Negligence
	Intuition	Rudeness
	Love	Spinelessness
	Modesty	Lack of commitment
	Receptivity	
	Sleep	
	Tenderness	
	Tranquility	
	Unconsciousness	

I suspect you have noticed that some qualities attributed to an element appear in both the positive and the negative columns; it all depends on how they are manifest in the individual and when they appear. I suggest to my students that they take four pieces of paper, one for each element, and divide each into two columns for listing the negative and positive traits they perceive in themselves. The important thing to remember is that no one else is going to ever see the lists — it's crucial to be as honest about yourself as you possibly can. There's no point in starting this process unless you're willing to look at yourself as closely as you would a cake in a baking contest.

I've suggested that you place these lists on separate pieces of paper so you can then clear some space on your desk and lay them at each cardinal point. Here's where we can get practical about dynamic balance. Read over the traits you have listed for each individual element: are some of the qualities you've listed in the negative column balanced by a positive quality that you evidence strongly? It's not that easy to change your personality once you've really become a grown-up, so sometimes it makes a lot more sense to develop controls for a negative trait and/or a positive one to reduce the potential harm to yourself and others. For instance, if you lack stick-to-itiveness (an Earth negative), perhaps you can combat it with organizing your time (an Earth positive).

However, our balancing act is not limited to working within a single element; we can look to the opposite element for help. We can attempt to use energy and strength from Fire to combat our difficulty in finishing projects. Or we can reach to all the elements and add fidelity from Water and optimism from Air in order to accomplish the same goal. Amazingly, after you manage to bring tasks to completion over a period of time, you will find that you simply finish things without having to call in the aids from other elements.

An individual's personality is made up of many different traits: some good ones, some bad ones. Both are necessary if for no other reason than without faults, there's little possibility of growth. Once perfection is attained, there's nowhere to go. Don't let shame (Water) or embarrassment (Earth) prevent you from being honest (Air and Fire) with yourself — just write those traits down in the proper column and proceed.

As part of your inner work, you will probably also develop some projects that you'll be eager to accomplish. These aspirations can also be sorted according to the elements. Again, I've provided some examples to get you going.

Element   **Project**

EARTH
- Finding acceptance of one's body (including body image, diet, exercise habit, health concerns)
- Projecting one's public image (with clothes, mannerisms, etc.)
- Developing self-identity
- Defining beliefs, values, ethics
- Exploring family or cultural roots
- Accepting personal history or redefining it
- Establishing a home, a safe place to reside
- Working for environmental concerns
- Practicing invocation
- Working on sensory development
- Understanding the cycles of the year

AIR
- Developing intellect, knowledge, ability to use logic
- Improving memory
- Expanding imagination
- Learning to use introspection, thought forms, ESP
- Cultivating spirit
- Developing spiritual goals
- Striving to achieve balance

- Developing right relationships with spirits
- Practicing invocation/evocation
- Understanding realities
- Aspecting

FIRE

- Channeling energy
- Finding clarity and strength of purpose
- Setting goals
- Encouraging passion
- Developing magical will
- Discerning which battles are righteous
- Controlling anger

WATER

- Exploring feelings and emotions (including understanding one's own emotions; changing, expressing, defining feelings; evaluating one's sensitivity to others; examining relationships)
- Exploring mental or physical travel
- Developing intuition and divination
- Practicing magic

If you'd rather use the Moon to seek personal growth and balance, you can approximately connect the traits listed above to the phases: Air to New Moon; Fire to Full Moon; Water to Waning Moon; and Earth to Dark of the Moon. I'm sure you'll make lot of changes before the lists fit well with your own private Moon mythology. Balance can be approached in much the same way as with the Elements. I suspect that you will want to bring in some of the Goddess myths, ones which seem to speak to who you are — or were. I can clearly remember my own "Diana phase" and have never considered putting it totally away.

Working with the Medicine Wheel to achieve transformation is similar to working with the Elements or the Moon. However, it does require that you be able to put yourself fully into an appropriate cosmology and have a deep understanding and sympathy for Native American life and spiritual practice. If you have studied this path only briefly, I recommend that you stay within the European mythologies. In my experience, the native sprits remain strong here on the North American continent and I must truly recommend against treating them lightly.

Working with the Medicine Wheel will involve your concentrating on each stone in the outer circle, the *Quarter* or directional stones, the moon stones, and working with the mythological qualities associated with each. With the Wheel you additionally have the red and black roads, which perhaps more obviously apply to personal growth than do the Elements or Moon. Since this book is mostly focused on Pagan paths of European background, I don't feel that I can devote enough space to a fuller discussion of working with the Medicine Wheel.9

Most of the various forms of divination or meditation exercises based on divination systems can also be valuable aids for exploring the mystery within. Choosing a single tarot card, one rune, or one throw of the I Ching as a theme for a meditation will serve the dual purpose of improving your divinatory knowledge and skills *and* give you insight into yourself. This can also be of great utility when you are going through a difficult patch in your life. Hopeful cards will make the day easier and disaster cards at least have the benefit of warning you that a particular day won't be the turning point.

Humans are infinitely clever in inventing ways to avoid being truthful with themselves. In order to get the most out of exercises intended to foster personal growth you need to make just a little time every evening to review your day. For each action or event which has occurred, you should check against the following list of avoidance techniques (defense mechanisms) to see if you are being honest with yourself.

- *Rationalization*: Explaining your actions using false motivations because the real motivation is rooted in an unacceptable emotion. Example: You claim you're helping another person as a part of your "exploration of the mystery within" rather than admitting you've wronged them in the past and are helping them now out of guilt.
- *Compensation*: Making up for some deficiency, real or imagined, usually where the deficiency cannot be corrected. Example: A sterile couple runs a boys' club to fill their need for children. (Which is not to say that compensation is *wrong*, just that you need to know when you're doing it.)
- *Displacement*: Moving emotion from its real cause to another that can be safely expressed. Example: A person feeling guilty attributes the guilt to some easy, but untrue, explanation.
- *Reaction Formation*: Masking a feeling with its opposite to avoid the emotional pain the true feeling may cause. Example: A person is rude to someone with whom they have unacceptably fallen in love.
- *Projection*: Attributing one's unacceptable emotion to another person(s). Example: A person disguises their negative feelings by accusing everyone else in a group of being negative.

A word of warning: The more you follow my suggestions and the more successful you are at seeing yourself clearly, the more strongly you will become yourself — and not everyone is going to like you. It's pretty easy to like wishy-washy people and to forgive them mistakes because, after all, the poor things really can't help but make them. A more realized personality, on the other hand, has very a definite and identifiable color, and others rightly judge that you *can* help yourself; their choice is not whether to forgive you, but whether to accept that you didn't consider what you did to be a mistake.

I've been discussing how to pursue inner development for most of the chapter but I have yet to say a single word about what your goals might be. Obviously, each person's goal in exploring the inner mystery is about the most personal objective anyone can have. It's also most likely a fairly misty idea, without definite edges or boundaries. It may approximate the figure of a Goddess or God as revealed in one of their myths. It may even closely approximate an actual person we've known, but its full extent cannot be known to the conscious mind all at once. Like the picture or reflection in a dark mirror, we can only see detail by concentrating on one small feature at a time.

"If you couldn't be who you are, who would you like to be?" In some ways this is the question you're asking yourself but in more important ways, it's the wrong question — you are not going to become a different person. At least it's my opinion that this is neither an obtainable nor a desirable end; I believe that the goal is to become *more yourself*. Sure, there are some habits or attributes you may want to discard but perhaps the most important goal of this journey is to learn to love all of yourself. Sometimes I believe this is the *only* appropriate place to practice unconditional love.

Unconditional love is a concept I am most uncomfortable with. It seems to me that if another entity loves me regardless of what I do, that's more undiscerning than unconditional. I spent thirteen years with an interesting and intelligent man who, every night at supper, told me, "That was the best [insert whatever we had for supper] I've ever eaten." It didn't take long for all the "compliment" to leave his remarks. In fact, that unvarying, unconditional compliment devalued all my work in the kitchen since he would have said it almost no matter what.

Let's ask of the God/desses and perhaps of a few people close to us for free and unconstrained love, but not undeserved and indiscriminate love. This is a love which can endure when we screw up, but notices when that happens and supports our efforts to do better. I suppose I'm a hard-ass but I do think that love must be earned to be meaningful.

The success of your inner work depends on your sense of balance. The balance I'm talking about isn't the quiet, static balance of the old-fashioned scale with two hanging pans filled with equal weights; it's a dynamic balance, always changing, always being readjusted. While walking, a human being is actually involved in the act of falling, only to catch and right themselves in a split second. Within reason, the faster you walk, the smoother and less wobbly the movement is because the speed reduces the number of split seconds spent falling. Take a two-legged dancer and send her moving quickly up a creekbed's shallow stream that flows around a million rocks — that's the kind of balance I'm talking about.

I used a dancer in that description because *confidence* is an important part of balance. It's actually good design or luck that humans evidently have a basic bias in favor of self-confidence. Despite all the things which life can do to us in an attempt to destroy our confidence (the advertisements which tell us we're too this or too that, the schoolmates who make us outsiders, even the parents who may react inappropriately to us in childhood), somehow most of us manage to scrape together enough self-confidence to function. And success — no matter how insignificantly the world measures it — works absolute wonders in helping us learn to feel good about ourselves. Digging up enough balance to take the first step provides a momentum which makes the second step smoother and easier — and thus it can go.

Does it come as any surprise when I say that at least half the stumbles you'll meet in this process you yourself created? Some psychologists claim that many of us fear success and this is one of their theories that I tend to believe. Having watched myself shoot off my own foot on occasion, I know that coping with success is darn near as difficult as coping with failure. With all the things that come up even in a lucky life, it's no wonder the balancing act is something which has to be reviewed and maybe assisted on a daily basis. After a while you begin to be able to tell right off when you aren't in balance, but the trick of fixing it doesn't necessarily get any easier.

There are times when you may want to change your balance enough to actually be out of balance for a time. While I've been writing this book, I've pretty much been out of balance in my ordinary life, as I do as little as possible which isn't focused on the writing. This is not a way to live for very long, although it may be necessary at times. (Just stay out of creekbeds while you are preoccupied with a significant project.) Even perfect balance changes daily, or hourly. Meeting with your class or coven requires a different balance than interacting with your boss or taking care of two toddlers. Thankfully, these adjustments can become automatic, although that can itself become a danger.

I suspect one of the worst habits we fall into is allowing ourselves to develop what I'm going to call *stereotyped behavior*. When this happens, we tend to adjust our behavior according to the *mask* we're wearing — Mother, High Priest, Network Engineer — without giving sufficient attention to the moment. Nine days out of ten we can welcome our kids home from school with the same words, without paying any *real* attention to them. The tenth time is probably on the day when the kid stole the family gun and took it to school. When you're dancing up the creekbed on the rocks, every bit of your attention is totally focused on what you're doing, but when you're walking through your own living room, your mind can be absolutely anywhere and you may have trouble remembering, say, which of the kids came in the front door first.

An important part of maintaining dynamic balance is always paying attention to what is actually happening *right now*. Sure, you're not going to reserve all of your introspection for designated meditation times; but you must cultivate sufficient awareness to note when something happens and to notice when what's happening now may not be quite what happened yesterday. I'm not going to try to tell you that this is easy or that it gets automatic. It never does. You have to kick yourself in the butt on a regular basis to wake up and notice. Part of the secret to reading people is just that simple: pay attention to them, notice them.

Well, that's a lot of work — enough to keep you busy until I write another book at least. It does get easier, although sloppiness and bad habits spring up like weeds. But when you're gardening, you quickly learn to tell the difference between weeds and vegetables. Likewise, it gets much easier to identify where work is needed for your exploration of the mystery within. But there is a great deal of satisfaction in realizing that you've had success in working with yourself and that, in part because of that work, you've been able to help others.

In Witchcraft, learning The Mysteries is an important part of the path. These mysteries can't be taught or written down — they just aren't that kind of secret. Part of the reason Craft education stresses spiritual growth is because it's part of the student's preparation for penetrating the mysteries. If you can't listen with the inner ear and eye, you may miss them.

POINTS TO PONDER

- It is said that the Goddess's gifts are always two-edged and that is why the traditional athame is sharpened on both sides of the blade. Her gifts to Her priest/esses are generous and awesome. The second edge of those gifts demands that we take full responsibility for all our acts, particularly those done with Her help. She never promised it would be easy.

- Take a few minutes every day to honor the God/desses and your own spirit.

- Let everything go for a moment now and then.

- Learn to achieve a static balance so you'll recognize the difference when you achieve a dynamic balance.

- Excepting meditation, balance is found in movement.

NOTES

[1] Judy Harrow, *Wicca Covens: How to Start and Organize Your Own* (Secaucus: Citadel, 1999), 23.

[2] FC 101: Feces Coagulation (i.e., getting your shit together). To the best of my knowledge, my first students created this term in 1986. There is no FC 102 because no one's ever completed 101.

[3] Change the elements to match your training. If you are on a Celtic path, divide things up to match the three elements of that way. What I've written is a suggestion, not something that is unchangeable.

[4] This name comes from the sci-fi convention term, big-name fan. The formal translation is Big-Name Pagan, but most people don't take themselves quite that seriously.

[5] *Apperception*: The process whereby perceived qualities of an object are related to past experience. (Source: Word Web, www.wordweb.co.uk/.)

[6] *Pastoral*: Relating to shepherds or herdsmen — those devoted to raising sheep or cattle. (Source: Word Web, see note 5.)

[7] The term *altar* is applied to the table set up in the ritual space to hold candles and other objects which are part of the ritual. For the purpose of differentiation, let's define *shrine* as a surface or place set aside to display objects relating to a particular deity and as a personal place to honor deity(ies).

[8] Harrow, *Wicca Covens*, 36.

[9] Check my Web site, www.greycat.cc, as I have a fuller discussion of the Medicine Wheel and its uses there. I also include URLs linking to materials that can aid you in learning more about Native American beliefs and practices. My book, coauthored with Medicine Hawk, *American Indian Ceremonies* (New York: Inner Light Press, 1990) is out of print at this time.

INDEX

abilities of god/desses 137
Absolute Ideal 69
abstract thought 55
academic disciplines, general knowledge of
    268
acts of God 139
advanced curriculum 280
"advanced magic" 184
Aesir 47, 105
"after-ritual air-walking" 214
Age of Reason, the 94
Agrippa 94
Air 329
alchemy 93
Alexander the Great 78
alphabet, Hebrew 93
altar 210
    layout 265
    permanent 323
    position 265
    quarter 210
Amazing Randy, The 54
Amber K 18, 171, 221
American Craft 17
amphiboly 50
analogies
    defined 57
    false 57–58
analytical thinking 42, 43, 44, 63
ancestors, gods seen as 144
ancient
    Masters 91
    matriarchy 76, 83
    Ones 106
    religions 298
anger, and magical workings 193
animism 91, 120
anointing 205, 209

Antagonists in the Church 267, 293
Aphrodite 147
apperception of the nonmaterial 322
apprentice mage 55
Ár n'Draiocht Féin 18
Aradia 71
Aramaic 75
archetypes 139
arguments 290, 327
    false 288
    premise of, questioning 61
Aristotle 48
Arrows Flight 185
Asatruar 203
Ash tradition 209
athame 171
    as symbol 72
atheism 90
Athena 148, 323
Atlantis 91
attitudes about deities 136
attributes
    list of, for elements 329–31
    of god/desses 137
August 1 101
avoidance techniques 336

Babylon 68
backlash 165, 177
Bacon, Roger 94
bad behavior 154
bad manners at festival 256–59
Bakker, Jim 24
balance 32, 131, 132, 324
    and Moon 334
    dynamic 338
    out of 339

balance (*continued*)
  dynamic, maintaining 339
  sense of 338
balancing act 321, 324, 332, 339
Baptists 288, 295
basic knowledge 264
Basic Civilized Life 269
Bear Tribe 16
beginners, ungrounded 203
behavior
  moral 155, 156, 163
  stereotyped 339
beliefs about deities 136
Beltane
  fires 86
  gathering 208
  ritual 208
Bennett, Rhiannon 256
Bible 56, 91
  as a word 55
  as ethic 153
Bierce, Ambrose 67
Big Three 124, 125, 132, 136
bigotry 295, 296
binary logic 138
black
  magic 159, 176
  pure 123
  road, with Medicine Wheel 335
black/white dichotomy 124, 138
Blavatsky, Mme Helena Petrovna 91, 102
body chemistry, and magic 175
bone-fires 86
Bonewits, Isaac 24, 96, 120, 137, 138, 172
Book of Shadows 264, 279, 298
Book, Protestant Christian 143
Boy Scouts 97
Briffault 96
Brittanica 101
brownies 141
Buddhism 100, 166, 289, 308
bulletin board, Internet 278
burning candle, visualized 180
Burning Times, The 81
burnout 29, 315

cake and cup 202, 205, 208, 212, 215, 217, 219, 220
call the quarter 210
calling East, West 210
candle-burning, formal 179
candles 189, 208, 210, 217, 219, 222, 317, 324

handmade pure beeswax 179
  tea light 209, 317
  votive 180
cantrips 176, 178
cardinal directions 329
Carter, Jimmy 44
casting
  generic 203
  sacred space 265
  sequence 203
  the Circle 213
Catholic Church 125, 142, 204, 288
Catholic priest 302
causes, false 62
celebrants 211, 216
  primary 206, 217
celebration, seasonal 214
Celts 78, 105, 106
Celtic
  deities 144
  festival 101
  religion 144
centering 181, 184, 186, 188, 316
central fire 207
Cerebus 145
ceremonial
  Magic 98, 105, 106
  magical schools 94
  Magician 93
  magic lodges 102
  magic rituals 95
ceremonies 316
chalice 212, 219
  bearer 212
channeling 120
  information 325
chants 176, 206, 214, 216, 217, 218
chaos 203, 207, 316
  magicians of 198
Charge of the Goddess 113, 124, 135, 162
charms 126
  love 92
  pregnancy 76
chemistry 93
Cherokee 328
Cherry Hill Seminary 27
chief, as role for deity 147
children of Pagan parents 291
choir 217, 218
Christian
  bashing 299
  book, the 296

Ceremonial Magician 289
Church 117
  denominations 204
  groups 300
  minority cults 94
  Pagan mixed marriage 304
  priest 29
  theology 298
Christianity 123–24
  and religious freedom 124
  as event religion 103
  as monotheistic religion 119
Christianization of Europe 97
chronic antagonists 267
Church
  of All Worlds 106
    as Pagan path 115
  of England 118, 204
  loss of its monopoly 88
Churching of America, The 31, 205
circle 29, 68, 143, 205, 207, 209, 210, 211, 212,
    215, 220, 222, 280, 301, 316, 318
  basic symbolism 265
  casting 190, 203
    rhyme 210
  magic 177
Circle 101 workshop 250
civilization's problems, solution to 60
class or group teaching 270
cleansing 183
  exercise 317
clear white light 123
clearing exercise 317
clergy 24, 25, 30, 128
  as counselor 32
  as teacher 32
  education of 31
  leading workshops 32
  Pagan 31, 304
  paid 31, 32
  perform weddings, funerals 32
  teaching basic classes 32
  visiting hospital, prison 32
code
  explained 162
  of Honor 266
  of silence 195
coercion 291
communication
  imperceptible 324
  internal 196
communion 204

with deity 202
  sacrament 118
community 131, 143, 226, 285
  service 273
  standards 291
compensation 336
complaints 301
concentration 177, 186
  meditative 186
  peaceful 187
  relaxed 186
concepts
  holistic 117
  immaterial 62
conceptual systems 196
confession 316
confidence 338
confrontation 290, 307
congregation 25, 205
conjuring 176
connecting with the God/desses 300
consciousness, facets of 196
Constantine 80
Constitution, the 307
context 51, 52, 54
  quoting out of 51
contract, deity and worshiper 141
conversation, with deity 120
Copernicus 142
correspondences, magical 178, 180
  information 183
cosmology 332
  building new 119
  containing magic 118
  natural 117
  Pagan 115, 132, 173
costuming the helpers 216
council of churches 306
counseling 27
country healers 95
coven 203, 227
  totems 265
  training 266
Coven Law 266
coven-trained leaders 299
covenant 141
coveners 160, 304
cow-houses 86
coyote 145
Craft, the 22, 115, 197, 275, 278
  brotherhoods 102
  community 267

Craft, the (*continued*)
  education 340
  family 268
  leader 292
  rituals 107, 204, 213
  teachers 264
cross-quarter days 101
Crowley Aleister 98, 99, 103, 104, 106
Crusades 89, 93
crystals 182, 183
cues, sensory 190
cult of the dead 102
cunning men 95, 104
cup and plate 206, 216, 219
cursing 177, 178
Cybele 91

dance 176, 206, 210, 212, 216, 217
  organized 213
  spiral 206
  totem 216
Dark Ages 93
Darwin 90
dealing with discord 267
death and rebirth, spiritual 127
death experience 175
dedicant 266
deductive logic 48
Dee, Dr. John 89, 94
defence mechanisms 336
defining sacred space 213
definition, lack of 54
Deification thought process 69
deities 83, 136, 197, 274, 305, 316
  adherents,culture of 323
  ancient 139
  and worshiper, contract between 141
  as balanced pair, transcendent 138
  as springing from singular force 139
  communication with 324
  communion with 202
  conscious connection to 315
  designing a pathway to 327
  direct experience of 205
  encouraging communication with 325
  figures 265
  for magic 181
  free choice of 145
  from history 323
  from mythology 323
  getting in touch with 328
  Greek 76

historical 323
  honoring 324
  immanent 120, 137
  indirect signs from 325
  individual 140
  invocation of 213, 214
  major 323
  nature of 327
  Pagan 131
  particular allegiance 324
  pervasive presence of 137
  prechristian 75
  sky 217
  specific, relationship to 324
  transcendent 120, 138
  tripartite 131
  unnamed 323
delegating 319, 320
Delphi, oracles at 175
Demeter 20, 148
demigoddesses, tripartite 145
demigods 141
devil 122, 124, 191–92
  worshiping of 79, 81
devotion to nature 92
diagnostic dream 175
Diana 79
  as Goddess 327
diluting the energy 215
directing power 215
directional stones, with Medicine Wheel 335
discipline 193, 194
displacement 336
distance, emotional 188
divination 17, 266, 272, 335
  improving knowledge of 335
  systems 335
  techniques 301
divine founder 100
diviner 174
divinity 74
diZerega, Gus 163
double helix 116
doubt 316
  and magical workings 193
drawing down the Goddess or God 325
Drawing Down the Moon 16, 214
dream-working 188
dreaming 123
dropout statistic 266
Druid 18, 92, 102, 106, 203, 213, 288, 295
  modern 98

traditional 24
drumming 176, 206, 218
  circle 253
  role in enhancing ritual 218
dualism 138
dualistic logic 138
Durkheim 74
dynamic balance 28, 274, 332, 338
  maintaining 339

early death 129
Earth 329
  centered 289
  Goddess 137
  magic 176
  Mother 77, 121
  negative 332
  positive 332
Earth Rising Inc. 260
earthquakes 129, 132, 327
East 329
Eastern
  Catholic priest 306
  Woodland tribes 328
ecclesiastic 23
Eddas, the 94
egg, universal 116
Egyptian, as Pagan path, 115
eight holy days 100, 101
eight
  steps 215
  Commandments 153–54
Elemental Cleansing Ritual 186, 317
elementary classes 280
elements 210, 211, 317, 329, 335
  for magic 181
  four classical 329
  individual 332
  list of attributes for 329–31
  negative qualities 331–32
  positive qualities 331–32
  projects associated with 333–34
  working with 335
elevation 128, 280
  to third degree 28
  refusing 275
Eliade, Mircea 127
embarrassment 332
emotional control 193
emotions, affected by magic 176
emperor 147
enchantment 176, 178

end justifies means 69
energy 220
  affected by magic 176
  ambiguous 182
  cleansing object of 183
  diluting 215
  flows, stabilizing 316
  from Fire 332
  magical 165, 214
  personal 165
Eneryes 146
Engel S. Morris 49, 58
entities 141, 326
entry-level teaching 280
Environment, The 133
environmentalism 121
Episcopal Church 29
equal, defined 26
Equal Rights Amendment 76
equivocation 54
Esalin 106
esbats 265
essays
  on ethics 279
  on the First Law 279
Essenes, the 94
ethical
  reality 122
  system, from First Law 154
ethics 140, 154, 165, 289
  defined 152
  essays on 279
etiquette 265
Europe, Christianization of 97
European
  Christianity 90
  mythologies 335
event 226, 227, 228
  "freestyle" 226
  local 234
  sponsoring 225
  sponsors, experienced 229
  regional 234
  weekend 235
evil 123, 129, 132, 133, 159
  as deliberate choice 138
  behavior 154
  eye, the 95, 104, 177, 178
  inherent 120
  intelligence 126
evoking the God/dess 328
exploring the mystery within 314, 318, 322, 337

faculties, nonverbal 180
failure 339
fairies 141, 142
fakirs 299
fallacy 54
    negates proof 63
false arguments 288
Farm, The 106
farmer, as role for deity 147
Farrar, Stewart 207
father gods 107
FC 101 266, 315
fear, and magical workings 193
female deity 125
fertility
    of crops and herds 79
    of fields and flocks 79
    religion 121, 122
festivals 203, 219, 288, 298
    organizing 225–61
fidelity, from Water 332
final judgment 130
fire 207, 210, 216, 217, 329
first degree 273
    course 278
    initiation 155, 278
    studies 194, 272
    training 265
First Law 153, 154, 156, 160, 161, 162, 191, 193,
        195, 326
    as scripture 162
    essays on 279
five points 131
flash burns 215
"floating population" 300
floods 129, 327
Flower Children 106
focus 189, 194
    magical 190
    of magical energy 214
folklore 95, 97, 98
folklorists 96
folkways 96
Force, the 140
formal initiation 21, 22
    third degree 21
formal
    grounding 215
    logic 48, 49
founder, divine, semidivine 100
four classical elements 213, 329
    plus spirit 131

fourfold imagery 203
Fox sisters 91
Frazer, J.G. 79, 87, 94, 96, 121
Freaks 106
free
    choice 129
    will 157
freedom of religion 307
"freestyle" event 226
Furies 146
fuzzy logic systems 138
Gaea Retreat Center 260
Gaelic traditionalist 295, 299
Gaia 121
Galileo 142
Gardner Gerald 68, 71, 80, 95, 97, 99, 100,
        101, 102, 103, 105, 106, 107, 109, 121,
        144, 286, 296
Gardnerian
    coven 144
    Wiccan practice 94
Gardner's Book of Shadows 164
Gaskin, Stephen 106
gathering 25, 203, 288
    Beltane 208
    with theme 209
    weekend 208
Gathering Pagan Spirit 216
generalizations 55, 58
    proof of 59
    the rule 58
    the specific case 58
    valid 59
"generic" Pagan 156
genetic manipulation 53
ghosts 141, 192
Gnosticism 93
God/desses within us 137
Goddess
    as muse 92
    as three 146
    concept of 124
    Great 77, 83
    Great Mother, cult of 76
    of Earth 137
    of Moon 137
    of the poets 146
    threefold 146
    tripartite 145
    within 197
God
    of the Jews 77

tolerant 91
vengeful 91
gods
as numinous 75
preferred faces of 137
triple 146
Golden Bough, The 19, 79, 94, 121
good 132, 159
versus evil 138
gossip 293, 294, 308
untrue 295
Graces, the 146
Graeme, Kenneth 102
grammar, ambiguous 49–50
granting initiation 275
Graves, Robert 46, 92, 146
gravity 89
Great
Beast 106
Masters 106
Rite 308
Greek
as Pagan path 115
first language 75
gods 145
green magic 176
grounding 181, 184, 186, 188, 215, 220, 316, 317
beginners 30
formal 215
techniques 301
group
charismatic 205
chats 278
dynamics 27
harmony 293
large 205
mixed-path 204
solidarity 293
guardians 208
gunpowder 89
Hades 147–48
hallucinogenic drugs 175
Hamilton, Edith 75
handwritten pledge 279
Hare Krishna 106
harm
defined 163, 177
potential for 163
harmony
idealized condition of 186
of the group 293
harassment, sexual 290

Harrow, Judy 24, 115, 285, 288
harvest ritual 214
hatred, and magical workings 193
Haugk, Kenneth 267, 293
Hawking, Steven 142
healing 174
arts 265
Lady Goldenrod 214
techniques 301
the earth 214
Heartland Pagan Festival 260
heat death 116
heaven 130, 154
Hebrew 75
Hecate 145, 146, 323
hedge
magic 176
witch 173
Hegel, George Wilhelm 69
helix, double 116
hell 130, 160, 167
helpers 217
costuming the 216
for magic 181
Hera 147, 148
herbalists 79, 95
herbs 180, 189
herding 79
heresy 81
heretics, Pagan 140
Herodotus 94
hexes 177, 178
high priest/ess 24, 29, 30, 339
skills, developing 314
high priest/essitis 320
high-power magic 176, 218
higher degrees 280
Hinduism 130, 166, 289, 308
Hippies 106
history 301
accuracy 298
awareness of 43
general knowledge of 267
how to read 83
objective, verifiable 68
of the Craft 265
perspective 43
History Channel 108, 173
Hitler's SS 47
hoaxes 44
Hobbes, Thomas 72
holidays, solar 101

holistic
  concept 117
  world 116
honesty 157, 158, 195
honor 158, 195, 273
  defined 158
honorable
  behavior 160
  person, described 161–62
Horned God 137
horse whisperers 102
HP/S 204, 207, 211, 215, 218
Hug in (memory) 41
hunting 79, 147
hurricanes 129, 132
Hutton, Lauren 47, 62
Hutton, Ronald 70, 79, 96, 100, 151
Hydesville NY 91
hypostatization 52

I Ching 335
ideal equality 26
imagery
  fourfold 203
  threefold 203
imagination, as tool of will 192
immanent deity 120, 137
immaterial entities 324, 325
incense 189
incorporeal entities 175, 326
individual action v government decree 60
Indus valley, and prehistoric civilization 82
ingredients, magical 178
initiates 28
initiation 20, 28, 97, 126, 127, 276, 316
  first degree 155
  granting 275
  in Witchcraft 280
  last formal 316
  quick 27
  refusing 275
  Ritual 164
  status 290
initiatory religion 20
inner
  development 337
  ear 273, 340
  eye 273, 340
  mystery 316
  sight 322
  work 333, 338

Inquisition 81, 90
inspiration 120
intelligence, defined 58
intentions, specific 324
Internet 286, 296
"Inter-Tradition Guidelines, The" 265
"Introduction to Paganism, Witchcraft" 266
introductory classes 268
intuition 322
invocations 203
  of the deities 214
invoking the Quarters and Deities 213
inward-looking process 272
irony 50
Islam
  and religious freedom 124
  as event religion 103
  as monotheistic religion 119

Janus 145–46
Jesus 91
Job 128
journal 317
joy, idealized condition of 186
Judaic religion 128, 129
Judaism 68, 127, 128, 129
  and religious freedom 124
  as event religion 103
  as monotheistic religion 119
Judea 77
Judeo-Christian God 136
Jung, Carl 139
Jupiter 148

Kabalism 93
karma 161, 165
  bad 130
  concept of 166
  defined 130
  good 130
  human 130
  Oriental interpretations 166
  retributive 131
Keep Wicca Traditional (Web site) 51
Kennedy, John F. 52
king 147
  Arthur 105
  of the Witches 106
knighthood, flowering of 105
Knights Templar 94
knotwork, Celtic 105

knowledge 194, 264
  oral tradition 78
Koran 127

Lackey, Mercedes 185
laity 25
Lammas ritual 214
language
  careless 298
  complicated 61
  meaning of 49
  sloppy 191
  stupid 298
  use and misuse of 63
Last Stand at Papago Wells 295
Latin, first language 75
Law of Three 161, 164, 166
Law, The 162, 163
lawmakers 23
leadership 272
  roles 319
left-hand path 159
  magic 176
legal problems 268
Leland, Charles 71
Lewis, Jerry Lee 189
"life skills" 269
life stages
  adult/parental/responsible 146
  older/retired/wise 146
  young/single/carefree 146
life, passages of 121
light trance 186, 187, 188, 189
litany 22
little people 141
Little Eagle 328
Living within the Moon 328
lobby groups 288, 320
lodges, ceremonial magic 102
logic 42
  deductive 48
  formal 48, 49
  informal 47
  lack of 45
  systems, fuzzy 138
logical
  absurdities 45
  methodology 43
Loki 145
Lord Cyprian's Creed 149
loss of faith 316

love
  charms 92
  free and unconstrained 338
  magic 323
  spell 191
  unconditional 337
  undeserved and indiscriminate 338
low magic 176
lunar celebrations 101
Lutheran Church 204
lying 195, 288
L'Amour, Louis 295

Mabigonian 94, 102, 105
MacBeth 171
mages 93, 314
  advanced 198
magic 16, 49, 79, 89, 98, 173, 175, 186, 197,
    272, 314
  advanced 198
  and powers of deity 118
  as fraud 54
  as protection 177
  black 159
  Ceremonial 93, 105, 106, 164
  defined 172
  divisions in 176
  ecstatic 193
  emotional 176, 177
  harmful 165, 193
  high-power 218
  ineffectual 155
  intellectual 177
  intent of 176
  list of skills for 184
  practices, family-based 80
  preparation for 181
  sexual 193
  sneakiness of 182
  unethical 164
  weak 154
  white 159
  word, science as 142
  workers 191, 195, 196, 198
  working of 172, 181, 190, 193, 194, 195
    emotional 193
    personal 196
    willed 193
magical 189
  energy 214
  hours, table of 178

magical (*continued*)
  jewelry 302
  lodge 103
  object 179
  persona 321
  thinking 44
  work 157, 191, 328
magicians 92
  black 289
  ceremonial 93, 184
  left-hand path 289
  teacher role 28–29
magick 171
maiden, mother, crone 145, 146, 147, 211
majority
  community 308
  culture 142–43
  society 290
marital discord 268
Martello, Leo 104
Mary 143
Masons 91, 93, 97, 98, 102
material elements 179
  burial at crossroads 183
  disposing of, in running water 183
mathematics 93
May Day 96, 101
maypole 210
mead 206
media 301, 302
medicine 93
Medicine Wheel 335
medieval pattern of life 88
meditation 123, 177, 188, 272, 301, 327, 335
  adeptness at 265
  guided 185
  learning 273
  seeking answer from Goddess 326
  theme for 335
  designated 339
meditative state 189
Memory raven 40
mental quiet 188
mentoring 272
Mercury 147
methodologies 329
  of religion 114
Middle Ages 80, 88
mime 210
minister 23
  Methodist 304
ministerial association 306

minstrels, traveling 105
miracles 118, 327
misinformation 46
mistreatment
  of students 290
  sexual 290
modern Witchcraft, sources of 68
monism 120
monoblock 116
monogod 137
monotheists 125
  philosophy 117
  religion 91, 119
moon 335
  and balance 334
  and personal growth 334
  and time of working 182
  cycles of 141
  Goddess 137
  phases of 121
  stones, with Medicine Wheel 335
  working with 335
moral
  behavior 153, 155, 156, 163
    from First Law 154
  guidance 163
morality 154, 157
  dependent on individual perception 140
morals, defined 152
Motel of Mysteries 70
Mother 211, 339
  Earth 217
  teacher role 28
Mother Teresa 159, 298
multi-media approach, teaching 271
mundane
  experience 268
  skills 268
Munin (thought) 41
murrain 95
Murray, Margaret 71, 97, 101, 102
music 210, 216, 218
Muslims 308
mysteries, the 264, 274, 340
mystery 126, 127
  element 274
  play 127
  religion 20, 47, 127, 140
  within 340, 335
    exploring 314
mystical truth 144
myth 147

as teaching tool 147
favorite of Witches 147
mythology 19
defined 67

natural world 117
nature 133
as part of deity 139
devotion 95
of religion 53, 114
Nazi death camps 90
needle and thread 180
negative path 159
neo-Celtic, as Pagan path, 115
Neopagan 16, 17, 18, 24, 29
clergy 17, 25, 315
defined 115
movement 25
seasonal rites 80
Web page 53
"never again the burning" 214
"new physicists" 142
New Forest 97
Coven 101, 105
New Age 106, 107
movement 24
newcomers 301
Newton 89
Nile, the 103
nine covens 98
Niniveh 68
nirvana 186
Noble Savage 19
non-European religious paths 308
Norse
as Pagan path, 115
men 105
mythology 146
North 329
North Wind
classes 280–82
workshops 282–83
November 1 101
numinous
gods 75
world 137

Oak tradition 209
oaths, keeping 159
objective
fact 144
reality 52, 197

universe 140
world, affected by magic 176
objects
empowered magically 183
enchanting 182
material, in spell 182
metallic 183
mundane 183
obscure, for a working 180
of focus 190
rare, for a working 180
sensory 189
obsession spell 191
occult 94–95
Odin, myth of 40
oils, scented 189
on-line teaching 277
one-on-one teaching 270
One True Right and Only Path 126, 296
optimism, from Air 332
ordination 128
organizational pattern 287
organized dancing 213
Oriental
philosophies 91
religions 90, 91
stories 105
original sin 120
Osiris 91
other 70
particular 163
"planes" 192
sight 185
out of balance 339
outer circle, with Medicine Wheel 335

pagan religions, Greek 91
pagan religions, Roman 91
Pagan Spirit Gathering 216
Pagan 20, 24, 25
clergy 23, 140, 304, 306
cosmology 132
defined 115
deity 131
"generic" 156
groups 31
leaders' jobs, listed 26
manners 250
nation 224
paths, of European background 335
paths, philosophy of 280
researcher 24

theology 301
top occupations 53
worldview 289
paganism 32
  ancient 95, 101
  classical 92
  Egyptian 91
  Northern European 92
paid clergy 24
pain 102, 129, 133
pantheism 120
panenthism 120
pantheon 138, 145, 147
  of god/desses 137
  of the tradition 265
Paracelsus 94
paradise 154
particular other 163
pastoral counseling 27, 316
pattern of life, medieval 88
penetrating the mysteries 340
pentacle 171, 302
peoples of the Books 137
"performance dance" 216
peripheral vision 186
Persephone 148
person, total 32
personal
  attacks 288
  communication with deity 204
  deities, devotions to 315
  growth 157, 314, 335
    and Moon 334
    and Medicine Wheel 335
  objectives 337
  relationship with deity 322, 323
  responsibility 273
philosophy
  monotheistic 117
  of the Craft 265
  of the Pagan path 280
  sorcerer's 173
Pickengill, George 98, 99, 104
Plato 94
pluralism 138
poetry 94
poisoning the well, defined 47
politics 287, 288
  toxic 288
polytheism 91, 115, 138, 289
Pomegranate: A New Journal of Neopagan Thought 108

poppet 179, 182
positive
  ethic 122
  path 159
possession 120
potential harm
power 192, 196, 197, 288
  brokering 288
  directing 215, 217
  how much 214
  issues 287
  kinds 214
  raising 214, 217
practice session 185
prayer 74, 316, 324, 327
  before secular meetings 304
  different from spell 118
  for rain 79
pre-Gardnerian coven 104
pre-initiatory training 265
pregnancy charms 76
prehistoric Judaic, as Pagan path, 115
prejudice 295
Presbyterian Church 295
Priest/ess 18
primary
  celebrants 217
  HP/S 211
Prime Mover 139
principle of balance 274
procession 209, 213
professional troublemakers 267
professionalism 19
projection color, definite and identifiable 336
promises, keeping 159
proselytizing 296
  defined 297
prospective students, questionnaire 268
protocol 265
psychic
  powers, as fraud 54
  senses 324
psychological
  confusion 324
  problems 268
punishment 130
purgatory 166
Pyramids 73
pyrotechnics, synchronized 207
Pythagoras 94

Quabbalah 127
qualities, mythological, with Medicine
    Wheel 335
Quarters 265
    altar 210
    calls 210, 265
    colors 217
    invoking 213
    with Medicine Wheel 335
Qur'an 127

rationalization 336
reaction formation 336
Real Magic 172
reality, scientific 68
receptive congregation 205
recipient of magical energy 214
reconstructionists 298
red road, with Medicine Wheel 335
Red Herring 63
Rede, The 177
Reformation 80, 88, 89
reincarnation 119, 130, 165, 166
religion 98
    as anti-intellectual 74
    defined 114
    ethnic 144
    false 68
    historical 144
    national 144
    organized 114
    progressing 91
religious
    "activity" 143
    comfort 304
    freedom 31
    professional 316
    truth 42
Renaissance 80
research 298, 299
    historical 323
responsibility, principle of 131
rest, idealized condition of 186
right behavior 154
right, defined 159
right-hand path 159
ring 211
    of power 214
ripple effect 118
ritual 25, 29, 83, 97, 98, 127, 143, 172, 185, 186,
    197, 204, 205, 207, 208, 209, 211, 212,
    217, 218, 219, 220, 221, 264, 271, 272,
    298
    adeptness at conducting 266
    area 209, 210, 212, 216
    as theater 218
    basic 265
    bath 18
    Beltane 208
    closing 215, 249
    communicating in 216
    community 225
    coven 209, 213
    Craft 213
    dedication 273
    demonstration, videotaping 279
    dismissal 210
    drumming as enhancement 218
    effective 203
    empty 204
    evaluation of 220
    expenses 208
    first 249
    group 203
    harvest 214
    home group 202
    individual dedication 272
    Lammas 214
    large group 207, 209, 210, 212, 214, 216, 217,
        219, 249
    leading 249, 295, 321
    learning 295
        to lead 272
        to participate 272
    local sabbat 226
    lunar 316
    magic 176, 177, 197, 214
    memorizing 273
    open 225
    opening 249
    outdoor 306
    outlining area for 222
    Pagan 213
    participants 207
    personal, altar for 324
    poetry reading in 222
    preparations 205
    public 202, 203, 204, 207, 214, 217, 218, 221,
        301
        stand-alone 203
    sabbat 316
    Samhain 216
    Satanic 305

ritual (*continued*)
  short 249
  site 208, 219
    Wiccan 305
  small group 203
  space 207, 213
  specific, selecting deities for 323
  story line of 216
  teaching 279
  trivialized 145
  understanding 272
  writing 316, 328
Ritual 101 workshop 203, 301
Ritual, Elemental Cleansing 317
ritualist 145, 202, 249
robe and badge of position 265
Robin Hood 105
Roman Catholic
  Church 29, 91
  sacrament of communion 118
Roman gods 145
Romanticism 72, 94
Romish Church 95
Rosecrucianism 98, 102
Rosecrucian Theater 98, 99
rote learning 272
rowan-tree 86
rules
  for gathering at festival 253
  of the universe, Pagan 116
Runes 40, 335
Russell, Jeffrey 81, 174

sabbats 265
sacred
  elements 265
  space 203, 208, 209, 213
    anchoring 213
    casting 265
    defining 213
    releasing the 215
  theater 214
sacredness of all things 137
sacrifice 324
safety 31
  issues 286
sample readings, Tarot 279
Sanders, Alexander 104, 106
sarcasm 50
Satanism 121, 124, 125, 302
satori 186
Saul of Tarsus 29

science, as religion 142
screening process, students 266
seasonal celebration 214
seasons 228
  passage of 121

second degree 128, 276, 316
secret passwords 97
"seeing" 190
self-confidence 338
self-consciousness, and magical workings
    193
self-discipline 193, 194, 273
  developing 273
self-knowledge 194
self-sufficiency 266
semantics 57, 159
semidivine founder 100
sense of balance 338
sensing energy 192
sentence structure, careless 50
sentry 322
Seth 145
seven, as magical number 182
sexual
  harrassment 290
  mistreatment 290
  techniques 176
sexuality 121
shadow-walking 123
Shakespeare 171
shaman, identifying traits 174–75
shamanic journey 326
shame 332
shape-changing 174, 175
  meditation for 185
shared participation 25
sharing food 212
shepherd 147
shrine 323, 324
signed charter 103
signs 325
silence 195
Silva Mind Power 186
simple receptivity 325
sin 140
  defined 152
Sisters of Charity 288
Site Repot 244–47
situational ethics 152
skills 264
slogans 52

smudging 205, 209
Society for Creative Anachronism 244, 300
solar holidays 101
songs 214
  leading 218
sorcery 74, 79, 173
  and superstition 174
  rural 104
sound bites 302
sources of information 45
South 329
space
  sacred 208, 209
  ritual 213
speaking-self 196
special effect 207, 218
spells 104, 126, 165, 176, 177, 181, 197
  bags 182
  "cookbooks" 183
  defined 178
  different from prayer 118
  object 181
spell-working 179, 180, 182, 183, 189, 195, 324
  materials, reusable 183
  on cattle 86
  on cow's milk 86
  the six parts 178
  traditional 55
Spinning with the Wheel of the Elements
    328
spiral 116
  dance 206
spirit 141, 192
  affected by magic 176
  essence of human 119
  self 196, 197
  shape of 166
spiritual
  growth 314, 340
  practice, purpose of 315
  realization 328
Spiritualism 91, 94, 98, 99
spoken parts 210
sponsorship 229
stabile lighting 207
stability, idealized condition of 186
staffing 228
standards of the community 291
Star, Ceffyl 278
"star stuff" 143
state versus individual 69
statement of purpose 214

status of women 78
  in Christian philosophy 143
stereotyped behavior 339
Stevens, R 263
stimulants, sensory 190
stones
  semiprecious 183
  with Medicine Wheel 335
Stonehenge 73, 92, 102
"story line" 217
strength, from Fire 332
students, training 264
studies, first-degree 194
substance abuse 266, 268
success 338, 339
suffering 129
suicide 129
Sumerian Goddess 323
Summerland 119
supernatural 114
superstition 173
  defined 174
support group 269
suspense 218
syllogism 48
symbolic cleansing 209
symbolism of Tarot cards 279
symbols 177, 196, 216, 298
  in logic 49
  power of 265
synchronized pyrotechnics 207
talisman 179
tantra 193
target 30
Tarot 279, 335
teaching 27, 227
  entry-level 280
  on-line 277
  technique, by example 160
  the Craft 274
techniques
  avoidance 336
  divination 301
  grounding 301
  healing 301
  of teaching 278
television 278
temple structure 83
ten commandments 153
thaumaturgy, defined 176
theater 210
  good 217

theater (*continued*)
  ritual 218
  sacred 214
Thebes 68
theme gatherings 209
theology 166, 280
Theosophy 91, 98, 99, 102
theurgy 118, 177
  defined 176
third degree 128, 276, 314
  elevation to 28
  initiation 316
third eye 185
Thorn tradition 209
thought
  form 190
  raven 40
thoughtful entities 274
three book religions 56
three Fates 146
threefold
  defined 165
  goddess, the 46
  imagery 203
  Law 131, 164
Times Square 117
tone of voice 50
tools 298
torches 211
totem 141, 326, 328
  animals 175
  dance 216
  spirits 274
towns
  development of 89
  growth of 88
tradition 227, 301
  ancient 100
  materials 271
  totems 265
traditionalists 298
training students 264
trance state 187, 188, 325
  light 186, 187
trance-working 174
transcendent deity 120, 138
  as balanced pair 138
transformation, achieving with Medicine
    Wheel 335
transubstantiation 118
traveling 123
tricksters 145, 218

tripartite deity 131
triple gods 146
Triple Goddess 145
Triumph of the Moon 100
true
  mysteries of Wicca 273, 274
  naming 179, 191, 195
  Will 287
truth, underlying 68
truthfulness, as desirable 157
tylers 208
  defined 207
Tyre 68

UFO sightings 273
unacceptable behaviors 291
unconditional love 158, 337
uncrossing spells 95, 104
unethical
  group 292
  means 288
universal egg 116
Universal Law 266
universe
  as mechanistic 94
  cyclical nature of 129, 137
unnatural world 117
unqualified teacher 292
unseen component 274
upper degrees 276
US immigration policies 308

Vacation Pagan School Classes 301
Valhalla 154
Valiente, Doreen 71
Vanyel 185
Venir 105
Venus 76
  of Wilendorf 102
violence 291
vision quest 272, 326
visitations 120
visualization 190, 321, 322
  positive 175
  specific 188
vocabularies 203

Walking the Medicine Wheel 328
wardrobe 217
Water 329
web-based learning facilities 278
weekend gathering 208